GETTING STARTED IN ACTING AND MODELING

Everything you need to know while avoiding all the scams and con artists

By Felicia Alexandria

MYSTIQUE PUBLISHERS

GETTING STARTED IN ACTING AND MODELING

Everything You Need To Know While Avoiding all the Scams and Con Artists

By: Felicia Alexandria

Published by: Mystique Publishers
P.O. Box 919
Newark, CA 94560

Printed and bound in the United States of America

Acknowledgements

Many thanks to all the actors, models, agents, photographers, teachers and other industry people for their generous time and contributions to this book. I also wish to thank my many friends who gave their kind support and encouragement.

TABLE OF CONTENTS

help promote their careers * When should a model move to New York? * How agents are paid * How models are paid * Vouchers * Model release * Understanding rejection * Drugs and alcohol * What agents expect from models * What you should expect from your agency * What you shouldn't expect from your agent

CHAPTER FOUR 79
UNIONS
The screen actors guild * The american federation of television and radio artists * Actors equity association * The american guild of variety artists * The american guild of musical artists * The screen extras guild * Joining the unions * Membership fees and dues * Miscellaneous items

CHAPTER FIVE 83
PHOTOGRAPHERS - ACTORS
Pictures actors use * Do's and don'ts for photo sessions * Hair stylists and makeup artists * Where photographers advertise * Photographers to avoid * Using an agency's photographer vs. your own * Questions to ask the photographer * Choosing photographers * Meeting the photographer * Verifying your photographer's legitimacy * Paying the photographer * The day of the shoot * After the shoot * Copyright law * Printers * Questions to ask the printer

CHAPTER SIX 102
PHOTOGRAPHERS - MODELS
Portfolios: why you don't need one until you have an agent * Pictures models use * Portfolios * Composites * Slides * Headsheet * Testing * How to find a legitimate modeling photographer * Pictures children need

CHAPTER SEVEN 109
TRAINING - ACTORS
Training actors need * Other sources of training * Where teachers advertise * What you don't know about agency classes * Questions to ask a teacher * Choosing a level: beginner, intermediate or advanced? * Before you meet the teacher * Auditing classes * Making sure your teacher is legitimate * Paying the teacher * What classes should children take

REFERENCE

Trade magazines * Theater directories * Directories * Film association * Talent books * Screen extras guild offices * Casting offices for extra work * Union credit offices * Screen actors guild offices * Casting offices for extra work * Union credit offices * Screen actors guild offices * AFTRA offices * Equity offices * SAG talent agents * Department of Labor offices * Federal information centers * Department of Education offices

WARNING - DISCLAIMER

This book is written to provide information on getting into acting and modeling. It is understood by purchasing this book that the author and publisher are not offering any legal or other professional services. If legal advice or other professional assistance is needed, the services of a professional competent enough to handle your situation should be consulted.

Every effort has been made to make this book as accurate and complete as possible. However, the acting and modeling industry changes frequently. This is why the information in this book should only be used as a guide and not as the sole source of information. In addition, there may be mistakes in both content and typography for which the author and publisher hold no liability or responsibility. Furthermore, this book contains information on the acting and modeling business only up to the printing date.

The case studies cited herein are based on the author's personal experiences and on extensive interviews with actors and models. Furthermore, to protect the identities of the people involved the case studies have been modified slightly.

The main purpose of this book is to educate actors and models to get into the business properly and not get ripped off in the meantime. The author and Mystique Publishers hold neither liability nor responsibility to any person or entity in regard to any loss or damage caused, or alleged to be caused, directly or indirectly by the information contained in this book.

INTRODUCTION

Every year thousands of potential actors and models are inspired to get into this business. Many of them are willing to do *anything* to get a piece of the action, only to find out later that it was the wrong choice.

I happen to be one of the people who made a wrong choice. I paid money into a fraudulent modeling agency which got me nowhere, except straight into a lawsuit. One of the main reasons I decided to write this book was to discuss all the fraud within the modeling and acting businesses. I'd like to help others avoid making the same mistakes.

After winning my lawsuit, I stayed in modeling for awhile. While it was fun and exciting, it wasn't as challenging as I thought it would be, so I left and instead went into acting. This venture didn't last too long, however, because what I really wanted to do was to write this book. Since both acting and writing are full-time careers, I decided to concentrate on this book. It is something about which I feel a lot more passionate.

I did learn one thing by going to all the acting workshops, seminars and auditions: many of the actors and models with whom I came in contact had been ripped off in one way or another because they either weren't familiar with how con artists operate or they had been unsuccessful trying to get into the business and thought that paying someone might improve their chances. Many of them also were ripped off by agents who sold them classes or had them go through their photographers only to find out that the agent had no intention of representing them and was *only* after their money.

There are many books on the market that can provide you with all the guidance you need to get into the industry including information on agents, pictures, auditions and so on. But you'll also notice that very few discuss in detail all the scams with the industry. This is probably because most of the authors of these books are casting directors, actors, models and other industry people. These are the same people who wouldn't want to be blackballed by making negative comments about their colleagues. So they keep silent because they fear they might cause problems for themselves if they revealed the truth.

A few of these books will tell you that you should make sure that you're with a licensed agency. Well, that's fine if you live in a state that licenses talent agencies. But what do you do if you're in a state that doesn't? There are quite a few of these. I guess those people are just out of luck.

Another thing is that many new actors and models aren't familiar with licensing, let alone whom they should call to find out whether a talent agency is properly licensed. So books that tell people to make make sure they're with a licensed agency should also tell them how to go about it.

Some books say you should run if a talent agency asks for any money up-front. But what they're forgetting to mention are all the agencies that don't ask for money up-front, but rip you off just the same by conning you into taking their classes or going through their photographer, from whom the agency takes a kickback. (There are discussions of this throughout the book.)

One of the main reasons that most new actors and models get ripped off is because they don't know where to begin or whom to talk to. How many acting or modeling schools do you know in which part of their curriculum educates students on different scams within the industry? I haven't seen any, nor have I seen any workshops that specifically address this subject. All the acting and modeling schools concentrate on is teaching students how to act or model. Which is great, but then when actors and models graduate they know all about doing runway turns and poses or how to do a monologue, but they know nothing at all about whom or what they should avoid.

By the time you finish this book, you will be well-informed on the the different scams, along with how to pursue your career as a model or actor. You'll also be guided step-by-step in every aspect instead of fending for yourself.

Whether you are pursuing acting or modeling, you should still read every section of this book. The reason I wrote a combination book is because many models get into acting once their modeling careers are over, and many actors will get sidetracked into modeling for awhile before pursing acting full-time. Then there are the people who are undecided and don't know whether they want to pursue acting or modeling.

In addition, I'm sure you'll find interesting the numerous case studies throughout the book taken from interviews with actors and models. To see how the con artists really operate, a couple of scams are closely examined so you can see how psychological and manipulative tactics are used to get people to buy whatever they are selling.

I hope you enjoy reading this book as much as I have enjoyed writing it. Let's get started exploring the exciting and glamorous world of acting and modeling.

CHAPTER ONE

LICENSING

Many actors and models who get into the industry know very little about licensing, such as which licenses talent agencies need, or why licensing is even important. To clear up this issue once and for all, part of this chapter has been devoted to explaining and defining it for you.

Even though you may not find this chapter as entertaining as the rest and are anxious to find out how to get into acting or modeling, it would be a good idea to take the time to read over this chapter. Many of the actors and models to whom I spoke had been ripped off by talent agencies that weren't properly licensed.

They were ripped off because many of the actors and models didn't know how to determine if an agency was properly licensed. Others didn't think it was important for an agency to be properly licensed.

Unfortunately, not all states require a talent agency to possess a "talent agency" license. For this reason, *everything on licensing in this chapter*, unless otherwise noted, will apply only to the state of California. However, you can still benefit from reading about licensing even if you're not in California.

In the reference section of this book there is a list of phone numbers for each state's Department of Labor, so you can contact them to find out what licenses, if any, your state requires talent agencies to possess.

Another reason to clarify this issue of licensing is that I have been to many talent agencies that were supposed to have a talent agency license. When I asked them if they had one, the agency would either lie and tell me "yes" (what agency do you think is going to tell you "no"?), or they would point to their business license on the wall. If you weren't familiar with licensing, you would probably think that an agency with just a business license is properly licensed. And they are to a point— but unless they also have a talent agency license, they are still not properly licensed.

BUSINESS LICENSE

A business license is designed for anyone running a business. It is an announcement to the city in which you are operating that you are conducting a business there. This license is fairly easy to obtain: you pay a small fee, fill out some paperwork, and if the business is operated from a commercial building, the fire department must inspect it for safety. There is no background check done on the applicants, nor do they have to provide references to vouch for their character or secure a bond.

BUSINESS TAX LICENSE

Companies must also pay an initial tax just to have their businesses exist. Like the business license, there is nothing more to this than filling out some paperwork, and paying a small fee.

STATE TAX LICENSE

If a company is selling a product in its business, then it needs to have a state tax license, also. So if a talent agency is operating a modeling school and selling makeup as well, even if they do not charge tax to their customers, they are still required to have this license.

TALENT AGENCY LICENSE

This license is only for talent agencies. A talent agency is defined by the Department of Labor as "any agency that either secures or tries to secure work for an actor or model and takes a commission." If the agency is only preparing you for the industry or referring you to agents, casting directors and other industry people, they don't need to have this license.

This is similar to some personal management services that charge for photography services and to complete their training program. Since they are not taking a commission, they are not considered a talent agency. So it doesn't matter what the agency is doing, even if they are getting work for you. If they are not *taking a commission*, then they are not considered a talent agency and don't need to have this type of license.

Talent agency licenses are more difficult to obtain than the other licenses. To apply, an agency must first fill out a basic application form. Then there is a personal record form that asks for everything from the social security number to places of employment during the last two years. Agents also have to present two affidavits from people who can act as character references.

12

Then there's the contract between the artist and talent agency that must be approved by the Labor Commissioner before the agency can use it. This also goes for the schedule of fees, which determines the size of the commission they will be taking. In the state of California, a talent agency is allowed to take up to 25 percent on nonunion jobs. If they try to get 30 percent approved, for instance, their schedule of fees may not be approved.

An agency also has to secure a $10,000 bond that will pay for all damages occasioned to any person by reason of misstatement, misrepresentation, fraud, deceit, or any unlawful acts or omissions of the licensed talent agency, or its agents or employees while acting within the scope of the talent's employment.

Then comes the fingerprint cards, one for each hand. After the agent's fingerprints have been taken by the police or sheriff's department, the cards are sent to the Hall of Justice in Sacramento, where a statewide arrest check on the agent's applying for the license is conducted. Finally, agents are required to pay the filing fees: $250 for a new agency and an extra $50 for each additional agency they own.

There are many reasons why an agency is refused a license. If an agent has been arrested for any crime related to acting or modeling, he or she will not be issued a license. For example, if they had been arrested for drunk driving, this would not disqualify an agent from getting licensed. On the other hand, if while operating a talent agency, they were selling drugs on the premises and were subsequently arrested, they would be disqualified.

If they were arrested for a crime involving money, such as embezzlement or extortion, you can bet they've destroyed all chances for getting a license. Other reasons for disqualification include child pornography, moral turpitude, the unsafe or unhealthy condition of the office or building used for the talent agency or if the agency's license was revoked within the previous three years.

These are just some of the reasons that an agency would not be granted a license. It's important for you to work with a licensed agency (unless your state doesn't have licensing requirements for talent agencies). If you don't, then you can't be sure who you are dealing with. For all you know, the agent could have been in jail for fraud and is now operating a talent agency. Would you want to do business with that person? Probably not. And it is doubtful that the agent will reveal to you the details of a crime they committed in the past. This is one reason why the Department of Labor does a background check on anyone who seeks to operate a talent agency.

In my opinion, there are many reasons why some talent agencies don't bother to obtain a talent agency license before opening up their doors to the public. They may have tried to get one but the Department of Labor found something objectionable in their background and denied them a license. Or the agent may not know he or she must have a certain type of license. There have been some instances in which a talent agency has all the other necessary business licenses, but wasn't aware that a talent agency license was also needed.

But it might also be that the agent couldn't get a license because of a lack of funds. Not only does an agency have to come up with a $250 filing fee, but it also has to secure a $10,000 bond. If they aren't able to secure a bond there is an alternative, such as substituting $10,000 cash in its place which is put in the Department of Labor's trust fund. If they can't come up with the money they won't be able to get licensed. The Department of Labor will simply not issue a license without a bond.

The other reason they may not be licensed could be that it's a disreputable, fly-by-night agency. Why would an agency that's planning on staying in town only long enough to rip people off bother to get licensed? Not only would the agency probably not qualify, but their fingerprints and personal information would be recorded, making it easier for law enforcement agencies to link them to possible past crimes.

When I did a comparison on the amount of licensed and unlicensed agencies for the Los Angeles area, about 40 percent of the agencies were *unlicensed*. That's a pretty high percentage. All of the franchised agencies were licensed, because the union will not franchise agents unless they are licensed by the Department of Labor.

The reason for problems with unlicensed agencies is that in the state of California it is not considered a criminal offense to operate an unlicensed agency. If an agency is caught, and turned in, all that will happen is that the Department of Labor will issue the agency a notice that grants 20 days to file for a license. If the 20 days expire and they have failed to do so, the case is turned over to the District Attorney or the Department of Labor's attorney. The attorney will then go to court and get an order from the judge requiring that the agency become licensed or the agent will be held in contempt of the court.

So where is the incentive for an agency to become licensed? There is none. This could be why some agents wait until they are caught before seeking a license. And since many new actors and models don't really know very much about licensing, some of these agencies go for months without ever getting a talent agency license, because no one ever turns them in. This may also explain why some of these agencies have a business license instead of a talent agency license—so that actors and models will think that they are properly licensed and not turn them in. This way for the time being the agency avoids getting bonded and paying expensive fees to get licensed.

When an agency finally does get a license, the Labor Commissioner can revoke or suspend its license when it is shown that the agency has

14

violated or failed to comply with the rules and regulations. (There is a free pamphlet you can get from the Department of Labor that has all the rules and regulations for licensed talent agencies.)

BONDING

One of the main reasons the Department of Labor requires an agency to obtain a bond is because if an agency took money fraudulently from actors or models, or didn't pay them for jobs they had done and skipped town, it would be difficult for the talent to get any of their money back from that agency. But since agencies are required to get a bond before they can get a talent agency license, the talent is a little more protected.

Applying for a bond is similar to applying for a loan. Most surety companies require that the applicant have some sort of collateral, good credit and a stable background. But each surety company varies in its policy; while some will work around a bad credit history, others will not.

It doesn't cost anything initially to get a bond, but there is an annual fee that varies with each surety company. One surety company I spoke to charges a 10 percent annual fee, so at the end of the year the agency that is bonded with them would owe $1,000.

An agency can lose its bond if there are so many complaints filed against it by the Department of Labor that the surety company considers the agency to be a financial risk. If an agency loses its bond, then it will either have to get a bond from a different surety company, post $10,000 cash in its place or lose its license.

So it's important for an agency to keep a clean slate, not only with the Department of Labor, but also with its surety company. Because if the agency is franchised and loses its talent agency license, it automatically loses its franchise. This means that the agency would no longer be able to represent actors or models. If that's the only way the agency earns a living, it would really cause a lot of upheaval for the agency to lose both its license and franchise.

Always confirm that the agency you are dealing with has a talent agency license (unless you are in a state that doesn't require it) and don't just take the agency's word for it, either. There was an agency that had ripped off hundreds of actors and models in several different states. While their newspaper ad said they were "licensed and bonded," they in fact were not. The Department of Labor had revoked their license several months prior to the ad's appearance in the paper. Some of the actors and models with whom I spoke who had been ripped off by this agency did not bother to confirm with the Department of Labor that the agency was licensed. They just believed what they read in the newspaper.

Don't ever let an agency try to intimidate you into not asking questions by making you sound foolish or stupid. You have every right to ask as many questions as you want. Most of the unlicensed agents with whom I've spoken became very annoyed when I would ask direct questions, especially about their licensing.

To give you an example of this: I responded to an ad that said a particular agency was looking for actors and models to do print, TV and catalog work; there were no experience or training requirements, and they were not a school.

When I arrived they asked me to fill out an application. Then 15 other actors, models and I were ushered into a room where we were introduced to the owner, who told us all about the agency. She explained that the actors and models weren't required to do any elaborate portfolios or have any training (although if you didn't have any photographs you could have some taken by their photographer for $300, but this was your choice). They were strictly a modeling agency and would be taking a 20 percent commission from each job the actors and models did.

Then the owner asked each of us a couple of questions, and after everyone had been questioned, we were told to call the owner the following day to see if we had been accepted into the agency. Well so far it sounded as if they were legitimate, but the big question hadn't yet been dropped.

After everyone had gone I asked the owner if the agency were licensed. Her expression changed from a smiling, happy one, to a surprised look. Then she said, "Oh yes, we definitely are," as she leaned down to pick up something—completely avoiding eye contact.

When I asked if it were a talent agency license another person came in and rudely asked what I wanted. When I asked her the same question, she avoided answering the question by replying that licensing wasn't important, and that what was more important is for the agency to get work for its models.

Then the owner asked my name and when I told her, she pulled out my application card and wrote on the back of it. I grabbed it out of her hand and read it. It said that I had been declined for asking "too many questions." So I asked her why she had written such a ridiculous statement. I said that models and actors are turned down because of their height or look, not because they ask questions. Instead of answering my question, she asked me if I had ever had an agent, and when I said "no," (I have had agents; I lied to make it appear as if I was new to the business), she told me that the reason was probably because I was too inquisitive. Agents may have thought I was stupid for asking questions, she said.

I saved the best part for last, and asked them why they had told me they were licensed when in fact they were not. By this time they probably thought I was some kind of investigator. They looked at each other as if I had discovered their secret, and the woman told me that their attorney was preparing the paperwork, so it hadn't been sent in yet. That's a far cry from actually being licensed. (They must have a slow attorney, because several months later the agency still hadn't filed for a license.)

My theory is that these two agents had said all those things to me (before I told them that I knew they weren't properly licensed) to discourage me from calling the Department of Labor and possibly turning them in. When I put them on the spot by asking them why they had told me they were licensed when in fact they weren't, they had nothing left to say except that their attorney was working on it. Why didn't they just tell me that in the first place? Because there probably was no attorney involved. This was just their way of making me think their agency was legitimate.

By the way, when I first started doing research for my book I would respond to an agency's ad just to see what they were all about, even though I knew the agency wasn't properly licensed when they were supposed to be. I also wanted to see if they would lie to me about having a talent agency license, which, as you can probably guess, is what most agencies did.

It will, however, be wise for you to check to see if the agency is properly licensed prior to visiting them rather than wasting your time on an unlicensed agency. (If you are in a state that doesn't have licensing regulations for talent agencies, there are suggestions in the following chapters to help you find the legitimate agencies in your area.)

The rest of this chapter will give you a brief description of businesses that will be able to assist you when doing a background check on agents, photographers and others, or if you need to file a complaint. Each of these businesses will probably vary in each state in the way they handle complaints and procedures. While one Better Business Bureau may not give out the details of a complaint, a Bureau in a different state may cooperate. If a business is not listed, it simply means that it wouldn't be able to assist you with your background checks.

BETTER BUSINESS BUREAU (BBB)

Any person running a business whether licensed or unlicensed, can register with the BBB. It costs nothing to be listed, unless the business is a member, then it pays a yearly fee and receives a plaque. Upon cancellation of the membership, the business is still allowed to keep the plaque. I've seen some unlicensed agencies displaying this plaque on a wall; usually we associate legitimate businesses with the BBB.

17

This could be another reason that some actors and models don't call to verify whether the agency is licensed.

For a person to list a business with the BBB or get a membership, a registration form must be filled out and sent to the appropriate board of directors for approval. Since the BBB is not a regulatory service like the Department of Labor, it does not have the authority to do an in-depth background check or run a police report on the business.

To receive approval from the board of directors, the business cannot have any legal action against them by the District Attorney or any other government agency (however, this doesn't include lawsuits against them in small claims or with private attorneys on other lawsuits), or any unanswered complaints with the BBB.

If a business has a lot of complaints against it, the BBB might delay approval for several months before registering the business to see if it will clean up its act so that complaints will stop.

Each BBB handles businesses for a particular city or county so if you want to find out about an individual business or file a complaint, you will need to contact the city or county's BBB of the business about which you are inquiring. (Phone numbers can be found in the white pages of your phone book.)

The business about which you're calling doesn't have to be a member or even listed with the BBB for you to inquire about it. Most BBBs can't release details of each complaint because this is confidential information, but if the business has a listing or membership with the BBB they can tell you when the business opened, how long the BBB has kept record of it and the status of its membership or listing with them.

If it's an *excellent* status, this means no complaints have been filed against the business within the past three years. If it's a *satisfactory* status, this means there could be a couple of complaints in the file within the past three years, but the complaints have been settled to both parties' satisfaction. An *unsatisfactory* status, could mean that the company doesn't answer complaints sent to them by the BBB or that it doesn't cooperate with the BBB. It might also mean that the BBB turned the business over to a government or law enforcement agency.

Keep in mind, though, that a lot of consumers don't complain about a business to the BBB. Instead, they go to small claims court or hire a private attorney (and sometimes they don't do anything at all), which neither the BBB nor any law enforcement agency will be able to report to you unless the information has become public domain. In my lawsuit, for example, neither I, my attorney, nor the District Attorney complained about the photographer to the BBB, so if you were calling to find out the status of his business (provided there were no other complaints within the past three years), the BBB would report an *excellent* status to you. And you would never know of the criminal lawsuit against him unless you checked at the courthouse.

To file a complaint against a business, you will need to find out the BBB's procedures to do so. The BBB will probably want your complaint in writing because this is one way it bases its reviews when a business seeks to register with it. Your complaint is kept on file for three years. You can renew it for another three years simply by calling the BBB.

The BBB does not get involved in matters concerning money; it does not collect bills, give legal advice, or handle a complaint if it's already being investigated by a government agency or is going to court (including small claims), help to assist or breach in voiding contracts made without misrepresentation or fraud, provide credit information on a company, give its opinion as to the price of a service or give recommendations of any kind.

CONSUMER FRAUD

The main job of a consumer fraud department in a law enforcement agency is to prosecute civil and criminal cases in each state. They also investigate and prosecute violations of state laws.

A consumer fraud department is similar to the BBB, in that they also mediate complaints. The difference is that consumer fraud is a law enforcement agency, so if there is a violation of law or if officials see a pattern of complaints and the business is not willing to mediate, they could prosecute. It is the public responsibility of the consumer fraud department to enforce the law, whereas the BBB does not have such an obligation or responsibility.

Even though the consumer fraud department handles fraud complaints, there are some complaints they do not handle such as embezzlement and bounced checks. The type of fraud they handle has to do with consumer disputes—the same complaints you would take to a small claims court.

Most consumer fraud departments don't give out information on the status of a business like the BBB, unless it's already a matter of public domain. In that case, you would be able to find the case in the appropriate section of the courthouse.

To file a complaint against a business with a consumer fraud department you need to find out the fraud department's procedures. Like the BBB, each consumer fraud office handles businesses in assigned cities or counties. You will need to contact the city or county's fraud department of the business you're filing a complaint against. (Check phone numbers in the white pages of your phone book.)

SMALL CLAIMS, CIVIL AND CRIMINAL COURT

You can sometimes learn a lot about a person's background by doing some digging in the courthouse. Unlike the BBB, you won't be able to call up and inquire about a business; you will need to make a trip to the courthouse.

To check on a business, you need to go to the city or county courthouse in the district in which the business is located. Each city and county's procedures vary, so it would be a good idea to call and check before going there. When I visited different courthouses, I was usually guided to a room that contained thousands of cases, and was given several thick books covering each year that I requested. When you do a background check on someone, it's always a good idea to review the previous two years, along with the current year. The books are alphabetized, and if you find the business you're looking for, you would go and pull their file according to its case number. That's all there is to it. You might even find something interesting; I sure did. This procedure is for small claims. To look up things in the civil or criminal sections, you may be directed to different places within the courthouse.

Phone numbers for the different courthouses can be found in the white pages of your phone book under "Government." If you have difficulty finding any of the above-mentioned phone numbers, or if you have a unique problem for which no one seems to be directing you to the right place, there is a list of Federal phone numbers in the reference section of this book for each state that you can contact for further assistance.

CHAPTER TWO

AGENTS — ACTORS

Most people who work at a nine-to-five job can often predict what kind of day they will have. Agents, on the other hand, can never do this because no two days are alike. One day it might be quiet and the next it's complete chaos. The average workday for an agent is from 10 to 12 hours. The majority of an agent's work is done on the phone. If they're not busy calling talent for auditions, they're phoning casting directors and other industry people, or booking actors for jobs.

When an agent gets a new actor, the actor's headshot will be sent to industry people (this includes anyone who is connected to the acting business) to promote his or her career. When an actor is booked for a job, the agent is the one who negotiates contracts and bills clients. And since agents are always looking for new talent, some of their free time is also spent going to productions, looking at new pictures and interviewing actors. The list doesn't stop here either.

WHAT ACTORS NEED BEFORE SEEKING AN AGENT

There are a couple of tools you will need before you can even interest an agent. Models can just walk in the door without training or headshots, except snapshots. Unfortunately, actors don't have that luxury; you must have a headshot and resume.

Child actors are different, they don't need a headshot and resume when starting out.

HOW TO FIND A LEGITIMATE ACTING AGENCY

One of the ultimate goals for an actor is to join the Screen Actors Guild (SAG) and obtain a SAG card, so it would be to your advantage to be with a franchised agent. Why? Because in order to join SAG you need to do union work, and this work is channeled only through franchised agencies. Without a franchised agent, you would only have access to extra and nonunion work. Furthermore, once you join the union, you can't be represented by a nonfranchised agent, anyway.

Also, an agency that advertises in either the newspaper or trade papers for new actors and models may not be franchised. So check with the union to see if they are if the agency wants to represent you.

Here are some suggestions to help you find a franchised agency, and to make sure it is properly licensed.

1) You can either use the list of franchised agencies in the reference section of this book or call your local union and ask them to send you one. If you live in a state that does not have franchised agencies, then compile your own list of agencies by checking the phone book, trade papers and asking around.

2) The next step is to find out if the agencies you're interested in are licensed. To find out, contact the appropriate Department of Labor located in the reference section. If your state does have licensing regulations, then ask the Department to send you a list of licensed agencies along with the rules and regulations they have to follow. If they don't have lists to distribute, wait until you find an agency that wants to represent you. Then follow the procedure under "Checking Out Your Agency's Background" in this chapter.

If your state *does not* license talent agencies, as long as you're working with a franchised agency you can be assured that you're with a stable agency. On the other hand, if your state doesn't have licensing or franchising for agencies you can still find stable agencies by going to Chapter 3, and following the suggestions under "How To Find a Legitimate Modeling Agency." (Ignore the first part about finding a modeling agency, and move on to the part where it discusses finding stable agencies.)

3) If you were able to get a list from the Department of Labor, check to see if the agencies you're interested in are currently licensed. If some of them are not on the list, then call the Labor Department to determine their status. These agencies may have recently filed and haven't been added to the list yet. If you see that an agency's license has expired, check to see that it has been renewed.

If any of the agencies you're interested in are not licensed with the Labor Department, cross them off your list and do not deal with them. (Of course this does not apply if your state doesn't have licensing for agencies.) If the agency is franchised and is not currently licensed, you may want to notify the union about this.

CONTACTING AGENCIES

There are many ways you can let agents know you are an actor, such as submitting your picture and resume to them or inviting them to a production in which you'll be appearing. If you are graduating from an acting school, sometimes the school will allow you to act out a scene in a performance to which industry people are invited. Agents also attend summer stock and showcases. (For more information on showcases, see Chapter 11.)

If you live in an area that has many agencies to choose from (such as Los Angeles, where there are about 280 agencies), rather than throwing your line into the water hoping to catch something, it would be better to get some opinions first from other actors or teachers you know who have agents. They may be able to make some suggestions as to which agencies might suit you best. If that's not possible, then just send your picture, resume and cover letter out to a small number of agencies at a time. It will be easier to keep track of 20 agents at a time rather than 100.

RESUMES

A resume gives industry people an idea of your training and experience as an actor. But you'll need something to put on it. If you don't have experience, then training can take its place. Actors' resumes follow a different format than a resume you'd send for a job as a computer programmer. (See the Appendix for a sample.)

Tips on Resumes

* Choose thick paper, such as 50-pound or 60-pound stock which all copy shops carry. Your resume will be handled by a lot of people, and thin paper won't hold up to all that wear and tear.

* Type, don't write, your resume. For a more professional look, try using either a computer or an electric typewriter, not a manual one. If you don't own either, copy shops usually do and will charge you a small hourly fee to use it. (When typing your resume, be sure to leave enough room on the paper, because you'll need to crop your resumes to fit your headshots.)

* Make sure everything is spelled correctly before getting copies made. (This also goes for all correspondence you send out.)

* Leave off your social security number, and unless you're a model, leave off your measurements.

* Leave off your age (unless you're a model) and age range. Casting directors don't usually cast according to age; they cast on appearance and ability.

* Resumes should be limited to one page. If you have a lot to list, include only your best experience and training. You don't want a cluttered resume. Not only is it difficult to follow, but some agents and casting directors refuse to struggle through a lengthy resume.

* For contrast, try using colored paper such as ivory or beige.

* When you have copies made, copy an amount equal to the number of headshots you have. Watch out for marks of any kind on your copies. (This is why you don't want to print them on cheap, low-quality printers. Kodak printers at copy shops make excellent, clean copies.) If there are marks, try a different machine or visit another shop altogether.

* Most agents advise against listing any of your extra work, unless you want to be typecast as an extra.

* Cut your resumes to fit the size of your headshots. If you don't, your resume will get torn when agents and casting directors pull it out of their file or when they refile them.

* Staple your resume to the back of your photo. Don't use tape or glue.

* It isn't a good idea to type your credits on the back of your picture. For one thing it's time consuming, and when you start dropping old credits and adding new ones, you'll have problems.

* Leave off the dates of any work that you've done, because unless you have current dates to list, industry people may wonder why you haven't been working recently.

Format

* Your name goes first in bold letters. (You can buy rub-on lettering at any art or office supply store for this effect.) If you belong to any unions, list this information below your name.

* Next list your agent's name, address and phone number. If you don't have an agent yet, it is not advisable to include your home address. Your resume and picture will pass through many hands (and may even end up in the trash). Instead, why not consider getting a post office box? They're inexpensive, and because it relates to your acting career, it should be tax deductible. If you are including your home phone number, it won't do you any good to delete your home address if it's listed in the phone book. If you have an unlisted address and will be using your home phone number, write "Machine" next to it if you're using an answering machine, or "Service" if you're using an answering service. (As an actor you should definitely have one of these items even before looking for an agent.)

* Last comes your height, weight, eye and hair color. If you sing, your voice type also should be mentioned somewhere in this area.

24

Credits

In New York, your theater credits would come first, including stock, Broadway, Off-Broadway, Off-Off Broadway, dinner theater and community theater. Then list your film (which includes student and nonunion films) and TV credits. In Los Angeles, it's the reverse. Your film credits come first, then TV, followed by theater.

If you have done commercials, never list them. Suppose someone is casting for Brand B detergent, and in the past you've done a commercial for Brand A. Since your contract with Brand A will expire in a couple of days, you will be free to audition for Brand B, but because you listed Brand A, the casting director will assume there are conflicts and you may not be called in for the audition. So just put "List and Tape furnished upon request." This also goes for voice-overs.

Training

If you've done different types of workshops, these can be broken down into separate categories, such as acting, commercials, improvisation, singing, voice or dance. You should indicate whom you have studied with, and how long you have studied with them. (You can leave off the dates if you've studied with a lot of different teachers in the same category.)

Special Skills

This category lists things you are good at and can still do. If you could ice skate 10 years ago, it is probably not something you could just pick up and do for hours on a commercial taping. Or if you are just learning French, don't put down that you can speak it fluently. Only list things you can do well now. Don't forget cooking, aerobics, surfing or karate: you never know when a part may come in for someone who can surf, and you're the only one qualified who can do it well.

CHILDREN'S RESUMES

Most children starting out do not have any experience or training and agents are aware of this. So if you don't have anything to put down for your child, don't even type up a resume. One agent with whom I spoke had this to say, "Many parents seem to feel that they need to send in a resume of their child. Many of these resumes have unnecessary clutter on them, and most agents don't have the time to sift out the good things. We've had some resumes that will say that the child waves bye-bye or makes sandcastles. You can tell that these parents are trying to make up for their child's lack of experience or training. I prefer that

25

children don't get any heavy-duty training right away until they have an agent. Then the agent can help the parent decide what type of training, if any, the child needs."

If your child has some experience and/or training but doesn't have enough to fill out a resume, just mention in a cover letter what they have done, along with any special skills (if they have any), their height, weight, hair and eye color (and clothes sizes if they model) along with the fact that you're a parent seeking representation for your child. Be sure to indicate what type of representation you're looking for such as acting or modeling and a phone number if an agent needs to contact you.

SHOULD YOU LIE ON YOUR RESUME?

If you don't have adequate experience to list on your resume, it can be very tempting to pad it. But if you do, this can backfire on you. One actor I interviewed said he listed a TV show, saying he had a part in it. What he didn't know was that the casting director who was interviewing him had also cast for the show. And of course knew the actor didn't have a part in the show. It was very embarrassing for the actor.

Then there was an actress who lied about her shoe size to get cast in a commercial. Well she got cast alright, but then she got stuck wearing the wrong size shoes all day and it was painful. Being honest can also work in your favor. If a director has to pick between you and another actor, he or she may just choose you since you have no experience. This has happened before. That's why it's important to get lots of training because it will make up for what you lack in experience. Casting directors and agents know who the good teachers and schools are. And since no actor was born with credits to his or her name, training can be just as valuable as experience.

COVER LETTER

A cover letter should accompany every resume and headshot you send out because it is useful as an introduction. Be sure it's typed and limited to only one page. Avoid using personal stationery or a piece of paper torn out of a binder or notepad. You're trying to come across as a professional. (There is a sample of an actor's cover letter in the Appendix.)

If one of your actor friends is signed to an agency to which you'll be sending your submission, ask your friend if you can include his or her name as a referral in your cover letter.

MARY TONRY - QUINN-TONRY AGENCY

"When actors are seeking representation, they really should look at the things they'll be sending out. We've had quite a few actors who have sent their pictures with the sticker of another agency on it. Or the only way you can reach the actor to set up an interview is through an old agent, whose name is printed on the resume they sent us. Or they put our address on it with another agency's name on it. These types of things don't go over very well with agents."

SENDING YOUR SUBMISSIONS

Before you send your pictures out, here are some other things you should do first.

* Confirm the name and mailing address of the agencies to which you'll be sending pictures.

* You should also find out who handles new actors' submissions. When you call, get the correct spelling of the person to whom you'll be sending your submission, and ask about their sex. For instance, the name "Lynn" could be given to a man or a woman. Some people get offended when you mistake their identity.

* If you are a parent getting your child into acting, make sure the agency handles that age group.

* You'll also need some envelopes large enough to hold your headshot, resume and cover letter, along with some mailing labels. For sending children's snapshots, you can use smaller envelopes. (For more on the kinds of pictures children need, see Chapter 6.)

Most agents prefer that actors *do not* drop off their pictures and resumes in person. So when you call to confirm the address, ask if you can drop your submission off in person. If they say "no," don't do it. Many agents have told me that it's irritating to tell actors not to do this and then have them do it anyway. Some actors will even go so far as to stand there while the agent is on the phone, trying to get an interview. It's good to be persistent in this business, but you should avoid overdoing it because this could work against you.

You are almost ready to send everything out. On the mailing labels, type the agency's name and address, along with the name of the agent who handles new actors' submissions and your return address. (Be sure to address the return envelope, also.) Write "Fragile: Photos Inside" on both envelopes and stamp both of them with the *correct* postage. One thing to point out is this: some people recommend putting cardboard inserts in the envelopes to keep the pictures from crinkling. But from what I've seen it doesn't help, except to add extra postage, so it's up to you.

Usually you'll hear from agents in about two weeks to tell you whether they're interested in meeting you. If you haven't heard from some of them in two weeks, it's best not to call because most agents prefer you don't interrupt them as anything can slow them down. If they're in the middle of a huge casting, your submission is considered low priority. So wait a couple more weeks and if you still don't hear back from some of them, then send them another submission. Most agents are very good about responding as long as you have included a SASE. It could be that some of your original submissions were lost in the mail.

The reason it's best not to call agencies that haven't responded, is that in the bigger cities, like Los Angeles, most phone calls won't get you anywhere. As one agent remarked, "Most agents are too busy to just drop everything and start looking for a particular actor's picture because he or she says it was mailed two weeks ago and they haven't received a response yet. If I were interested in the actor in the first place, I would have contacted them. So when they call, unless their picture is sitting right in front of me, most of the time I just tell them to send me another one."

On the other hand, some agents to whom I spoke said they don't mind actors calling and inquiring about their submissions. So it's your choice.

RICK MARTEL - MARTEL AGENCY

"Sometimes it can be to an actor's advantage to follow-up on a submission if they haven't heard anything from the agency. Sometimes the agent may hear a voice with personality that wasn't picked up from the picture, which makes the agent want to meet the actor. When you call, make sure there is energy and enthusiasm in your voice. A bland personality saying, "I mailed my submission a week ago. Do you want to see me?"—will get you a flat NO."

You might want to keep a logbook to record to whom you sent your submission, the date you sent it, the response generated from it, any follow-up that was done, whether the follow-up was by mail or phone and what type of response it generated.

If you get nothing back but rejections, remember that this often happens when you're sending pictures and resumes to agents for the first time. See the section titled "Why Actors Have Difficulty Getting An Agent," in this chapter.

BEFORE THE INTERVIEW

You finally received that call for an interview and now you're going to go meet the agent and dazzle him or her with your personality. But getting that call doesn't necessarily mean they want to represent you, they may only be partially interested. It's similar to when you respond to an ad for a computer programmer. Just because someone calls you in for an interview doesn't mean you're hired. The person at the computer company thinks you can do the job based on your resume, or they were impressed with your cover letter. (By the way, you can't convince an agent in a cover letter that you can act.) Well now they want to see what you're made of. It's the same thing with agents.

Before going to see the agent, look these items over carefully. Agents will be looking at:

YOUR OVERALL APPEARANCE - For women, it's best to wear either a dress, pantsuit or skirt and blouse. Men should stick to slacks and a shirt or a suit and tie. Both men and women should avoid wearing jeans, which don't look professional. Children should wear something that's clean and pressed, even jeans are OK as long as there are no patches or rips in them.

Your appearance is *very* important. If you come in wearing an outfit that's wrinkled or dirty (or you are wearing too much makeup) the agent may think, "If this is how he or she looks when trying to get an agent, what will this person's appearance be like when sent out on an audition or interview?" It won't give them much confidence in you, because if they send you to an audition and you're not dressed professionally, it's a reflection on the agency. No agent, I repeat, no agent wants to look bad.

YOUR HAIR - Is it clean and well styled? It may have been months since you got your headshots taken. So if your hair looks a little ragged, get it trimmed before meeting the agent. Remember to look exactly like your pictures. So if you get a new hairstyle or hair color, you'll have to get new pictures done.

YOUR FACE - Does it match the face in the picture? If your face is blemish-free in your pictures, it should also be clear in person. Your pictures shouldn't have been airbrushed to remove *anything* permanent. If the pictures have been airbrushed, the agent won't be pleased, and may ask that you do new pictures.

* *YOUR WEIGHT* - If you say on your resume that you're 110 pounds, you don't want to come walking in weighing an extra 20 pounds. You won't be weighed in as the models are, but the agent will be able to tell you've put on weight, and overweight actors don't work as much as slim actors. Also, keep in mind that the camera will add an extra 10 pounds to your original weight. NOTE: Before going on any weight reducing or gaining diets, be sure to consult your doctor first.

* *YOUR PERSONALITY* - Your personality can make or break you in this industry. A bad personality can get in the way of you getting work or agents.

TONY FERRAR - L. A. TALENT

"An actor's personality, along with good acting ability, is very important in this industry. Especially when you're talking about commercials, because they're really based more on personality. Obviously they want good actors, but if an actor has a certain sparkle and vitality, that's very appealing. But if actors walk around with chips on their shoulders because they're not getting an agent or work, then that's not productive."

MEETING THE AGENT

When you arrive, you will usually be asked to fill out a form that asks for basic information, or the agent may just ask you in person. Then you'll be ushered into the agent's office when they're ready for you. (Every agency is going to be different; some agents don't have a separate office and everything is out in the open.)

If the actor is a child, the child should be told in advance that the parent will have to wait out in the lobby. One of the reasons for this is because if a child has a hard time leaving his or her parent for an interview, then the child sure isn't going to want to be alone in a room with complete strangers on an audition. Some agents do not have a lobby, so if that is the case, let the child speak and be themselves. Many agents have told me that some parents completely take over the interview, which is ultimately the child's. Agents are interested in hearing from the child, not the parent, unless a question has been addressed to them.

When you walk in to meet the agent, turn on the energy and sparkle. Don't just walk in, plop down in a chair and expect the agent to go crazy over you without some effort on your part. They see tons of actors, and what will make you stand out from the crowd is a unique personality that's filled with energy, sparkle, a deep desire to act and an inner drive to succeed at it.

It would also be a great benefit to remember your manners by shaking hands and saying that you're glad to meet him or her. Wait to sit down until you are offered a chair. Every little thing you do stands out, and if you leave a good impression, you will be remembered well.

There are a couple of different approaches the agent may take. Since he or she called you in, he or she was either impressed by your picture, resume—or both. But now he or she wants to see what you can do. So be prepared to do either a monologue or a cold reading with the agent. There are many good classes on these two items. Since you'll be doing quite a few cold readings for auditions, you may want to enroll in a class or two. (For more on this, see Chapter 7.)

For a child actor doing a monologue or cold reading depends on the age of the child and on the agent. If the agent does have your child read a copy of a script, he or she will be looking at the child's talent, ability to take direction and speaking voice. (For more on the type of training children need, see Chapter 7.)

The agent may just talk with you and not have you read anything at all. They'll talk about your training, what type of acting you're interested in, when you're available for auditions, what you've been up to lately, why you chose their agency, etc. So be prepared with some interesting answers. For instance, if the agent asks what you've been up to lately, a bad answer would be, "Well, I've been working a lot at my computer programming job." A better answer would be to say that you've been auditioning for plays and taking acting classes. Say that your life has been consumed with acting. You need to make it look as if acting is your life, even if it isn't. They know you don't eat, sleep and drink acting, but you need to convey the impression that you do. If the agent has a partner they may introduce you and have you talk to him or her for awhile.

Beware of agents who recommend that you take their classes or get your pictures done through their photographer. For more on this, see Chapter 5, "Using an Agency's Photographer vs. Your Own." And in Chapter 7 see, "What You Don't Know About Agency Classes."

For some more tips on what to do when meeting the agent, see "Do's and Don'ts When Meeting an Agent" in Chapter 3.

WHAT YOU CAN EXPECT AFTER MEETING THE AGENT

Here are some of the possible outcomes you can expect from the agent after you meet with him or her. Even if you didn't receive the answer that you were wishing for, you should still thank the agent for his or her time.

* The agent may decide to represent you.

* You may be referred to a different agent if your interests are not compatible with the agent's. It's possible that you two don't see eye to eye on certain things.

* You may be asked to come back and meet another agent, if he or she has a partner who wasn't there or was busy at the time of your interview. The person you met may just screen potential actors and not do the actual approving of new actors.

* The agent may also ask you to let him or her know if you're doing something locally so he or she can check out your acting ability. They may see some potential but want to see you in action.

WHY ACTORS HAVE DIFFICULTY GETTING AN AGENT

It can be frustrating to send your pictures and resumes out to agents and receive rejection slips, but it will happen. Most of the time it can be cleared up just by doing new pictures or acquiring additional training. But sometimes there are other reasons that are out of your hands, so look over these different items to determine what you might be able to improve.

* PICTURES - Acting is a visual industry and your picture can make or break your career. Your resume and picture go hand in hand. If either one of them is bad or lacking, you're unbalanced.

First of all, make sure you're sending out an 8" by 10", black-and-white headshot. Unless you're a child actor, don't send out snapshots or agents will not know where you are coming from. One agent told me that she once received a picture of a bunch of people, and the actor had circled his face, drew an arrow pointing to it and wrote, "This is me." She said she almost fell off her chair laughing at how ridiculous it was. (No, he didn't get an interview.) So stick with an 8" by 10", black-and-white headshot.

It's possible that you picked the wrong photo from the contact sheet to be enlarged. You see yourself every day and it's hard to be objective about which pictures to select. Instead, retrieve your contact sheet and get a professional opinion from someone in the industry. If it is recommended that you get new pictures, then you should probably do it. This could be what's holding you back.

GAIL JONES - LOS LATINOS AGENCY

"You wouldn't believe some of the pictures we receive. Some of them are so bad I can't believe these people actually think that someone would be interested in them. The photography or the quality is bad, or the person looks terrible. It could be their hair, teeth, smile or clothes. And then to top it off, they have no experience or training on their resume. It's very hard to get into this business without training or experience."

In certain areas, (like Los Angeles), make sure you're sending a theatrical headshot to a theatrical agency, and likewise with the commercial headshot. A good idea would be to send a commercial and theatrical headshot to each agency. It won't hurt and will give the agent more to look at, which may improve your chances. (For more information on theatrical and commercial headshots, see Chapter 5.)

If you're a parent doing snapshots of your child, it's not really necessary to run out and get opinions from industry people. The reason it's a good idea for headshots, is because it's more expensive and time consuming to reshoot headshots than to reshoot snapshots. Also, the snapshots may not necessarily be the problem.

You may instead want to look over the snapshots of your child and ask yourself: Do the pictures compliment the child? Can you see the child clearly, including the face and body? Is there too much clutter in the background so that it takes away from the child? If the view of the child is distorted or you're only getting the side view of the child, then it's too difficult for the agent to ascertain whether or not the child has a good, salable look. If you feel new snapshots are in order, by all means take some. But avoid going to a professional photographer. It's a waste of your time and money to get professional pictures done before getting an agent.

* TRAINING - Actors with little or no training sometimes try to get an agent. You need to reverse that thinking quickly. In Los Angeles especially, most agents won't even look at you unless you have had some training. This is how it works: most agents only make a living off a 10 percent commission for each union job and 20 percent for each nonunion job they secure for an actor. If actors don't get work, the agent gets no money. If the agent gets no money, they can't pay the rent and other bills, which means they are in trouble.

It's also hard for an agent to convince a casting director to see an actor with little or no training, because few actors can act naturally without adequate training. So when an agent looks at a resume that lists little or no training, an eviction notice may pop up in his or her mind. That's why agents can't afford to take on every actor wanting representation, just the ones they feel can make money.

So even though rejection slips can be frustrating, believe it or not, they're actually doing you a favor by not representing you. Some other reasons why you may be having difficulty getting representation could be that they don't handle your particular look, ethnic type or age group. Or if they do, they may already have too many people that look like you, and don't want to take on any new actors for the time being.

So if your resume has little or no training, go sign up for a couple of classes, put the new training on your resume, and send your pictures and resumes out again. You don't have to wait to complete the classes, but if the agent asks how long you've been in the classes, don't lie.

If you're a parent having difficulty getting an agent for your child, don't run out and get training for your child. There are many reasons that children have difficulty getting an agent. It could be that the agent doesn't handle children or that they have too many children who look like your child. It could also be that your child is at that awkward stage where he or she needs braces or is in an age group for which the agents aren't getting too many casting calls. But it's better not to sit around trying to evaluate the reason. Persistence and patience are absolute musts in this business.

* WEIGHT PROBLEM - Overweight people are used in the acting industry, but not as much as slim people. So if you're overweight you might want to try losing some weight, get new pictures done and send them out.

There are other reasons why actors get rejected. Unfortunately these are out of your hands:

* TALENT POOL - Each agency receives up to 20 submissions from actors daily, and out of these pictures, only the best will get representation. Once the agent has a certain number of actors in his or her pocket, he or she usually won't take on any more. But that doesn't last forever, because actors are always switching agents or getting out of acting to get married or start a family. If the agent takes on too many actors, some actors will get less attention than others. So most agents like to keep it to a certain amount. They also have established categories like leading ladies and men, ingenues and children. Sometimes if an agent is lacking a certain type or age range, they'll take on new actors.

* STRIKES - Strikes don't happen very often, but when they do, most agents won't take on new actors. However, I did hear from sources that during the writers' strike, some agents kept taking new actors and getting them to go through their classes. This would make sense in my opinion because during a strike there isn't as much money being made, so many of these agents had to do something to make ends meet.

* AGENCY EXPANSION - The agency could be expanding and taking on a new partner or moving, or maybe the agent you want is going into casting or directing and is selling the business. There could be delays because of these big changeovers.

These are just some of the reasons why you could be having difficulty getting an agent. But keep trying, and in the meantime, stay in training. Do plays, take a variety of classes and keep in shape physically by working out. You don't want to finally get an interview with an agent and be 10 pounds overweight.

OTHER WAYS TO GET AN AGENT'S ATTENTION

If none of the above ideas work, put your mind to use and invent some really innovative ways to get the agent's attention. I've heard of actors sending messengers to deliver boxes of candy with the actors' picture and resume on the top layer or a bottle of wine with their picture and resume wrapped around it. Get some of your actor classmates together and brainstorm on ideas. You'll be amazed at what you come up with.

Theater

Agents frequently spend some of their free time going to showcases and the theater, which includes Equity productions, 99-seat equity waiver and community theater. If you're going to be in a play and will invite industry people, make sure that you have a big enough part which really shows your acting range. You also want to be working with a choice director and cast. You don't want to invite industry people to a badly organized play with actors who act only as a hobby. It's possible that they could make you look bad.

To invite industry people, get some flyers made up (see if the entire cast will contribute toward the expenses), announcing the date, time and title of the play, the name of the theater, address, and a phone number that the agent or casting director can call for more information, along with directions and a couple of tickets to the play. Industry people will usually not show up if they have to pay for admission.

A couple weeks before the play opens, send the agents and casting directors your picture, resume, a cover letter and a flier. Tell them about the play you're appearing in, the part you are playing and in what sets. (They will want to know if you'll be in one, or several, sets.) If this is the first time you've made contact with them, also include in your cover letter that you're looking for representation, or an interview if writing to the casting director.

Make sure that you have seats reserved in the front rows for them. You wouldn't want them to sit in the back where they can barely see you. After the show, introduce yourself (but refrain from asking how you did because that could show that you lack confidence in yourself), and tell them you'll get in touch to set up an appointment for additional discussion.

Then send thank you notes to the casting directors and agents who attended, and request a convenient time for an interview. If you don't get a response from some of them in a couple of weeks, you might want to call and remind them that they saw you in a particular production, and add that you'd like to set up an interview.

If you don't get an interview for any reason, keep in touch by mailing photo postcards and continue to remind them that they attended one of your shows, and ask them to keep you in mind for future auditions and interviews.

You can use this format for anything in which you'll be performing, as long as the part and the cast and crew are good. And make sure that your acting ability is top notch. If you prematurely invite an agent to your performance, you may have a difficult time getting representation from them. So play it safe. If you're not sure, get the opinion of an acting teacher or even the casting director or director of the play before inviting anyone.

DO ACTORS NEED AGENTS?

LOS ANGELES

In Los Angeles, you will have a difficult time trying to get auditions and work without an agent; there are just too many actors. A casting director would rather deal with three or four agents when casting a project than 400 free-lancing actors.

One of the agent's jobs when they get a casting call is to send the actors they feel can properly fill the role. You wouldn't be able to go directly to the directors or producers because they almost never deal directly with actors until after they have been screened by the casting director.

JACK SCAGNETTI - SCAGNETTI TALENT AGENCY

"If actors want their careers to go anywhere they need to have an agent, especially in Los Angeles. Most casting directors pay much more attention to a submission sent in by an agent as opposed to a free-lancer because they figure the actor has already been screened by the agent."

Even if you had access to the agent's tool, the breakdown service, it would still be difficult to get an audition without an agent. In Los Angeles, many casting directors work on studio lots, and you need a pass, which an agent can supply, to get past the guard.

OTHER CITIES

In other cities, such as New York, free-lancing is more accepted and making rounds is an acceptable practice. I've gone to many auditions where there were two or three other actors who didn't have agents. They found out about the audition through a friend who had an agent. This might sound like a good idea, but keep in mind that many casting directors won't let you audition unless you've been submitted to them by an agent.

No matter what city you live in, your career won't go very far without an agent. Agents have access to the big jobs, and a casting director isn't going to advertise in the trade papers for the casting of a part in a major movie. Do you know how many actors would show up for the audition? Even though the casting director might include a specific type, age and look in the casting call, the wrong actors could still turn out for the audition.

Agents do much more than just send actors to auditions. If you were cast in a TV show, would you know how to negotiate your salary and billing? Billing refers to the titles you see on TV such as "Starring Mary Joe," "Special Guest Star Joe Brown." Agents sometimes will negotiate better billing in place of a higher salary. You need to get seen and it is very beneficial to have top billing. Most new actors don't even know how to interpret a contract, let alone negotiate salary or billing.

Agents also have contacts with the people who do the actual hiring of actors and can promote you to the right people. They also book auditions for you and bill clients. They make sure the people you're working for are legitimate. After all, the agent wants money, too. They don't want clients skipping town. They advise you on pictures, makeup, wardrobe and much more.

Now if you had to do all this plus much more, you'd have little time to go to auditions, acting classes, update your pictures and all the other little odds and ends that are involved in an actor's career. It would be too difficult to concentrate on all areas. Most actors also have to work part-time to support themselves. Very few actors make a living from acting in the beginning.

GETTING ACCEPTED

So your wish has come true and an agent finally wants to represent you. Now only good things will happen to you: your phone will be ringing off the wall, Spielberg will be dying to sign you to his next three movies, you will be invited to all the Hollywood parties, the Tonight Show will want to interview you. You're thinking limos, champagne: Stop! You're dreaming.

I was so happy when I first got an agent because I thought that my phone would be ringing all the time with calls for endless auditions. I thought I didn't have to really do anything to promote my career because my agent would be doing it for me. I had some fancy visions. Was I in for a big surprise.

I got my first audition three months later; my phone didn't ring like I thought it would, and I went to auditions only two or three times a month. I also found out that if I wanted to get my career going, I had to do something about it and not leave it to my agent. I also spent a lot more money than I was making on my career. So all this brought me back to reality quickly. Just getting an agent doesn't mean that you're on Easy Street. In fact this is just the beginning of a long and winding road.

QUESTIONS TO ASK YOUR AGENT BEFORE SIGNING CONTRACTS

Here are some questions to ask your agent before signing any contracts. Of course, feel free to add anything else.

* How will the agency be promoting my career? What can I do to help?
* What are my obligations to this agency?
* What are the agency's obligations to me?
* Do you want me to call and check up on my picture and resume supply?
* Can I check with you for auditions? If so, how often?

CONTRACTS

Your agent may sign you either exclusive or nonexclusive. In Los Angeles, expect to be signed exclusive to one department in an agency, even if you're with an agency that handles commercials, film and TV. In other cities you may also be signed either exclusive or nonexclusive.

If you don't live in Los Angeles, I would think twice before signing exclusively with an agent because it means that you can't work with any other agency. And since no one agency gets every single casting call, an exclusive contract means you don't have the advantage of getting additional auditions from other agents. One of the advantages of being exclusive is that the agency will usually take more of a personal interest in the actor and will work a little harder trying to find auditions for him or her.

If you're with a franchised agent, the contract that you'll sign will be a union-approved contract. In my opinion it really isn't necessary to take it to an attorney to review, but you should take it home and look it over carefully. You can also call your local union and order a copy of a standard union contract to look over, even before you start looking for an agent.

Don't feel like you have to sign it right then and there in the agent's office. If you don't understand something, ask the union or your agent, but don't sign *anything* until you completely understand. If it's not a union-approved contract (for a nonfranchised agent), then you should have either an attorney or someone who's familiar with contracts look it over. I heard about one agency that had a nonunion contract with actors and models who signed it which said that all classes and pictures had to be done through their agency. If you don't thoroughly read and understand things, especially contracts, you may find yourself in some undesirable situations.

Some agents will wait until the actor gets their first job or to see if things work out between the agent and actor before signing any contracts. If the agent doesn't want to sign you to a contract, they will usually have you sign a power of attorney. (See Chapter 3 under "Contracts" for more on this and on the outclause.)

CHECKING OUT YOUR AGENCY'S BACKGROUND

Another thing you should do before signing contracts with an agency is to check out the agency's background. Someone told me about an agency that was licensed and franchised but was taking advantage of actors by having them take their classes and use their photographer. The union was even considering taking away its franchise, so if you had called the union, you probably wouldn't have gotten a good report on this particular agency. Even if the agency is licensed and/or franchised, it would still be in your best interest to check on some of the items below before signing contracts. This also applies if the agencies in your area don't have to be licensed and/or franchised.

* If you're with a franchised agency, call your local union and check on the agency's status with them.

* If the agency has a talent agency license, check on its status with the Department of Labor. (Be sure to ask if it's licensed if you weren't able to obtain a list of licensed agencies.)

* Call the Better Business Bureau to see if there are any complaints against the agency.

* Check with small claims court. (If the agency is franchised and/or licensed, sometimes the union and/or Department of Labor is notified if an agency has been taken to court, however, many times they aren't notified. It's up to the actors and models to notify these businesses. Most of the time they don't and just take the agency to court, so you may want to check on this one.)

HOW AN AGENT PROMOTES AN ACTOR'S CAREER

Depending on your area and agent, there are many ways an agent will promote your career. The majority of the agents with whom I spoke said that what they will usually do when they first sign a new actor is to notify different industry people by sending the actor's pictures and resumes announcing his or her availability for auditions and interviews. Some agents, to cut down on their time and postage, will have you do most of the legwork. Then there are the agencies that publish a newsletter announcing their new actors, which is sent to industry people.

There is also the breakdown service they scan to see the roles for which their actors could audition. This is a service offered by a company in Los Angeles to agents and personal managers, but not to actors. The majority of the auditions are in the Los Angeles area, with some auditions going on in New York.

The service provides a summary of all the roles that have been taken from scripts about to go into shooting, and includes a small description of all the characters, as well as how big each part is. If your agent feels you're right for a part, you'll be submitted for the audition, or the agent will submit your picture and resume to the casting director first.

HOW ACTOR'S CAN HELP PROMOTE THEIR CAREERS

Even though your agent will be helping out on some of the initial promotion, it will be up to you to keep it going full speed in the long run. Remember that your agent has lots of actors to look over. An agent is not a publicist, so he or she doesn't have extra time to heavily promote each actor. In the beginning you won't need or be able to afford a professional publicist anyway, so here are some ideas:

Many cities have trade papers in which an actor can make announcements, such as getting signed to an agency or being cast in a movie or TV show. Some trade papers will also print your picture. The only drawback is that ads can be quite expensive, and announcing that you're acting in "Little Red Riding Hood" at the community theater would be a waste of money.

But look around. There may be some trade papers that have agent sections which will list your signing to an agency without charge or at a reduced rate. Your agent should be able to give you some information on which trade papers in which you could advertise. Before going out and placing any ads, get an issue or two of the trade papers you're thinking of advertising in and read them to get an idea what's inside before spending any money.

Another suggestion would be to get some of your acting friends together and have monthly meetings. (If you're a parent getting your child into acting, you could do the same thing by getting other parents of child actors together to talk shop.) It's a lot easier and fun to come up with ideas with other actors rather than by yourself.

These meetings can also be used to exchange information such as knowledge of auditions or information on good teachers, photographers and agents. You can even use them for group therapy. Lord knows, acting can be frustrating. Rather than go to an expensive therapist, everyone could take turns expressing personal feelings to other actors rather than to a therapist who may know nothing about what actors go through. If you're looking for a scene partner, you may find one within your group.

For actors in New York, there is a network group called "The Actors' Information Project" (AIP) that offers counseling for every aspect of your acting career, such as marketing, interview techniques, seminars, and much more. You can reach them at 311 West 43rd Street, New York, NY 10036 or (212) 245-4690.

One other idea is to ask your agency for a list of all its clients and then send a photo, resume and cover letter to each of them, announcing who you are and that they should keep you in mind for future auditions or interviews. Mention that you can be contacted through your agent. Every once in awhile send a photo postcard of yourself reminding them of your existence and availability for auditions or interviews. It's *not* advisable to call, because if they're interested, they will contact your agent. Besides using your agent's client list, there are other lists that can be compiled by utilizing some of the books listed in the reference section of this book.

THE BREAKDOWN SERVICE

They won't provide audition information to actors, but they do have two other services for actors in the Los Angeles area. Tired of typing labels to different industry people? They sell preprinted labels. The service for a fee will also hand-deliver announcements and invitations to casting directors, producers, agents and personal managers.

These ideas are good if you're going to be in a play and don't want to do all the running around yourself. If you don't live in the Los Angeles area, your agent may know of a similar service in your area, or maybe you could start one of your own for added income.

Even if you do have this type of service in your area, this is something you can do yourself for less money. Why shell out the extra money when you don't need to? Delivering announcements and invitations has great advantages. Just think of all the agents and casting directors you'll be meeting in person, instead of just mailing it to them. But a word of advice: don't wear out your welcome by hanging around trying to get the agents or casting directors to notice or interview you. If they start up a conversation with you, great; if not, just drop off your flier and move on to the next ones on your list.

There are hundreds of things you can do to promote your career. Space does not allow listing all of them here. When your career finally does take off and you have the money, a publicist can sometimes do wonders for your career. (See Chapter 10.)

WHEN SHOULD AN ACTOR MOVE TO LOS ANGELES?

Since Los Angeles is *the* capital for film and TV work, you will eventually need to move there if you want your career to really take off. But don't pack up and move just yet.

Almost all the agents with whom I spoke in Los Angeles had one thing to say to actors: "Don't come here unless you have your SAG card

41

or lots of training and/or experience." About 80 percent of all jobs that come across casting directors' desks are for union jobs. So the majority of actors that agents send to auditions have their SAG cards. But even so, many agents accept new actors without SAG cards, if they have lots of training and/or experience. (You'll be hearing this a lot; you may even have nightmares about it.) Experience can come in the form of doing plays and nonunion work such as student and nonunion films, commercials and industrials. Without any of this, your chances of getting an agent are pretty slim no matter where you live.

Here's an explanation to give you a better understanding of how it works everywhere, not just in Los Angeles. Actors who aren't well-trained usually lack good audition skills to secure jobs. This is something that's weeded out in acting classes, not at auditions.

Casting directors cannot afford to continually audition bad or un-developed talent because their boss, the producer, or director, will start going elsewhere for castings. When the actor looks good, so does the casting director. Then the boss is happy, and so is everyone else. This is why most casting directors will be very hesitant to audition actors who lack training. So do yourself a favor and get lots of training first before deciding to move to Los Angeles. If you think it's competitive in your hometown, just wait until you arrive in Los Angeles.

Besides, if you don't have any money saved up, how do you plan to move anyway? Your best plan would be to stay in your hometown, get a local agent, and acquire some experience, training and your SAG card. (If you live in a state that doesn't have franchised agencies, then just concentrate on training and experience.) It's advisable to save lots of money for all those expenses such as rent, utilities, phone bills, food, gas, pictures (the pictures you had done in your hometown won't be right for the Los Angeles market), acting classes, postage, wardrobe and much more. Once you have your money, training and/or experience and possibly your SAG card, it would be a better time to move. You'll be more welcome in Los Angeles.

For parents who are contemplating a move to Los Angeles or New York, your child doesn't necessarily need training, experience or a SAG card before moving. It would be quite helpful, but this can be discussed with your local agent.

Starting out with an agent in your hometown can be very beneficial. Many small town agents deal with agents in some of the bigger markets and a recommendation from your agent could really give you an edge on the competition. Plus your agent can help prepare your child for the bigger markets and help them to get experience. Your child would be earning money at the same time to help finance the move.

HOW AN AGENT GETS PAID

The maximum commission an agent can take on a union job is 10 percent. On nonunion jobs, it's up to 25 percent. (The 25 percent may vary from state to state so check with your local Department of Labor on this, even if they don't license talent agents.) Agents *never* get paid fees for registration, interviews, auditions, etc. The only money that your agent should ever receive from you is a commission on jobs you've done (unless you're paying for agency classes or photo sessions).

There are agencies that try to charge actors and models registration fees to sign up with their agency. I heard about some licensed and franchised agencies that tried to avoid calling it a registration fee by saying the fee was for an audition, interview or screen test. Some of these agents were charging fees *before* you could even meet with them!

Whether the agency is franchised and/or licensed, they are not supposed to charge registration fees. If the agency has a talent agency license in California, they are not allowed to charge a registration fee to *register* talent with the agency, but they can charge a fee for expenses to *obtain employment* for the talent. Like many of these modeling agencies that charge a small fee to include the model in the agency's headsheet, they are only supposed to charge the model a fee for "printing costs," and nothing else. Notice the difference between fees for expenses and fees for registration? In the event the actor or model fails to secure employment, or get paid for work done, the actor or model can take the problem to the Labor Commissioner. In most cases, the agent will have to repay the actor or model any fees for expenses given to the agency.

HOW AN ACTOR GETS PAID

When you are booked for a job, you will sign a contract and your agent will have told you in advance all the details of the job. The contract will serve as a binding agreement and to confirm everything. So read it over carefully to be sure it includes everything your agent has told you before signing it. This also includes the amount of money you were quoted. Be sure you also get a signed copy of the contract.

After you have done a job and the agent has received the money (when he or she will receive the money depends on the type of job you did), he or she will log it in their book the amount you were paid and the amount of the agent's commission. If your agent is franchised, he or she has five working days on a union job and 15 working days on a nonunion job (this time limit will probably vary in each state) to turn the money over to you, minus the agency's commission, after he or she has received the money.

On the other hand, if the check is mistakenly sent to you instead of the agent, be sure to give the agent his or her commission right away. Remember that the commission is the only way that most agents make their living. If it hadn't been for them you probably would never have heard about the audition, landed the job and made the money.

WHAT AGENTS EXPECT OUT OF ACTORS

Now that you have an agent who wants to represent you, you are going to have to keep up your end of the bargain. Your agent has many other actors who are making excellent money for them, so don't expect an agent to hold your hand.

GAIL JONES - LOS LATINOS AGENCY

"People who make it in my agency are willing to do whatever it takes. If I call and tell them I need 10 more resumes, they mail them that same day, instead of three weeks later. Some actors don't communicate with me. Most of the people who really make it in this business are those who are serious actors. Acting is their top priority."

Here is a list of things that agents say actors need to keep tabs on.

* *KEEP YOUR PICTURE AND RESUME UPDATED.* If you change your look or get new training, it is your responsibility to get new ones done and send them off to your agent.

* *ALWAYS KEEP YOUR AGENT INFORMED OF YOUR CURRENT ADDRESS AND PHONE NUMBER.* If they have an audition for you, they don't want to play Sherlock Holmes trying to track you down. If you just got a job during the day, make sure they are notified of the phone number and the hours and days that you're available for auditions. (This is why most actors have jobs waiting tables rather than nine-to-five jobs. There isn't much flexibility in an office job.)

* *HAVE YOUR OWN ANSWERING MACHINE OR SERVICE.* If it's a machine make sure that it's on at all times and working. You should also make sure that your answering machine will allow you to play back calls from another phone, so you can call and check for messages. (You should do this several times a day if you're away from home.) Some actors have even gone so far as to carry beepers so that it's even easier for their agents to reach them.

A good thing to keep in mind when you're recording a message for your answering machine is to keep the message brief and to the point. Agents don't want to call and listen to five minutes of a song or a clever impersonation. If agents wanted to hear this, they would either turn on their radio or have you come in and do a talent show.

44

If you're always over at a friend's house, you might want to have "Call Forwarding" put on your phone. "Call Waiting" is also another good thing to have, even if you don't spend a great deal of time on the phone. If your agent gets a busy signal, he or she may just move onto the next actor, and you'll lose out on auditions.

KEEP YOUR SKILLS HONED. Keep yourself active in classes, theater and anything else that involves acting. Acting is like a muscle. If it's not used all the time it gets weak, and you want to be strong at your auditions.

BE ON TIME FOR EVERYTHING. Being late for interviews and auditions is not only rude, but many times it holds other people up. A client may have flown in from another state and may have to be back on the plane in a couple of hours, and the auditions have been scheduled so that every actor gets a turn to audition. If you show up late, you may lose your turn. And you start showing up late more than once, you may be tagged. Even though this industry is big, it's actually quite small in some ways, and when word gets around that you're always late, your career could take a nose dive. So leave plenty of time for weather problems, accidents and road construction, parking problems and to find the casting location.

SHOW UP FOR AUDITIONS. It's amazing, but some actors have actually not shown up when their agents send them out on auditions. *Always* go to your audition and make sure you carry enough money so that if your car breaks down you can take a taxi or use public transportation. If you do need to cancel an audition, try to give your agent at least a 24-hour notice, longer if possible.

DRESS APPROPRIATELY FOR EACH AUDITION. If you're not sure what to wear, be sure to ask your agent so that you dress right for the audition. One actor didn't, and went to an audition for a jeans commercial dressed in a three-piece suit. Bad move.

KEEP IN SHAPE AND YOUR COMPLEXION CLEAR. You want to look your best at all times and like your pictures. When the casting director calls you in for an audition, if you've gained 20 pounds and have blemishes all over your face, but didn't in your pictures, you'll probably blow your chance right there. So keep in shape and your face clear, or have new pictures done.

BE PROFESSIONAL AND COURTEOUS TO EVERYONE. You are representing your agency, so be proud of it. If your agent feels you're damaging the agency's name, you'll be dropped like a hot potato.

KEEP ACTIVE IN THE BUSINESS. Send your pictures and resumes to industry people and keep your listings updated if you're in a book such as "The Academy Players Directory." Go to auditions for stage, student films, and so on.

WHAT YOU SHOULD EXPECT FROM YOUR AGENCY

There are things that you should legitimately expect from your agency. If you feel as if you are not getting them, talk it over with your agent. If nothing happens, go to the union or the Department of Labor to complain. (If you live in a state that doesn't have a union or licensing for agents, and nothing happens, think about getting a new agent.)

__HONESTY__ - Your agent should never lie to you about anything, just as you should never be dishonest with them.

__ADVICE AND PROMOTION OF YOUR CAREER__ - When your agent calls you for an audition, he or she should advise you on every aspect of the audition, such as what to wear, whom you should see when you arrive, and anything else that will ensure you doing the best possible audition.

Your agent is expected to do a reasonable amount of promotion of your career at all times. However, he or she is not expected to do everything while you just sit back and relax. You and your agent are a team, and as a team you have to work together to accomplish your goals.

__TO BE PAID ON TIME AFTER EACH JOB__ - Depending on whether it's a union or nonunion job, agents have a deadline by which to pay you after they've received the money; so you should expect prompt payment. Just as they'll expect prompt payment from you if you happen to receive the check.

__PROFESSIONAL AND COURTEOUS SERVICE__ - Agents are busy all the time and may seem a little rushed on the phone when you speak to them, but they should never be rude or abrupt with you. They should also be expected to return your phone calls within a reasonable amount of time, and you should do likewise.

WHAT YOU SHOULDN'T EXPECT FROM YOUR AGENCY

There are things that agents are not obligated to do for you:

__GIVE ADVANCES__ - In the modeling world some agencies do give advances but not for actors. Your agent is not Bank of New City and will not give out loans of any sort.

__BE A PSYCHOLOGIST, MOTHER, FATHER, ETC__ - If you need a place to crash, do not expect your agent to put up a tent for you. Your agent also doesn't want to be called in the middle of the night because you had a fight with your boyfriend or girlfriend.

__GIVE YOU A RIDE ANYWHERE__ - If your car doesn't work, don't expect to borrow the agent's car to go to an audition. And don't expect them to call taxi services or tow trucks for you, or to pick you up anywhere.

These are just some of the things you shouldn't expect, but every agency is different. Some agents may do some of these things for you if you are in trouble, but don't always count on it.

EXTRA WORK

There are pros and cons to doing extra work. So let's start with the pros first. If you've never been on a movie or TV set, this is a great way to familiarize yourself with what goes on behind the scenes. It can be frightening to get your first real movie or TV job when you have never been on a set before. As an extra, many times you can watch different scenes being filmed, so when you get your first job, everything won't seem foreign to you.

Since you'll spend *a lot* of time waiting to be called onto the set, use this time to meet other actors (who are extras) and continue building up your network of acting friends.

Now for the cons. From what I've heard no one in this industry, including working actors, thinks highly of extras. Anyone can be an extra; it takes no skill at all. Sometimes people are just pulled off the street for atmosphere if additional extras are needed. The amount of time that extras wait can be absolutely boring. Then you may not even be used because they've decided to use other extras instead. You still get paid whether or not you work, but it can feel like a waste of your time.

The money isn't all that great, either. I once did an extra job and was quoted $40 for an eight-hour day. Well, by the time I subtracted money for taxes, taxi fare plus tip and public transportation, I was left with a scant $15. Union extras are paid more, but then there are membership fees and dues to be considered, so unless you are constantly doing extra work, I don't think it's a good move financially to join the Screen Extras Guild.

Sometimes extras are treated poorly. I've heard two different stories relating to extras. The first story is about an actor who was talking to an extra on a movie set but didn't know the man's role. The actor asked the man what part he was playing in the movie and he replied that he was an extra. When the actor heard that, he had a completely different attitude toward the extra, stopped talking to him and left.

Normally on a movie extras are allowed to eat the same food as the principals (speaking actors). Well on this particular production, one of the assistant directors told the extras that they would have to wait to see if the principals wanted second helpings before the extras could help themselves. One extra said he was so insulted that he just went to a restaurant for lunch.

I think one of the reasons many actors do extra work is in the hope that a director or producer will spot them among the hundreds of other extras and upgrade them to a speaking role. That doesn't happen very often. Here's why: say you're on a movie set as an extra and out of nowhere, the producer walks over to you and tells you that he wants you to speak a couple of lines. Last minute changes, he tells you. Well, of course, you are elated because now you'll be able to get your SAG card since it was a union job. (See Chapter 4 for more on the unions.)

But let's say that someone finds out about this and complains to the union. Now the producer has to explain to the union why he hired an extra, rather than one of their 70,000 out-of-work union actors. If he doesn't have a good reason, he'll be fined. He can't just say that you looked fantastic for the part. On the other hand, if the same movie was shot in the jungle, and they used you, the producer would have a better reason for hiring you. They wouldn't necessarily have been able to shut down the set and audition union actors for a two-word part. It costs too much money to shut down a set.

If you have done extra work, remember to leave it off your resume, otherwise you'll be typecast as an extra and won't be taken seriously as an actor especially in Los Angeles. Also it wouldn't be a good idea to spend a great deal of time pursuing extra work if you want to be a serious actor. Even trying to get extra work is time consuming, and usually not very profitable. You may want to do a couple of extra jobs until you get a feel for movie or TV sets, but keep pursuing your *real* career.

In the reference section there are listings for businesses that cast for extra work. It is for the Los Angeles area because this is where most of the movie and TV work is cast. If you don't live in Los Angeles, a lot of times you can find extra work in the trade papers or newspapers. If you're a member of the union AFTRA or SEG, many times extra castings are routed through those channels.

There are some extra casting offices that will charge you a fee to register with them. They will generally guarantee you work. Since anyone can work as an extra, it's easy for these offices to guarantee work, so it's up to you whether you want to pay this fee. If you're going to do only one or two extra jobs, it wouldn't be a good idea financially to pay to get work that would be easy to get on your own. Instead register with agencies that don't charge for finding you this work or just find extra work on your own.

CHAPTER THREE

AGENTS - MODELS

Many books start out by talking about all the glamour and money that's involved in modeling. But you'll get neither glamour nor money if you end up in the wrong hands. There are lots of stories of young girls and guys who travel to Los Angeles or New York in the hopes of being a model. Then they either end up in pornography, prostitution or get ripped off. Many of these models didn't really know whom to talk to or where to begin.

An agent will be the first person who can help get your career going in the right direction. But if you're not familiar with the proper way of getting an agent or the requirements needed to get into modeling, you may have a frustrating time. So let's start from the beginning.

BASIC REQUIREMENTS NEEDED TO
BREAK INTO MODELING

Maybe you're an attractive person and have thought about putting those good looks to work. But unless you are a certain height, weight and so on, you'll have a better chance at becoming a doctor or lawyer than trying to be a model.

There are many reasons why models have to be a certain height and weight. One of the main reasons is that if outfits had to be altered for each model, photo shoots and fashion shows would take forever to get off the ground. So it's easier on everyone if models are a certain height and weight.

But over the past years the fashion industry has also come to realize that not every consumer who buys clothes is tall and thin. To accommodate them, there have been some changes, such as adding petite and full-figured lines to different designers' collections. Even so, the high fashion models still get the majority of the work, but hang in there because you never know what will happen in the years to come. In the meantime, though, you still need to possess certain requirements to get anywhere in your modeling career. Here is the breakdown of the requirements you need to break into modeling.

49

Height

HIGH FASHION: 5'9" to 5'11" for women, and 6'0" to 6'2" for men.
JUNIOR: 5'2" to 5'7" for girls, and 5'11" to 6'2" for boys.
PETITE: 5'4" to 5'7" for women. No height for men is listed because there really isn't a demand for petite men.
PLUS SIZE: 5'9" to 6'0" for women, and 6'0" to 6'2" for men.
CHILDREN: There are no heights listed because usually when a client calls looking for child models, he or she doesn't ask for a certain height. Instead he or she asks for children who can fit into certain clothes sizes.

Weight

HIGH FASHION: 110 to 125 pounds for women, and 160 to 170 pounds for men.
JUNIOR: 100 to 110 pounds for girls. Junior boys see "Look" interview below for your weight requirements.
PETITE: 105 to 115 pounds for women.
PLUS SIZE: See below on Clothes section.
CHILDREN: There are no specific weight requirements, as each child is different, but they shouldn't be overweight. (Although some agents have been known to take plump children, these agents are few and far between. They are the exception, not the rule.)

Also, keep in mind you don't want to be the heaviest weight on this chart in your category if you are also the shortest height. So if you're a high fashion model and 5'9", you wouldn't want to weigh 125 pounds, just keep it in moderation. And before going on any weight reducing or gaining diet, be sure to consult your doctor first.

LOOK AGENCY

"Junior boys should be able to fit into a size 38 to 40 jacket. Usually when a boy outgrows a size 16 jacket he's really out of work until he fits the junior level which is 5'11" to 6'2". Sometimes exceptions are made if the boy is really handsome, but there really isn't enough work for a junior model between 5'5" to 5'10", says Al Lacayo.

"As far as weight goes, it's just what size they're wearing. A boy can work up to a size 16, then he needs to graduate to the junior department because there is little work in between sizes 16 and 38. So in order to keep working, boys need to move up to fit into a size 38 to 40 jacket," replied Brad Fox.

Measurements

* Women and Girls - Your waist measurements should be 10 inches smaller than your bust, and your hips should be the same size as your bust.

* Men - You should have broad shoulders (not as wide as a football player's but you look good wearing a jacket or shirt), and a narrow waist and hips.

* Children - There aren't specific measurements for children.

Clothes Sizes

The clothing industry has changed over the past years. Pants, dresses, shirts and jackets used to all be different sizes. Now that has changed, so when an agency says that a model has to fit into a size 8, they mean for pants, dresses, shirts and jackets.

HIGH FASHION: Size 6 to 8 for women. Men should be able to wear a size 40 jacket along with a 32" to 34" inseam. For shirts the sizes are 15 1/2, 32, 33 and 35, depending on the height of the model.
JUNIOR: Size 3 to 7 for girls.
PETITE: Size 5 to 7 for women.
PLUS SIZE: Size 12 to 16 for women (although some agents have been known to take models all the way up to size 22). Men should be able to fit into a jacket size of 44.
CHILDREN: One agent with whom I spoke said that the sizes for children depend on the clients' needs at the time. Most of the sizes are anywhere from a size 3 for toddlers, and sizes 5, 8 and 10 for girls. For boys, the sizes are usually 12 and 14 with a jacket size of 10 or 12. Little boys sizes are usually 4 or 5 with a jacket size of 5 or 6.

Advice to Men: Although it's nice to work out and keep in shape, remember that overworking on the weights to increase your muscle mass is OK only to a point. If you can't fit into the jacket sizes mentioned because you're too buffed, you'll probably have to lose some of it or you won't be working as a model. So if you can't fit into the sizes mentioned above, tone down a little before you start looking for an agent.

Age

Agents have told me that models can start their modeling careers as early as possible, since the modeling industry thrives on the youthful look. But they also advise against starting your career too early unless you can handle the demands of both school and modeling.

51

This is why some models wait until they're out of high school when they are about age 18 to get their careers going. Which is actually the perfect age, because instead of having to concentrate on the following day's history test, you can concentrate on your modeling career. For parents getting their child or baby into modeling, you can start them out as young as you like. Some agents take babies as young as 3 months old.

Keep in mind that not all agencies have the same requirements as mentioned above for height, weight, measurements and clothes sizes—even in New York. For instance, one New York agency with whom I spoke said that they take high fashion female models starting at 5'8". But for the most part the majority of the big New York agencies said that the ideal high fashion model height starts at 5'9" for women and 6'0" for men. Even so, you may want to do a survey of the agencies within your area to see what their specific requirements are.

OTHER REQUIREMENTS

Before you start taking pictures to send to agents, there are a couple of things you should look over and take care of, if necessary.

Hair

If you're thinking about getting a new hairstyle, it would be a good idea to wait until you have an agent. What if you get your hair cut short and the new trend is long hair? If your hair is ratty looking, just get it trimmed for now, and once you have an agent, you'll be told if you need to do something different to your hair. If you dye your hair, make sure the roots aren't showing, and if you have premature grey hair, cover it.

Complexion

If your face has any blemishes, clear them up. If the blemishes are out of control, consider going to a dermatologist. You want to look your best in these pictures. Don't worry about warts, moles or scars. Many models you see in magazines have had airbrushing done to remove imperfections. Women: if you have any facial hair (like a moustache), you should bleach it. (There are specific products on the market that will take care of this.) This should be done before taking snapshots.

WHAT MODELS NEED BEFORE SEEKING AN AGENT

When you look your best, that's when you'll be ready to take pictures. Some models may be surprised to hear this, but *you don't need a portfolio or a composite to get the attention of an agency*. All you need are a couple of unretouched snapshots done with a Polaroid camera taken by a friend, relative or anyone who knows how to operate a camera.

When shooting snapshots there are three different poses you will need to include. A headshot, profile, and a full body shot.

Headshot

This picture shows the agent what your face and neck look like, so it should be taken from the waist or neck up. Show as much enthusiasm and energy as you can in this picture. And be sure to smile! If you don't, they may wonder about the condition of your teeth.

Leave glasses and contact lenses off (they reflect light). Don't wear jewelry, hats or shades. Make sure agents can see your eyes and eyebrows. If you have long bangs, either cut them a little or comb them back.

If you're wearing makeup, be sure to go light on it. Flip through some of the magazine ads and see how natural looking most of the models look. You want agents to notice your face, not your makeup job. By the way, it's not really necessary to hire a professional makeup/hair stylist. Agents can judge your potential as a model without that extra help. So save your money until it's time to do professional pictures.

Profile

There's nothing to this one except turning to the side and clicking the camera. If you have long hair, you might want to pull it up, or brush it to the side that's away from the camera lens, so that agents can also see your neck.

Full Body Shot

Women and Girls

This picture needs to show off your overall body structure including arms, shoulders, waist, hips and thighs. Stay away from baggy clothes. Try a one-piece bathing suit (you don't need to be tanned), tennis outfit, miniskirt and blouse or any other outfit that shows off the body structure. Agents need to be able to see how well you can wear clothes. However, stay away from lingerie or revealing clothes.

If you are a plus model, you don't need to bother with wearing a bathing suit or miniskirt, instead stick to pants and shirt combinations or a flattering dress. Agents are more concerned with how you wear outfits than in your body structure.

Men and Boys

Agents want to see what your body structure is and how you wear clothes, so keep this in mind when selecting your outfits.

Children

You don't need to put your child in a miniskirt or swimming trunks because agents aren't as concerned with the body structure as they are with adults. A clean pressed outfit will do.

Everyone

When you're doing your headshot, profile and full body shot, you should take enough pictures, so that you have several shots of each pose to send to agents. Agents generally have enough experience to judge a model's potential based on one picture. But you should give them at least two or three pictures of each pose to give a little more information on which to judge. You don't need to be posed in your full body shot, so have fun and be creative, but make sure that the agent can clearly see you.

Also, avoid wearing black, white, or red clothes in your pictures. Black makes some people look harsh, white can give you a washed-out look and red can take away from you too much. Instead, choose colors in the medium-to-light range. Avoid shirts that have turtlenecks, textures, patterns, shiny fabrics and fur-lined necks. You don't want your clothes to upstage you. Whatever you do, don't run out and buy a new outfit for this photo session. You will look better wearing something you've worn before and feel comfortable in.

TIPS ON SHOOTING PICTURES

* If you're shooting outdoors shoot either early or late in the day. Avoid shooting in direct sunlight, it can cause you to squint.
* Try out as many different hairstyles, makeup, clothes and looks as possible, so you have more from which to choose.
* Use color film rather than black-and-white.
* Don't get fancy using mists, elaborate lighting or background features. You don't want anything to draw attention away from you. Keep it simple and conservative.

When you're doing your pictures it would be to your advantage to take them with a Polaroid camera because they'll develop right in front of you and you can keep shooting until you like what you see. If you don't have this particular camera, it would be a good idea to take at least several rolls of film at once. You don't want to keep running to

54

the print shop getting pictures developed.

When you're looking over the finished pictures, examine them closely and ask yourself:

* Are the pictures clear and sharp?

* Do you have any bruises on your arms or legs that you didn't notice before?

* Is your hair in your face or eyes?

* If you're wearing makeup, is it natural looking and not caked on? Is it too lightly applied? (There's a fine line between wearing too much and not wearing enough.)

* Is there something in the background that will distract attention from you? (Brother Bob mowing the lawn in the background isn't going to help the focus to remain on you.)

* On the headshots, will the agents be able to see your face clearly or were you too far away from the camera lens?

If you're not satisfied, either keep taking pictures or try again in a couple of days. Remember, these pictures may get you an agent so you want them to compliment you as much as possible.

When you have satisfactory pictures, go to the print shop and have several sets made, according to the number of agents to whom you'll be sending them.

HOW TO FIND A LEGITIMATE MODELING AGENCY

Unlike actors, models don't have to be with a franchised agency. What you should be looking for is a legitimate, stable agency. Below are some suggestions to help you achieve this:

1) The first thing you should do is to get your phone book (use several different cities if you need to) and flip to the modeling section. But watch out for agencies that don't represent models in the traditional sense, such as porno agencies and escort services. (For more on this see the "Pornography" section in Chapter 12.) Next, make a list of all the agencies to which you want to send your pictures.

2) To find out if the agencies you're interested in are licensed, you would follow the same procedure for Number Two and Three in Chapter 2 under, "How To Find A Legitimate Acting Agency."

If your state doesn't license talent agencies, you will have to take a different route to find established agencies. Your first choice is to try to get representation with a franchised agency that also handles models, provided you have franchised agencies in your area. Then you can be assured that you're with an agency that's pretty dependable because the union isn't going to franchise a fly-by-night agency.

But since this route may not always work for any number of reasons, what you'll then need to do is to take the list of agencies you have compiled and call as many of the businesses mentioned below as possible to find out what agencies they deal with. For example, it would be better to call many ad agencies rather than just one because the one ad agency you call may only deal with one or two agencies. If you have 20 agencies on your list you want to make sure you're not excluding legitimate agencies. Be sure to contact each business below. You don't want to call just ad agencies and photographers; you want your survey to be thorough.

What you'll want to do after doing your survey is to start matching the agencies the businesses deal with to the ones on your list. Don't be surprised if your list dwindles substantially because legitimate agencies will be known within your community, whereas fly-by-night agencies won't.

* Try local advertising agencies.
* Check with photographers.
* Call major department stores.
* Check with local casting directors; they're always dealing with agents.
* Local television stations may be helpful because sometimes they hire from local agencies for fashion shows or commercials.
* If you have any trade papers in your area, call them to see if they can recommend any agencies.
* Some of the bigger cities have Convention Centers. (These are located under "Convention" in the phone book.) Call and ask the Center if they can send you a list of the different vendors who participate in the shows. Then contact these vendors and ask which agencies they deal with. Not all vendors hire talent for their shows, but there are some that do.
* If your state has franchised talent agencies, ask around to see if they can recommend some modeling agencies for your area. Even if they don't handle models or you aren't able to get representation through them, they can still help recommend other agencies.
* Check with modeling schools.

When you are looking for agency representation and come across an agency advertising in the newspaper or trade paper looking for models (either because they need new faces or have work available), proceed with caution unless the agency is licensed and/or franchised. Many ads to which I've responded appear to be making a profit from the money they collect for registration, portfolios, classes or other fees. Many of them skip town with everyone's money, never to be heard from again.

CONTACTING AGENCIES

There are two ways to meet an agent: "Open Call" and "Mail Submissions." If you are a petite or plus model, or a parent getting your child into modeling, make sure that the agencies you're interested in handles your type before going to open call or mailing your pictures. Not all of them do, or they may only handle a small number.

Open Call

Most agencies allocate several hours each week just to look at new models. Call the agencies on your list (the ones that you have previously checked out) and ask if, and when, they have open call. If some of these agencies don't have open call, see below on Mail Submissions.

When you go to an open call be sure to take your snapshots. If you have a resume take it. Don't worry if you don't have a resume because most agencies will ask you to fill out a form that will ask for your height, weight, clothing size and additional information.

When you finish filling out your form, you'll wait with many other models until it's your turn to see the agent.

Mail Submissions

For agencies that don't have open call, you'll have to send your pictures along with a cover letter. Below are some other things you may want to do before sending out your pictures.

* Call and confirm the name and mailing addresses of the agents to whom you'll be sending your pictures.

* You should also find out who handles new models' submissions. When you call, get the correct spelling of the name and the sex of the person to whom you'll be sending your submission. For example, the name "Lynn" could belong to a man or woman, and some people get very offended when you misspell their name or address them by the wrong sex.

* You'll also need to get some envelopes to hold your snapshots, a self-addressed, stamped envelope (SASE), cover letter and resume. If you have mailing labels, type on it the agency's name and address, the name of the agent who handles new models' submissions and your return address. (Be sure to address the return envelope, also.) Then write "Fragile: Photos Inside" on both envelopes and stamp both of them with the *correct* postage.

Sometimes the cover letter and snapshots have a way of separating, so it would be a good idea to include your name, vital statistics and a way for the agency to contact you on the back of each photo. You don't want an agency that wants to set up an interview with you to be without a way of contacting you.

Depending on the agency's schedule, you'll usually receive a call or letter within two weeks telling you whether or not they're interested in meeting you. Most agents prefer that you don't call them if it takes longer, because lots of things can slow agent's down. You will hear from them one way or another. If you don't receive a response from some of them after a couple of weeks, try sending those particular agencies another submission. Some of your original submissions might have been lost in the mail.

PAUL NELSON - CITY MODELS

"Normally we try to get to our mail submissions within one to two weeks, depending on how busy we are. Sometimes we even have to take them home to do it. We don't want pictures sitting around for a month or so, because if there's a model in the pile who is really good, we want to catch that person. But models really shouldn't call to see why we haven't responded because we get up to 20 submissions a day, and it's difficult to remember all the people who have sent in pictures. If a model calls and says he or she sent a submission a week ago, it would take us forever to go through the pile and see who the model is. Then we would also need to look over the pictures and decide if we wanted to represent that model. This would be too difficult to do over the phone, so we usually just tell them that if we're interested, they will hear from us."

A good idea would also be to keep a record of each agency to whom you send pictures, including the date you sent the submission, what type of response you received, whether or not you did any follow-up and what type of response was generated. This way you won't inadvertently call an agency that you called the previous week and try to get an interview with them. You might already have an appointment with them for the following day. Then the agency might wonder just how organized you really are.

RESUMES

The object of a resume is to tell the reader about your vital statistics, training and experience. If you don't have any training or experience, don't worry, practically all new models starting out don't have a resume. Yet models can still interest an agent without having one.

If you have enough training and experience to fill out a resume, there is a sample of a model's resume in the Appendix you can review. For some helpful tips on resumes, see Chapter 2 under "Tips on Resumes," but disregard the last five tips and the format because they only apply to actors.

If you have a small amount of training or experience—say you've just graduated from a modeling school or are a member of your school's gymnastic or cheerleading team—mention that along with your vital statistics in your cover letter. There is a sample of a model's cover letter in the Appendix. (For Information on children's resumes, see Chapter 2.)

COVER LETTER

A cover letter introduces you to the agent and tells him or her that you're looking for modeling representation. In your cover letter, or on anything you send to potential agents for that matter (such as your snapshots), you should use caution when giving out your home address or home phone number. Your pictures will pass through many hands and may even wind up in the trash can and in the wrong hands. So if you have a post office box and an answering service, by all means use it. Be sure you check your service and mail frequently if you choose this route.

BEFORE THE INTERVIEW

Whether you're meeting the agent in person for open call or for a personal interview, you still haven't been signed to the agency yet. Besides asking questions, agents have other reasons for wanting to meet you in person, rather than just signing you off a photograph. So study these next items carefully. Agents will be looking at:

  *** *YOUR OVERALL APPEARANCE* - For women, a dress, pant-suit or skirt and blouse will do. A pair of slacks and a shirt, or even a suit and tie will do nicely for men. Both men and women should avoid wearing jeans because they don't look as professional. But children can wear anything, even jeans, just so long as there are no rips or patches on the jeans.

  The above were just suggestions. If you come up with different ideas for an outfit make sure that it's clean and pressed. If you're dressed sloppily or unprofessionally, the agent will think that this is how you'll be representing their agency on go-sees and jobs. Plus you will be competing with many other models, and you don't want to stand out by wearing an outfit that's dirty or wrinkled. In the modeling industry, especially, because you are constantly being judged on your appearance.

  *** *YOUR HEIGHT, WEIGHT AND MEASUREMENTS* - Agents will be rechecking these statistics so keep in shape. You don't want to write in your cover letter or on the agency's form that you weigh 120 pounds, if your weight is 130 pounds.

* **FOR WOMEN** - Is your makeup flattering and natural looking? You don't need to be a professional makeup artist, but you may want to enlist the opinion of friends or family. Ask them what they think of your makeup job.

DEANNA ALLEN - J. MICHAEL BLOOM AGENCY

"One thing models need to check out before visiting an agency is their appearance. Modeling is a business based on looks and appearance, and if the models are going to walk into an agency looking like they've slept in their clothes, it's not going to make a very good impression. Women should also watch their makeup usage, many models come into our agency with way too much on, and it looks unnatural."

* **YOUR HANDS AND NAILS** - Are the nails well manicured and polished? (If you don't have a color that complements your outfit, stick with clear polish.) Men: you also should take notice of your hand-and-nail condition. Are your hands chapped and rough looking? Could your nails use a manicure? They aren't just for women.

* **YOUR HAIR** - Is it clean and well styled? If your hair has grown out since you last took your pictures, and the style looks ragged, have it trimmed. And watch out for oily hair, dandruff, roots that show, or premature gray hair.

* **YOUR COMPLEXION** - Is your face clean and clear looking? They will be scrutinizing your face so make sure that it looks good. You might even give yourself a facial the night before (men, too). Your face will look better, and for women, makeup will glide on easier.

* **YOUR PERSONALITY** - Many agents told me that this is an area in which many models are lacking. Some agents have received pictures sent in by models who have a lot of potential, but when the model comes in to meet the agent, he or she has no life or enthusiasm to them. Usually the model just kind of sits there and has no personality at all. Even if you're a shy person, you can still drum up a little bit of zest and energy. If you come across as dull and lifeless, you might prevent yourself from getting an agent.

JOANNE GUNTON - ZOLI AGENCY

"Personality plays a big role in a model's career. Some clients book more based on personality than they do on looks because they'd rather work with a fun loving, outgoing model, than another with a bland personality. Most agents look for energy and aliveness because that's what sells clients. Modeling does not just entail being 5'9"; there are other qualities involved. There are thousands of models out there but it's the ones who stand out from the crowd that make it."

DO'S AND DON'TS WHEN MEETING AN AGENT

Don't

* Wear lots of jewelry. This is distracting for agents, and they can't see your neck and hands if you look like a jewelry shop.
* Be pushy, rude or obnoxious to anyone. (The receptionist could be the agent's daughter just filling in for the day.) Treat others as you would want to be treated.
* Smoke cigarettes, wear shades, eat or chew gum. Since you want to look as professional as possible, sitting there eating a ham sandwich while chugging a soda isn't going to go over too well.
* Go to see an agent, or any industry person in the acting or modeling business, after you've been drinking alcohol or taking drugs. They may get the impression that you have a drug or alcohol problem. It's OK to be nervous, industry people will understand this, but don't go out and get intoxicated because of it.

Do

* Be on time if you have a specific appointment. If you're late, the agent will wonder whether you'll be late to go-sees, auditions and jobs. If an emergency comes up, call and explain the situation, and reschedule the appointment.
* Bring whomever or whatever the agent tells you to bring. And if you're not sure, ask, because if you are under 18, they may want one of your parents to be there.
* Leave all personal problems at home, or go on another day.

MEETING THE AGENT

When you are ushered in to meet the agent, be friendly and smile, show that you're happy to be there not as if you forced yourself to go. Be prepared to talk a little bit about yourself and answer such questions as, "Why do you want to be a model?" "What do you like to do in your spare time?" "Would you be willing to dye or cut your hair if we accepted you?" "Would you be willing to travel overseas?" "Why did you choose this agency?" Agents like to hear more than one-word answers, but on the other hand, they don't want you to spend 20 minutes answering one question. Most appointments with agents will only last about 10 minutes, so you want to make the strongest impression in the shortest amount of time. When you're answering questions, be sure to direct the answers to the agent, not to the ceiling or the floor or the picture hanging above their head.

As was said before, they will be checking out your personality, so from the moment you walk into the agency till you walk out the front door, turn on the energy. Remember that looking good is not the only reason models are successful in this business. A client would much rather work with a less experienced model who has lots of energy, enthusiasm and is fun to work with, than another model who's been all over the world and has lots of experience, but is dull, boring and treats modeling like just another job.

Along with checking out your personality, they will also be looking at your sales ability and how you come across at the interview. If you're enthusiastic, outgoing and have a charming personality, they'll figure you'll come across this way to the clients. And since most clients see literally hundreds of models every day who have similar appearances and personalities, every little thing you can do that's different from other countless models will make you stand out and leave a good impression.

But don't go against how you really are. If you're shy and reserved, don't force yourself to be extroverted. Sometimes it's just the reverse with clients who have seen bubbly, outgoing models all day and then you come along and you're different. So your reserve could be very refreshing to them. Whatever your personality, just turn it up a couple of notches.

WHAT YOU CAN EXPECT AFTER MEETING THE AGENT

After you meet the agent, there are many different things he or she might say to you. Below are just a few of the possible outcomes. Even if you don't receive the answer that you want to hear, you should still thank the agent for their time.

* The agent may decide to represent you.

* You may be asked to come back and meet their partner or other colleagues. The person you met may initially screen all potential candidates and not do the actual signing of new models.

* The agent may recommend you try a different agency with which you might be more compatible.

* The agent could tell you to do something different—like cut or grow your hair—then take new pictures and come back. This is a good sign. An agency wouldn't have you do this if you didn't have potential.

* The agent could also just thank you and tell you that he or she will get in touch if interested in representing you.

If you are accepted into the agency, make sure that there are no strings attached, such as fees for registration (see Chapter 2 under "How an Agent Gets Paid"), classes or portfolios. (For more on this, see Chapter 7 under "What You Don't Know About Agency Classes," and Chapter 5 under "Using an Agency's Photographer vs. Your Own.")

62

WHY MODELS HAVE DIFFICULTY GETTING AN AGENT

It's easier to get answers from agents when you meet them in person. But since that may not always be the case, here are a few of the main reasons why you may be rejected.

* *YOUR LOOK* - Just being a certain height doesn't mean every agency will want to represent you. Each agency handles a particular look and style. While one agency may handle models with slender bodies, another may handle more athletic-looking models.

* *YOUR TYPE OR AGE* - Agents who represent models on the side such as petite, plus and children, may handle only a few models. So the agency may have enough and is not presently looking for new models.

* *YOUR FACE OR BODY* - It could be that you have a big nose, crooked teeth, your eyes aren't set wide enough or your body isn't well-proportioned. But until you have an opinion from an agency, don't run out for plastic surgery or the dentist just yet, because you don't know if this is the problem and it could be a costly mistake.

* *YOUR SNAPSHOTS* - You may also want to look over the pictures you are sending out. Are they flattering? Do they show you off the best way? How is your choice of outfits? Is your weight where it's supposed to be? How is your complexion?

There are many other reasons why getting representation may be difficult. So hang in there and keep trying. This industry is strange: one week you are rejected by everyone and the following week you're in demand. If you feel new pictures would help, then take some and send them out. The main word in the entertainment business is "perseverance."

PAUL NELSON - CITY MODELS

"If models are having difficulty getting an agent, many times it has to do with their look. Of course there are eighty million other reasons. Sometimes it's the personality. The agent could have in their possession a fantastic-looking guy or girl, but maybe they're real jerks or stuck on themselves. Sometimes the agency tries to work with them for a couple weeks or months and see what happens. A lot of the other reasons have to do with the height, hair, eyes, nose or the mouth."

But let's say you send out new pictures and you still get negative responses. If none of the agencies in your area provide open call where you could at least get an opinion, the other possible alternative would be, provided that you have the right requirements to be a model—down to your weight—would be to personally seek the opinion of an agent. Sure, maybe the agencies in your area don't want models just walking into their offices unannounced, but if you were to call and try to set up an appointment with them, they would just tell you to send in your

63

pictures. So dress as professionally as possible and, using your charming personality, go into an agency and try to get an opinion.

If this suggestion doesn't work, you could try getting the opinion of a fashion photographer, because they are usually in tune with what the agencies like and what types of models the industry is currently using.

When you do go asking for opinions, my advice is stay away from agencies that have schools attached. Otherwise they may tell you that you have a lot of potential, but that it needs to be developed and then they may try selling you a course at their school. Even if you do go through their school, most of the time you still don't get representation by that agency. Then you are not only back at Square One, but you're out all that money.

I know it may be difficult to find an agency without a school attached. In some areas every agency has a school. If that's the case, you can still visit these agencies, but if they try selling you a course at their school, then you might want to stick with getting opinions from fashion photographers. They are second best to an agent's opinion. But watch out for photographers who tell you that you have lots of potential, and then try to sell you a portfolio. You don't need a portfolio until you have an agent.

If you are told that you have potential, then keep trying. If you really want to be a model then sooner or later you'll get an agent. And in the meantime:

* Keep on top of your appearance, such as the condition of your weight, hair, hands, nails and complexion.

* Read fashion magazines to keep abreast of the different looks and styles.

* Practice different sitting, standing and reclining poses. Many photographers with whom I spoke said that most new models have no knowledge of posing. So it would be to your advantage to learn some poses, which can be found by looking through different catalogs and magazines.

DO MODELS NEED AN AGENT?

NEW YORK

In New York you won't work unless you have an agency behind you. Ad agencies, photographers and other industry people are too busy to deal with free-lancers when all they have to do is call an agency and tell them specifically what they are looking for and the agency takes care of the rest. The way that some of the clients have set up their bookkeeping will prevent paying anyone without a federal ID number or who does not have an agency behind them.

If you want your career to thrive you need an agency. They have access to all the big jobs, whereas a free-lancer would never have that kind of information. Even if you did, it would be difficult to book a go-see. Let's say, for example, a friend of yours who is a model told you about a big print job for a jeans company. So you called the ad agency and told them you wanted to set up an appointment to show them your portfolio. They don't know what you look like over the phone, and even if they did, they may wonder why you don't have an agent. Some of the things that might occur to them is that you're not tall enough or you're not "model material." Or maybe you did have an agent but got thrown out for not showing up on time for jobs. Plus most free-lancers do not have the knowledge of billing or negotiating contracts that an agency has. It would be wise not to expect an ad agency or client to take the time to explain it to you.

Most agencies also have contacts overseas and in other modeling centers such as Los Angeles, Chicago, Miami, Atlanta, San Francisco and Texas. The more a model travels, the more money he or she makes. Agents are sure to be very aware of the latest and future trends in the fashion industry. They will negotiate a model's earnings to make sure the model gets paid fairly. In addition, they book appointments, bill clients, promote a model's career, make sure that the people a model works for are legitimate and gives advice on makeup, diet and wardrobe. The list goes on and on. If you were to free-lance, you have to take care of all these details yourself—and that would leave you precious little time to focus on modeling.

OTHER CITIES

Even if you do not live in New York, eventually you will need an agent to help launch your career. Just because you live in Wyoming or North Dakota doesn't mean that you would not reap benefits from having an agent. Many small town agencies do business with their counterparts in other markets as well as overseas locations. Some of the smaller cities don't have a great deal of modeling work, and if agents had to live on just the commissions they received from model's local work, they'd quickly starve. (I believe that this is another reason that so many of them also run schools.) But the agent can earn more money by promoting models to their agency contacts throughout the country and overseas.

By the way, your agency should never attempt to charge you a referral fee when dealing with their contacts overseas and in other cities. Legitimate agencies don't charge "referral" or "finder fees" to get interviews for their models with other agents.

GETTING ACCEPTED

When you are accepted by an agency, the first thing they will usually ask you to do is sign contracts or a power of attorney. Then you may be asked to go through an orientation to introduce you to the bookers and other staff. They will also explain to you such items as vouchers, model releases, go-sees and other industry items. Most agencies won't send you out on go-sees for the first couple of days until you've had a chance to build up your portfolio. Then over the following days the agency or you will arrange to meet with different photographers to test. (For more on Testing and Portfolios, see Chapter 6.)

CONTRACTS

Agencies differ when it comes to the issue of contracts but most of the larger ones in the major modeling centers will exclusively sign their models. Smaller agencies may either sign you exclusive or nonexclusive. The agency may even wait to see if you progress past the testing board. They may want to hear the feedback from other clients and people with whom you work before making any kind of commitment.

If you are not asked to sign contracts, they may request that you sign a *power of attorney*. Be sure you read this as carefully as you would read over all your contracts before signing any of them. Most powers of attorney are quite straightforward and allow the agency to act in matters such as collecting and endorsing checks received. They then turn the money over to you after taking their commission. They are also allowed to book appointments and interviews as well as negotiate rates and contracts. But keep in mind that not all powers of attorney are this straightforward and may give the agency power to do things you may regret.

If an agency wants you to sign exclusively with them and you live in a small town, you might want to think twice before doing it. Why? Because if you are signed exclusive to one agency, you won't be able to get go-sees from others. That is fine if you are signed with an agency in a city that's a center of modeling work. But if you live in a small town that doesn't have very much modeling work to begin with, you may be cutting yourself off from extra jobs if you sign an exclusive contract, because no one agency gets calls for all the jobs. But if you sign a nonexclusive contract, then you are still free to receive go-sees and jobs from other agencies as long as you are also not exclusively signed with them as well.

One of the advantages to having an exclusive contract is that the agency will usually work harder to get you bookings since they are your only agency. On the other hand, if you are not exclusively commited to

66

an agency, they may not work as hard.

If you want to add or delete *anything* from your contracts, it is recommended that you consult an attorney before doing it. Attorneys can help you with all the legal formalities. They can also help you to understand every word of your contract by pointing out the pros and cons of what you'll be signing and explaining the sometimes difficult "legalese."

If you do sign a contract or power of attorney, be sure to get a copy of it to keep in a safe place.

Outclause

When you sign a contract, you are signing yourself over to the agency for a certain amount of time, usually anywhere from one to three years. What the outclause does is allow you or the agent the opportunity to withdraw from the contract after a specified amount of time (usually 91 days) if either party is not satisfied.

For actors, the outclause on union contracts states that if you are signed to a theatrical agent you or your agent may terminate the contract if you don't get 15 days of work in any 91-day period. The contract with a commercial agent can be terminated if you don't earn $2,000 in any 91-day period.

If you are signed with an agency across the board the theatrical outclause would be used. For instance, if you're signed for commercial, film and TV work (across the board) with one agency and you haven't received 15 days of work in any 91-day period, you or your agent can terminate the contract. Even though you are also signed with the commercial department in the same agency, the theatrical outclause would be used in this case.

If you do terminate the contract, be sure to put it in writing to your agency. Don't forget to send one copy to the union if you are an actor and are with a franchised agency. You should, however, refrain from telling the agents how lousy they are, you may work with them again in the future. It's a good idea not to burn any bridges.

QUESTIONS TO ASK YOUR AGENT BEFORE SIGNING CONTRACTS

The best time to ask any questions you may have is *before* signing any contract(s). This way everything can be clarified before the ink dries on the paper. Ask as many questions as you like, and don't feel intimidated about it. Agents often find it refreshing when models ask questions because when you are well-informed you'll often achieve more in your career.

The following questions may not cover everything that can be asked, so feel free to add to this list. Problems always arise when there is a lack of communication. If you have two agencies that want to represent you, asking questions will enable you to compare offers so that you can make an informed decision.

* What will the agency expect from me?

* What can I expect from this agency?

* How will the agency promote my career? How can I help this process?

* Does the agency give monetary advances? If not, how will I be paid? If they do give advances, do they charge interest on them? (See "How Models are Paid" in this chapter.)

* How much of a commission will the agency take from my jobs? If I earn a small amount, will the agency take the same percentage or do they adjust it? (See "How Agents are Paid" in this chapter.)

* Will the agency put any portion of my money into a reserve fund? Will I get interest on my money? (See "How Models are Paid" in this chapter.)

GO-SEES

After you've built up your portfolio, the agency will start sending you to "go-see" different clients, such as art directors, magazine editors, catalog houses, casting directors and fashion coordinators of department stores. A go-see is to a model, what an audition is to an actor.

Your agency will help to prepare you for each go-see, by giving you all the information you'll need to help you do your very best. You will be going out on lots of go-sees until you get established and known in the industry, then clients will call and book you by name. But until then, you will need to go on go-sees in order to get bookings.

Here's what happens at a go-see. (Of course they won't all be the same, but this will give you a basic idea.) Clients will call an agency about a job they're doing, and tell them the type of model they're looking for. Then the agency will send the appropriate models for the job.

The go-see is usually for a specific time, so be sure to be on time and take all necessary tools especially your portfolio and some composites to leave with the client. Expect your visit with clients to be brief; many times you won't be the only model they're seeing. Make a good impression by being friendly and polite. Don't forget to turn on all your energy, charm and sparkle. At the end of your visit, be sure to thank the client for his or her time before leaving a composite as a reminder of you.

It would also be a good idea to keep a record of all go-sees—to write down the date, time, address and phone number, whom you saw, how it went, the type of assignment it was for, and the results: whether or not you got the job. Include anything else you feel is important such as whether you left a composite, what you wore, the time you arrived and left and even directions to the place. This way when your agency calls up about a go-see at the same place, you'll have all the information at your fingertips.

BOOKERS

Another person who acts as a vital link to the agency and model is the booker. This is the person you will frequently be contacting throughout the day. Bookers have many functions to perform in an agency including knowing a model's whereabouts at all times, negotiating rates and contracts for the model, handling client problems, booking jobs, go-sees and auditions, screening calls, making appointments for models with hair dressers, makeup artists and photographers, and sometimes, if necessary, even acting as someone the model can complain to. The list of their duties doesn't conveniently stop there, either. Develop a good working relationship with bookers and remember them on holidays and birthdays.

CHECKING OUT YOUR AGENCY'S BACKGROUND

Before committing yourself to an agency you should check out their background first. Use the same procedure that is in Chapter 2 under "Checking Out Your Agency's Background."

WHEN WOULD A MODEL JOIN THE UNION?

If you get a speaking role on a union job, you would be required to join the appropriate union if the job lasts longer than 30 days or if you receive your second union job 30 days after your first one. If you live in a right-to-work state, you have the right to work without having to join any unions at all.

If you want to pursue acting as well as modeling, you will need to be with a franchised agency provided there are some in your area. So unless you are already with a franchised agency you will need to get a separate agent. You will also have to sign contracts with the acting agency, which you should read over and make sure you get a copy of anything you sign.

PROMOTING A MODEL'S CAREER

Each model is promoted differently according to age, the market your look currently fits and other elements. Promotion also depends on how the model does with testing and if you have enough good pictures for the agent to start sending you out on go-sees.

Some agencies will ship new models off to Europe or Japan (this doesn't apply to children) to build up their portfolios since there are more magazines and opportunities to do so abroad. In the modeling centers such as New York, it is difficult for a new model without a good portfolio to be seen by clients. This is one of the reasons that many agencies have models shoot with a wide variety of photographers. A European photographer is going to have a much different style and technique than an American photographer.

Expect to be traveling a lot as a model, as clients always want to see new pictures, and you won't really be able to accomplish that by staying in your hometown. It is much more exciting for a client to see the same model after he or she has come back from Europe or Japan with new tearsheets and pictures. Agents have told me that sometimes a model will be a hit in a particular city for a certain amount of time, then clients tire of him or her. But after the agency sends the model overseas to shoot some new photos, the model many times finds that he or she is in demand upon returning to the United States.

If your look is the current trend in another city, then your agency will probably ship you there. The average model's career lasts only about five years, so the agent is going to want to promote you as much as possible. Since most models can't make as much money sitting in their hometowns. Expect to be spending a lot of time away from home.

HOW MODELS CAN HELP PROMOTE THEIR CAREERS

The way that models will help promote their careers is different than the way actors would do it. Your best bet would be to get suggestions from your agency as to how they want you to be involved in the promotion aspect of your career.

One thing I should mention here is that if you are scouting the "Help Wanted" sections of newspapers looking for additional bookings, as many models do, a word of caution is advised. Ask yourself this question: why would clients advertise in a daily newspaper for models, when all clients have to do is call up an agency and put in an order? My conclusion is either:

A) The clients aren't going to pay the models or if they do pay it is minimal. Or the models will be given something in exchange for their time, such as a discount on clothes in the clients stores or free samples of cosmetics, shampoos, etc.

70

B) The ad could be a front for a school or a photographer who wants to sell portfolios to models or another type of rip-off scheme. The ad is made to sound as if legitimate work is available. I don't want to imply, however, that all classified ads you see in the newspapers are false and misleading. Just use caution and check things out.

To be on the safe side, tell your agent about any ads, and let him or her try to book you. Your agency is there to help and protect you. Besides, you'll need to notify your agency before accepting any jobs, anyway, in case it already has a booking for you on the same day. You may as well let them call for you. My experience has shown that most modeling jobs advertised in the newspaper aren't worth the time it takes to pursue them.

WHEN SHOULD A MODEL MOVE TO NEW YORK?

It wouldn't be a good idea just to pack up your bags and move to the Big Apple unless you have a New York agency behind you. For one thing, most New York agencies receive anywhere from 10 to 30 pictures per *day* from people all over the country who want to be models.

A smarter and safer way would be to stay in your hometown, get a local agency so you can get experience and make money to help finance a trip to New York. Have your agency promote you to the other markets. You'll get a lot farther if your agent promotes you to agency contacts in New York than if you were simply to move to the city and compete with thousands of unrepresented models.

In addition, there are many living adjustments to be made in New York that models from other cities have never had to deal with. For instance, if you're used to driving everywhere, good luck in New York. You don't drive there, you either walk, take a taxi, subway or bus. It's also expensive and crowded: more than 8,000,000 people live in New York. If you move there you'll need an apartment, which could cost anywhere from $600 to $800 a month for rent, and this would be an apartment to share with a roommate in a fairly decent, safe neighborhood. There's snow to think about in winter and, if you're from a state like California where the weather is warm, this would be another big change.

I'm not trying to put New York down or discourage anyone from moving there. But many models don't look at all the details and end up moving there and fail to get an agent. Then they wind up without money for a plane or bus ticket to return home. Before you move to New York, you'll need money for things like rent, food, transportation, clothes, makeup, phone bills, entertainment and much more. So you will need to save some money before relocating there.

HOW AGENTS ARE PAID

In some states, the agent is allowed up to 25 percent of the model's earnings for each job the model does. If you're not sure how much commission the agencies in your area can take, contact your local Department of Labor. Even if your state doesn't have licensing for agencies, the Labor Department can still help you. Some agencies may adjust the commission depending on what the model earns on a job. So if you make $200 on a job, they may take just 15 percent commission instead of the usual 20 percent.

HOW MODELS ARE PAID

The way your agency pays you depends on its operation. Some agencies will take a percentage of your earnings and pay you right away, with the remaining amount being put in a reserve fund. This money is used as a "rainy day" account and is helpful if the client won't be paying for several months and you need money for the rent. Some agencies, however, don't have reserve fund accounts.

If you opt to keep the reserve money in the agency's bank account, you should make sure that you are receiving interest on it. If not, you're better off collecting the money as soon as it becomes available and putting it in your own bank account.

There are agencies who give advances when necessary but they may also charge a percentage for that luxury. Here's why: say you do a job for $5,000 but the client won't be paying for 45 days. In the meantime, your rent is due the following week. So when you ask the agent for a $1,000 advance against that money, the agent has to go into the bank acount and withdraw the money to give to you, therefore losing interest on the money until the client pays the agency. So they're actually only charging you for the interest they are losing. But make sure that the interest they are charging you is reasonable.

VOUCHERS

Each time you do a job, you will bring a voucher along to be signed by the client, photographer, ad agency, or whomever is in charge. When the job is booked, verify who's supposed to sign it. It's the model's responsibility to fill out the voucher correctly, have it signed by the appropriate person, give a copy to the client, keep one for themselves and turn a copy over to the agency in order to be paid. As one agent said: "No voucher, no money." Jotting down wrong or inaccurate information can cause problems and also hold up your getting paid.

MODEL RELEASE

At the bottom of the voucher it will say something like: "In consideration of the sum stated hereon, I hereby sell, assign and grant to above or those for whom they are acting as indicated above, the right and permission to copyright and/or use and/or publish photographic portraits or pictures of me in which I may be included in whole or in part or composited or reproductions thereof in color or otherwise made through any media at their studios or elsewhere for art, advertising, trade or any other similar lawful purpose whatsoever, for a period of one year, unless otherwise specified."

What this release means is that it gives the client or photographer the right to use the photographs that you're getting paid to do, in the manner and for the length of time specified in the release. If they wish to extend the agreement or change anything on the agreement, they have to renegotiate with the agency.

So if you happen to be at a department store and see your pictures on hanger tags on clothes, and the release you signed gave that client permission to use your pictures only for the Sunday edition of the newspaper, go and tell your agency. Now the client will have to pay the agency and you more money because the pictures are being used in a different way than was specified on the release. This is part of the protection of a model release, but sometimes people will try to sell your pictures in other forms to get more money, without renegotiating with the agency. This doesn't happen too often, however.

If the model is a minor, the parent or guardian will also have to sign the release.

This section is to give you a general idea of what a voucher and a model release are. Since each agency is different, you should have them review its procedure for filling these out and interpreting them when you start working with an agency.

UNDERSTANDING REJECTION

It can be very frustrating to go on go-sees or auditions when you keep getting rejected. Doubt starts creeping into your mind and you start to wonder if you are cut out to be an actor or model. You should persist because you wouldn't have an agency if someone didn't believe you have what it takes. A little understanding of how the industry works might shed some light on the matter.

Here's the scenerio: a company has decided to launch a new perfume and has a particular image in mind for the model or actor it wants to have represent the fragrance. The company at this point will usually turn the model or actor selection over to an ad agency with its suggestions or let the ad agency come up with the whole advertising concept on its own. Let's say the ad agency decides that a blonde, sensuous woman would do justice to the perfume ad. They call up the modeling agencies they deal with and tell them specifically what they're looking for. The agency sends over composites of different models it thinks would fit the part. The ad agency would then pick the models they want to see and call the modeling agency and inform them of its selections.

Each model who is sent on that go-see has a good chance of getting that job. Otherwise the models wouldn't be there. With the image in mind, the ad agency looks over each model and her book and finally picks one model for the job.

Here's another way to think of it: let's say you've been invited to a party and you don't have anything to wear. You mull it over in your mind about who will be there and what kind of party it will be. Finally you come up with an image of what you'd like your outfit to look like— even down to the colors. You picked this image because you felt that it would show you off in the best way much like the ad agency decided on the concept of the blonde model showing the perfume off in the best way.

So off you go to the store to buy the outfit. With the image in mind you go from store to store looking at racks of clothes. Even though they all look good and someday you may even buy them, right now they don't fit the image you have in your mind—like the ad agency or casting director looking over each model or actor. Sometimes you may even settle on something else instead because you feel it will show you off even better—much like clients or casting directors. Many times they have an image in mind of whom they think they want. But then another actor or model comes in, and they end up changing their minds and decide to go with an image they weren't even considering. So instead of that red and black outfit you were so intent on having, you found a green one that would improve your appearance even more. Since you can't wear two dresses to the party, you have to settle on one—just like the ad agency or casting director.

These two different scenarios can be used for both actors and models in understanding rejection a little better. Just because you get rejected doesn't necessarily mean that you're a bad actor or model, it may mean that you don't fit a particular image, like selecting an outfit. And maybe when the ad agency or casting director goes shopping again, they'll pick you.

DRUGS AND ALCOHOL

Modeling and acting are tough businesses to get into, and once you're in, it can be just as tough and frustrating. You need to arm yourself with a lot of resiliency and be able to bounce back from

74

rejection and go on to the next audition or go-see. But many models and actors have a hard time dealing with the lifestyle and get into drugs and/or alcohol. You will kill your career by doing this. Do you think that an ad agency or casting director will want to hire you if you smell like a winery or you're high on drugs? No they won't, and when they start reporting this to your agency, you may be kicked out before you give them a bad name.

Not to mention the fact that it will eventually destroy your looks, stamina, personality and devour your finances. Some models and actors are so hooked on drugs and alcohol that they spend practically all their hard-earned money buying more of these substances. And if you think it will get easier once you become rich and famous, you're wrong. If some of these famous, wealthy actors and models are so happy, then why have so many died of drug and/or alcohol abuse? There's even more responsibility once you become rich and famous. So do yourself and your pocketbook a favor and stay far away from substance abuse.

WHAT AGENTS EXPECT FROM MODELS

Getting accepted by an agency is not the time to start slacking off. Many models don't make it past the testing board of an agency because they don't treat modeling like a business or act professionally. There are literally thousands of models who would love to take your place, and they will replace you if you treat your agency or the industry without respect.

Here are some things told to me by different agencies that are overlooked by models.

KEEP YOUR WEIGHT UNDER CONTROL. A lot of clothes in modeling fit a certain size and if you let your weight go up and can't fit or can barely fit into the clothes, you won't work at all or very little. A model who is not working is not an asset to an agency or to themselves. Also remember that the camera puts an extra 10 pounds on you. This is another reason models have to be so slim. (Of course this depends on what type of model you are.)

* *KEEP YOUR SKIN CLEAR AND CLEAN LOOKING.* Facials at least once a week are necessary if you're modeling quite a bit. Models, especially women, wear layers of makeup even though it doesn't appear that way in pictures. After awhile, all that makeup will clog your skin and cause blemishes if you don't steam open the pores and wash it away. If you're having a problem with blemishes, you may want to see a dermatologist.

* *BE ON TIME.* Leave extra early if you have to, you never know if there will be a traffic jam, the subway will run late or your car will break down, and you'll need to get a ride or catch a taxi. To ensure that

you arrive at your destination on time, when you get booked for a job, be sure and get the directions to the place, phone number of the job site, the name and address of the place and the person you'll need to see when you arrive. Then reconfirm everything: call the place and check their address again, the company might have recently moved and forgot to tell the agency. So then you go to the old address and you're late. (This has happened before.)

To deter a model from being late to jobs some agencies deduct money for each minute the model is late. Sometimes models are put on probation. If the client is paying everyone by the hour, they don't want to have people standing around waiting for the model to arrive.

BE PROFESSIONAL AND COURTEOUS TO EVERYONE. Getting rejected can make you feel resentful and if you start letting it show, you could lose jobs and maybe even your agency. So be pleasant to be around, and more people will want to work with you.

DRESS PROPERLY. This goes for each job or go-see. The way you dress is a reflection on you and your agency, and if something goes wrong, the agent's reputation is on the line. So bring whatever items your agent or booker has told you to bring. If you're not sure, ask.

Another thing that many models tend to overlook is the importance of sleep. Get enough sleep the night before a job or go-see. Save partying until the weekend or when you don't have a job or go-see the next day. Bags underneath your eyes can be airbrushed out, but without sufficient sleep you will lose your vitality and energy which are needed for good pictures.

TAKE YOUR AGENCY'S ADVICE. If an agent tells you to cut your hair, change your makeup or lose weight, you should do it. This isn't to say that you should go against your own morals and values. If you don't want to cut your hair or shoot with a certain photographer because he or she yells at you, discuss this with your agency.

Your agent will only make suggestions when they feel you could make more money. But you shouldn't withhold your true feelings. An agent isn't going to throw you out because you express an opinion. Maybe in the hair situation they will tell you that by cutting it they can send you to Europe where you'll make double the amount of money that you presently make.

CHECK IN WITH YOUR AGENCY. They will tell you how often you should check in for messages. You may lose out on jobs or go-sees if they have booked you and you don't call in when you are supposed to. If you forget to call you won't show up for the job or go-see. It is your responsibility to call when you are supposed to and to notify your booker when you won't be available for bookings or go-sees. You're in this business to model, and if the agency can't get ahold of you or you don't call, they may drop you.

76

ALWAYS KEEP YOUR AGENCY INFORMED OF YOUR CURRENT ADDRESS AND PHONE NUMBER. If they have a job or go-see for you, they don't want to have to try and track you down. If you have a day job, make sure the agency has that phone number. Also make sure that they are notified of the hours and days that you're available for go-sees and jobs.

KEEP YOURSELF IN TIP-TOP CONDITION. We've already talked about your weight and skin, but you should also keep on top of your hair and hand-and-nail condition. Everything from the top of your head all the way to your feet should always be in good shape. After all, you are what clients buy, and if something isn't in shape you could lose out on jobs. You wouldn't buy a dress that had a rip in it, even if you like the dress, would you? So why should a client hire you if everything is in shape except for your hair or skin?

This also means keeping on top of your diet. Remember the phrase, "you are what you eat?" If you fill up on foods that are low in nutrition but high in calories, your face and body will show this sooner or later. If you need help with choosing nutritious, low-calorie foods, ask your agent for advice.

LOYALTY. Most agencies don't like their models secretly booking jobs on their own. If you see a job that you're interested in, tell your agency and let them book it. Because your agency might work very hard to book you a job, only to find out that you've already booked the same job for less pay. That's being disloyal to your agency.

WHAT YOU SHOULD EXPECT FROM YOUR AGENCY

There are things you should legitimately expect from your agency, and if you feel as if you're not getting them, talk it over with them. If nothing happens, and they're licensed, take your complaint to the Department of Labor or think about getting a new agent.

Instead of repeating another section of this book, go ahead and look over "What You Should Expect From Your Agency" in Chapter 2.

WHAT YOU SHOULDN'T EXPECT FROM YOUR AGENT

This is not going to be the same as in Chapter 2. In fact, many of the things quoted in that section are just the opposite in some modeling agencies.

For petite and plus models, it would be wise for you to also get into something else that interests you. Because very few petite and plus models make a good living just off modeling. I know several petite and plus models who are with an agency that handles both acting and modeling, and when the agency doesn't have any go-sees to send the models out on, they go out on auditions for commercials and movies, and this helps supplement their income.

It's just that there's more work for high fashion models than for petite or plus models. This is not to say that if you don't work really hard that you can't live off the money you make from modeling, it just depends on how hard you are willing to work, and what type of lifestyle you're used to. Eventually you will need to move to New York if you want to make good money because there are more opportunities for those types of models there.

CHILDREN

Children can do just about everything in modeling but unless the child keeps growing and advances to the junior and the high fashion market, your child may have to do something else when they reach a certain height and age. But when the child does reach that point, this can be discussed with your agent.

CHAPTER FOUR

UNIONS

There are three unions that actors should mainly concern themselves with. They are SAG, AFTRA and AEA. When you start getting union jobs in acting, you will need to join the appropriate union. Here is a brief description of what each covers.

THE SCREEN ACTORS GUILD (SAG)

Covers actors performing in motion pictures, prime time TV programs, most TV commercials, industrial and educational films, student and experimental films and anything else shot on film.

THE AMERICAN FEDERATION OF TELEVISION AND RADIO ARTISTS (AFTRA)

Covers live and taped TV shows, some TV commercials, announcers, disc jockeys, newspersons, singers and specialty acts, sportscasters, stuntpersons, all radio commercials, soap operas, and anything else shot on videotape.

ACTORS EQUITY ASSOCIATION (AEA) (CALLED "EQUITY")

Covers live stage performances, stage managers, and under some contracts, covers choreographers and directors as well.

THE AMERICAN GUILD OF VARIETY ARTISTS (AGVA)

Covers live performances in musical variety shows, performers in Las Vegas cabarets and club showcases, comedy showcases, magic shows, dance revues and amusement park shows.

THE AMERICAN GUILD OF MUSICAL ARTISTS (AGMA)

Covers performers in operas and other classical music productions and concerts and dancers.

THE SCREEN EXTRAS GUILD (SEG)

Covers extras (nonspeaking roles) mainly for SAG.

JOINING THE UNIONS

AFTRA

AFTRA will be the easiest to join as there are no prerequisites to join. You just fill out an application and pay the hefty membership fee and you're a member.

SAG

There are several ways to get into SAG. The first is to get a speaking part on any production under SAG's jurisdiction where a signatory employer has signed a collective bargaining agreement with SAG.

For the time being, you will be working under "Taft Hartley," and so you do not have to run out and join the union. However, you will need to join the union if the job you are hired to do will run more than 30 days or if you're hired for your second union job 30 days after your first one. (You are not required to join the union in right-to-work states.)

Another way to get in is if you get an unscripted line. Let's say a director is in the middle of shooting a movie and he needs you to say a line that wasn't in the original script, you would be eligible to join SAG, provided it's a union job.

The other way you can join SAG is if you are a member in good standing of an affiliated performer's union such as AFTRA, AEA, AGVA or AGMA, have been a paid member for at least one year and have worked at least once as a principal performer (not as an extra) under that union's jurisdiction. But a lot could happen in a year, so if you need to get more experience in the form of community theater, joining any union, will deny these opportunities. (This policy, may vary from union to union however, so it would be best to check with your local union to be sure.) It would be best to hold off joining until it is necessary.

When you do join SAG you will need to show proof of employment, which can be in the form of a signed contract, letter from the company on letterhead stationery or a payroll check or check stub. The proof of employment must list your name, the name of the production or the commercial (the product name), your social security number, the specific date(s) worked and the salary paid in dollar amount.

Your proof of employment and application to SAG will be investigated and you will be denied membership if anything has been falsified or if you have not worked with a signator employer. SAG will also look

80

into whether the work you did was actual work or if you just created it to gain membership.

When you join SAG you will be prohibited from working on any production for which the employer doesn't have an agreement with SAG. If you do, you could be censured, suspended, fined or even expelled from the union.

If you do get hired for a SAG union job, your agent or the casting director is supposed to check with the union to see if the employer is a signatory and also to get clearance from the union for you to work. (So keep your dues paid up because if you don't, then the job may be given to someone else.) To be on the safe side, if you do get hired for *any* union job, find out from your agent whom your employer will be, then call the union and verify whether they are a signatory employer before you sign any contracts for the job.

When you join SAG or AFTRA you will not be able to deal through any agent for representation unless the agency is franchised.

EQUITY

There are several ways to join Equity. Like SAG, you can join if you're a paid member of one of the affiliated unions (including SEG), and have worked on at least one production under that union's jurisdiction and have written proof of it. With SEG, you would either need to have a letter from SEG or proof that you worked three days as an extra.

Another way in is if you get hired to work as an actor or stage manager on an Equity show.

The other way in is to work in the Equity membership candidate program. You're not eligible for this program if you're a working member of AFTRA or a member of SAG. To find a list of Equity theaters who participate in this program, contact the closest union office. Once you get accepted into an Equity theater, you'll need to send a completed registration form to Equity. There is a fee to join, but it can be deducted when you join Equity.

Depending on the theater you'll be working in, you could work as an understudy, actor or work on the set itself. After you've done 50 weeks of this work, you can join Equity. The 50 weeks don't have to be consecutive or at the same theater. Equity also has a plan in which if you pass a written examination, you can go from 50 weeks all the way down to 40 weeks.

MEMBERSHIP FEES AND DUES

When you join the union you must pay for your membership and dues altogether. No personal checks are allowed for payment, only cash, cashier's check or money order.

UNION	MEMBERSHIP FEE	DUES
SAG	$796.00	$42.50
AFTRA	$600.00	$32.50
AEA	$500.00	$26.00
SEG	$600.00	$55.00
AGMA	$500.00	$26.00
AGVA	$300.00	$24.00

You may want to check on the procedures for joining the different unions, including membership fees and dues, as they vary from union to union. Also, SAG and AFTRA have been discussing a possible merger, and so by the time this book is published requirements to join these unions may have changed. To be on the safe side, call the union in your area (if you have one) and ask about their procedures.

MISCELLANEOUS ITEMS

For parents getting their children into acting, there's a free handbook called "The AFTRA-SAG Young Performer's Handbook." It discusses child labor laws, parental do's and don'ts, information on different work forms your child needs, questions and answers regarding working conditions and much more. Call or write your nearest union for a copy.

SAG and AFTRA also provide to members other services such as a credit union, which provides low-cost loans (see the reference section for addresses), relief funds for performers with financial needs, a health, pension and retirement plan and scholarships. For more information on these and other programs, contact your nearest union.

CHAPTER FIVE

PHOTOGRAPHERS - ACTORS

Photographs are the first introduction industry people have to you and one of the most important items to remember you by. And yet some actors neglect this area. You can possess all the talent in the world, but unless you also have outstanding pictures of yourself, you won't get very far in your career.

PICTURES ACTORS USE

Each city has different headshot requirements. In San Francisco, for example, a commercial headshot can be used for every field. In Los Angeles, the criteria is different. You will need to have both commercial and theatrical headshots. But when you're starting out a good, commercial headshot will get you in the agent's door. (Except in Los Angeles, don't send a theatrical agency a commercial headshot.) Then the agent will advise you on any additional pictures you'll need.

Listed below are several tools you and your agent will use to sell you and get you an audition. Depending upon your area, you and your agent may use all, or just one of these tools.

Commercial Headshots

These are mainly used for commercials, so your expression should convey lots of energy and enthusiasm. There's nothing deadly serious about these pictures. So smile! Otherwise, industry people may wonder if you're hiding something.

Theatrical Headshots

These pictures are used for film, TV, stage and soaps. Your expression will be different in these photos. They show your style, image and personality. So if you're serious, sexy, dangerous, etc., this is the expression that will come across in your theatrical headshot.

Composites

These are also used for commercials. There's a headshot on one side and four to six smaller pictures on the back that portray you in different environments, outfits and looks. Composites are especially useful for someone with a "rubber" face who can look totally different in each picture.

Since composites are complicated to arrange and can be quite expensive, it would be wise to wait to get the guidance of your agent. An agent's advice can be cost effective and valuable. Also, in some areas a headshot is preferred over a composite.

There was an actor who, before getting an agent, went out and got a composite, commercial and theatrical headshot done. He felt that if he were well-prepared, it might improve his chances for getting an agent. He did get an agent, but not because anyone was impressed by his preparation. He had a great deal of training and a good, salable look. His agent told him that he really didn't need the composites because his commercial and theatrical headshots were good enough. So the actor had wasted both time and money doing composites, when he might have waited to be advised by his agent.

Photo Postcards

Photo postcards come in two sizes. The first is postcard size and has your headshot on one side, along with anything you want printed on it such as name, union affiliation and your answering service or phone machine number. The reverse side is blank. These can be helpful when you want to remind industry people of your existence or thank them for attending one of your shows.

The other size you can get is business card size. It also has your headshot on one side, along with anything you want printed, and is blank on the reverse side. Since this size is harder to write on, many actors send these cards to industry people to keep in their rolodex.

When you get your pictures produced at the printer, you should also get about 200 photo postcards in both sizes run off at the same time.

DO'S AND DON'TS FOR PHOTO SESSIONS

Don't

* Wear accessories of any kind for headshots: earrings, necklaces, nose rings, hats or sunglasses. You're trying to sell yourself and it

84

distracts attention from you if you're wearing shiny earrings.

* Get anything new done to your hair right before your shoot. If your hair looks ratty around the edges, get it trimmed. But if you decide to try a new hairstyle, and then you either don't like it or haven't quite adjusted to styling it, you won't feel confident at the photo session. If this happens, the pictures may not turn out as well.

If you want a new hairstyle for your pictures, do it several months before the photo session. If you color your hair make sure that the roots aren't showing. If you have premature gray hair, you either want to dye it or highlight it. You don't want to look older than you are.

* Get your pictures airbrushed to remove *anything* except blemishes. If your face is full of blemishes, either try to get rid of them yourself or see a dermatologist before taking any pictures. If a casting director wants you to audition and your face is clear in your pictures but then you walk in with blemishes all over your face, it may create problems.

CLAUDIA QUINN - QUINN-TONRY AGENCY

"Actors shouldn't airbrush permanent things like wrinkles, scars and moles. Because if they've been selected on the basis of a photo, and then at the audition they look 15 years older than their picture, it doesn't reflect well on the actor. We've had actors come into our agency and I'd have to do a double take because they didn't look anything like their picture. It's misleading and usually creates problems for the actor."

* Men should avoid sporting a beard or moustache in their commercial headshots (how many actors in TV commercials do you see with one?). If having one is part of your image, leave it for your theatrical headshot.

* Wear solid black, white or red in your commercial headshots. Instead choose colors in the medium-to-light range. You can wear any color you want for theatrical headshots. But keep in mind that black is harsh on some people, and white makes some people look pale. For both types of headshots, avoid shirts with textures, patterns, shiny fabrics, fur-lined necks or turtlenecks; they take the focus away from you.

If you're not sure what to wear, take along a selection of clothes. Photographers are usually in tune with what colors and styles will look best in the pictures.

* Get fancy with elaborate lighting or background features, unless you're a model doing professional pictures. You don't want to be upstaged by these tricks. You should be aiming for a simple, conservative look.

* Get color headshots. They are more expensive and very rarely

85

used in the acting world.

* Style your own hair or do your own makeup, unless you are very good at it. Remember: this is your selling tool for agents, casting directors and other industry people; you want to look your best. Splurge and hire professional people.

* Take your friends to the photo session. If someone is giving you a ride, have them return to pick you up instead of waiting around.

* Tell the photographer how to do his job, such as how your face should be lit or what the lighting should be. Many photographers with whom I spoke said they are tired of actors and models trying to direct the show. You can suggest ideas but in the long run you should let them make the final decisions.

DO

* Your hair and makeup before the photo session, if you're doing it yourself.

* Try to exercise before your photo session. You'll feel more alive, relaxed and vibrant, which will come across in your pictures.

* Make sure to give yourself plenty of time to prepare for the photo session and arrive on time.

* Get plenty of sleep the night before. It's true that the photo lab can airbrush bags under the eyes, but you may lose the sparkle and vitality in your expression.

* Try to schedule your shoot in the afternoon instead of the morning. The reason for this is that when you first wake up there's fluid in your face and sinus area that causes your face and eyes to look puffy. If you wait until the afternoon to shoot the pictures you allow all the fluids to drain.

* Give yourself a facial or have one professionally done the day before your shoot. Men will benefit from this, too.

HAIR STYLISTS AND MAKEUP ARTISTS

There are several places where you can find professional artists and stylists. One way is to call the cosmetics sections of major department stores for artists and finer hair salons for stylists. You might also find them through the trade papers or by asking actors, models and other industry people. Some people do both hair and makeup for a flat rate, usually from $75 to $150 per hour or per shoot depending on the artist or stylist and your area.

Before deciding to hire a makeup artist you should ask to see his or her portfolio. If they don't have one, I'd reconsider whether or not to hire them. As a general rule of thumb, most professional makeup artists have books that show their work. You want to work with someone who does makeup frequently for acting and modeling pictures, not someone who does it only a couple times a year.

Anyone can be a makeup artist but it takes a certain expertise to do makeup for photographs, especially for different levels of lighting and film situations. The artist could volunteer to give you a free demonstration, but the makeup job you see may not necessarily be the same thing you'll see in your pictures. If the artist has a book of their work to show you, however, then you'll be able to see how well he or she applies makeup for different lighting, film and environments.

Professional makeup artists will cost more than one who does this as a hobby, but you don't want to wind up with good pictures and a bad makeup job just because you worked with an incompetent makeup artist. This may also result in having to reshoot the pictures, which will cost you more money and time for another photo session and makeup artist.

Like anyone else, your makeup artist should have referrals. Books can look good, but the artist might have purchased the pictures from someone else and now claim them as their own work. They work closely with photographers and agents, so these will be the main referrals they'll probably give you.

If the makeup artist doesn't do hair, you will need to hire a hair stylist, who should also have a book of their work along with referrals.

The other place you can find makeup artists and hair stylists is through the photographer with whom you'll be working. Many fashion photographers work with several makeup/hair stylists. Sometimes the photographer's price will include not only the photo session, but the makeup/hair stylist's fee as well. Many times this can be cheaper than booking everyone separately. If you go this route, make sure you meet the makeup/hair stylist and see a book prior to the photo session. Just because the photographer loves the makeup/hair stylist's work, doesn't mean you will. Photographers who do pictures for actors usually don't work as closely with makeup/hair stylists as fashion photographers do, but they usually know of one or two who they can recommend.

After you have found an artist/stylist you want to work with, it would be a good idea to get the business arrangement in writing.

The artist may ask for a deposit up-front to ensure your booking, but you shouldn't have to pay the full amount prior to the shoot.

If you pay in cash, make sure you get a receipt. (Remember those tax write-offs.) I would advise against paying the artist/stylist any money at all until you have checked their referrals and gotten a copy of the business arrangement. If an artist or stylist doesn't want to put anything in writing, it wouldn't be a good idea to hire them.

WHERE PHOTOGRAPHERS ADVERTISE

Photographers for acting and modeling usually advertise in the trade papers. Actors can also check with other actors, agents, acting teachers, bulletin boards of acting schools, the union and casting directors. Models can check with agents, other models, ad agencies and modeling schools.

PHOTOGRAPHERS TO AVOID

Many photographers will specialize in one area such as composites or headshots, while others do not limit themselves and shoot everything in the acting and modeling field. You should avoid using photographers who don't specialize in actors and/or models *only*. Many of these photographers advertise as shooting weddings, family groups and portraits as well as model portfolios and headshots. But would you hire a bricklayer to fix your plumbing problems? Of course not, so why hire a photographer whose expertise is out of your area?

Photographers who earn a living shooting weddings and portraits, but shoot actors and models on the side do it to make extra money. You need a photographer who focuses solely on actors and/or models because these areas require a certain expertise. Just because a photographer can shoot weddings doesn't mean he or she can shoot models or actors well enough to meet industry standards. Besides, most photographers who don't concentrate on shooting actors and models are not intimately involved in the entertainment world and often don't have the slightest idea what the industry is looking for in pictures.

One of the reasons that new actors and models hire these photographers is because they aren't aware of the differences. And because the ad says that the photographer does actor or model pictures readers tend to believe that the photographer is competent in these areas. Sometimes these photographers can be lower in their prices compared to the ones who specialize in entertainment. But if you want to sacrifice your look and waste money, then go ahead. You'll be saving money but wasting your time, however. The same photographer who shoots weddings or portraits uses a certain style and technique that will carry over to your headshot or fashion shot. Generally you will not be after that type of photographic style.

One example: a model who was building up her portfolio before she had found an agent, was going through the phone book and calling different photographers to see if they were doing any testing. She called up a photographer who did weddings, portraits and modeling portfolios, and he agreed to test her. They set up a photo session.

He shot several rolls of film indoors and on location, but when she

88

got the contact sheets back, she wasn't pleased at all. The pictures didn't look high fashion at all and the quality was bad. She told me that the photographer was charging her only for the film and any prints she wanted enlarged. Of course, she chose none. She also compared the photographer to a fashion photographer she had previously worked with. She said that this one didn't know anything about the modeling world or how to do high fashion pictures. She hired this photographer because he was cheaper than fashion photographers, and she thought she could save some money.

USING AN AGENCY'S PHOTOGRAPHER VS. YOUR OWN

There are advantages and disadvantages to using an agency's photographer. The disadvantage from what I've heard is that some of the agents (or bookers) take kickbacks for referring actors and models to certain photographers. I have heard about one agency that would always set up appointments for actors and models with its photographer. Then the agency would ask the actor or model to write the check out to the agency for $200 to pay for the photo session. The agency would then turn around and write a check out to the photographer for $150, giving the agency a profit of $50 for each actor and model who was referred.

One actor discovered this scam through another actor who had called the same photographer and was quoted a $150 fee instead of $200. When the actor went to his agent with this story, the agent was surprised and gave the actor back his $50.

The other way that some of these agencies take kickbacks is that the agencies will give the actors or models a list of different photographers with whom they work. Then when the actor or model calls the photographer and says that they're from this particular agency, the photographer makes a note of that. At the end of the month he tallies up the actors or models who are from the agency or agencies he deals with and slips the agent or booker some money for sending those people his way.

I have also heard from reliable sources that some agencies also over-charge actors and models when proofs which are to be made into composites and headshots are sent to the printer. What usually happens is that after you shoot with the agency's photographer, the agency will have you write a check out to the agency for the cost of the printing, which many times is more than what the printer would normally charge.

There are some agencies that will get a reduced rate for models on a photo session, by booking a photographer, hair and makeup artists, photo assistants and stylists for a day, and then splitting the cost over four to six models. This can be a great money-saving opportunity for models, but it can also be a good way for some agents to take a piece of the action. They could quote a price that would be divided among several models, then have each model make out a check to the agency for his or her portion. The agency could then turn around and write checks to each person who worked on the set that day, while keeping a small profit for themselves.

The advantages of working with agency photographers is that the photographer will sometimes give a discount to models and actors who were referred to him or her by the agency. Photographers who work with agencies are also quite competent, and are in tune with what the industry people like. An agency is certainly not going to work with a photographer who doesn't produce excellent work because if a model's or actor's pictures are bad, they will have a hard time getting auditions, go-sees and jobs. So an agency can't afford to work with incompetent photographers.

Of course, the advantage to finding and booking your own photographers and printers is the assurance that some agencies won't charge you more than they should. But some agencies will probably give you some resistance about finding and booking your own photographers and printers. This is more likely with the modeling agencies, because actors are supposed to have pictures prior to getting an agent, whereas a model doesn't need professional pictures to get an agent. Most modeling agencies work with several photographers whom they feel capture the look of the models the agency represents. So many of these agencies don't want models booking their own photographers. This is understandable because most new models aren't knowledgeable enough to select whom they should shoot with.

This entire situation can be tricky so I really can't tell you what to do. I can only point out the pros and cons of the situation and then it's up to you to make a decision based on what you think is right for you. The way I see it: if you can't trust your agency, find another. You are better off with one you can trust. There are lots of agencies that work very hard for their models and actors and are honest in their dealings. But like everything in life, there's always a good side and a bad side.

QUESTIONS TO ASK THE PHOTOGRAPHER

You should talk to at least five photographers, get prices, check referrals and see their portfolios before making a decision. Of course, if you hit it off with the first one you meet, like his or her prices and portfolio, and his or her referrals check out, then by all means book him or her. But there may be someone out there whom you like just as much whose prices are even lower. Just as when you buy a car, you usually don't purchase the first one you see. You shop around to see if you can find a better, cheaper automobile.

Here are some questions you can ask photographers. Of course, feel free to add to this list.

* Do you have any referrals?
* How much do you charge?
* Do you require deposits? If so, how much and when would it have to be paid? (If they do, ask if you would get back some or even all of your deposit if you give advance notice to cancel your appointment.)
* How many outfit changes are permitted?
* Does the price include any free prints? (Some will include one or two in the fee, and you pay for the additional prints.)
* How much is charged for additional prints? (The average rate for this is from $10 to $20, but some have been known to charge as much as $50. This is an important question to ask, as you can see from the story below.)
* Does the price include a makeup artist or hair stylist?
* Can I keep the negatives? (Most photographers won't give or sell negatives. One of the reasons for this is to make extra money. Each time you order additional prints from the contact sheet they charge you an extra $10 to $20.)

You should still try to get ownership of the negatives because when you take your original print to the printer for copies they will need to duplicate it to produce the necessary negative to print your pictures in bulk. In the process of doing that your pictures won't come out as well. It's not that your pictures won't look professional, you're just better off dealing with the original negative instead of the copy.

* Will you be posing me or am I expected to pose myself? (Most will guide you along throughout the session, but some others do nothing but focus the camera and shoot. Consider getting your pictures done by one who will guide you, especially if you're not used to posing. A photographer can see what you look like through the camera lens, whereas you can't, so he or she should be guiding you. If you're a model, it will be helpful if you are familiar with posing.)
* How long is the session?
* When will I get my proofs (also called contact sheets) back? Are they mailed to me or do I have to pick them up? (Proofs are the first things you'll get back from your shoot. These are about 16 small pictures about the size of a high school yearbook photo that run down the sheet in strips. So if you shot 32 exposure film, then expect to get two sheets back. Two weeks is usually the maximum time to wait until you receive them.)
* Do you guarantee your work? If not, what if I don't like my proofs? (This can be touchy because who likes to be told that their work isn't up to par? But you're paying for these pictures, so be picky. On reshoots, some photographers will charge you for film and the pictures that you select for enlargement. Some will charge you half the original

price of the shoot, while others may charge you for a completely new shoot.)

* When will I get my prints back? Will they be mailed to me? (These are the pictures you selected from the contact sheet to be enlarged. It usually takes about two weeks to get your prints back.)

* Do you go on location or do outdoor shooting? (This is good to ask if you're a model doing a portfolio or an actor doing outdoor shooting.)

One of the first questions you should ask is for the photographer's referrals, with the location of each one. If he or she has none, there's no sense in continuing the phone call and wasting your time. It's better to get the phone number of the referrals yourself, rather than get the number from the photographer. He or she could give the number of a friend who will pose as the referral. I've heard of some elaborate scams in which a dishonest photographer or other industry con artist who will have a separate phone line in their home or a friend's home, which will be answered under a different, assumed name. This is so people will think that he or she is well-known in the industry, when he or she actually isn't.

The referrals he or she gives you should consist mainly of agents or casting directors. Here's why: before you can get an acting job you have to get past two people, the agent and the casting director. You need an agent first to get auditions and you need a casting director to go to them, so if they don't like your pictures either because the photographer is inadequate or the quality is bad, then you've got problems. So look for photographers who are approved by agents or casting directors.

If the photographer's ad says that he or she is agent or casting director approved, you should still ask for the names of the agents or casting directors and verify whether the photographer's claim is true. Even if your acting teacher or friend thinks a certain photographer is great, it's more important that agents and casting directors like his or her work. You need to impress agents and casting directors, not friends or teachers.

If you're a model the referrals should be the same. Models also have to get through industry people to get work. But in your situation there are other people whom he or she can recommend like ad agencies, magazines and catalogs.

After the photographer answers the questions and you've written down the answers, it's a good idea to repeat your notes back to him or her in case you've misunderstood something. Then call the other photographers on your list and ask the same questions.

CHOOSING PHOTOGRAPHERS

Take a day or so to review the prices and answers you've received from each photographer. Then ask yourself some of these questions: Were some more helpful? Are some more lenient about outfit changes and reshoots? Did I have more rapport with one than with the others?

Call back the ones in whom you're interested (or keep searching) and make appointments to see their portfolios. It would be a good idea to get the business arrangement in writing and signed before paying a photographer any money. Ask the ones you'll be meeting whether they would be willing to put the business arrangement in writing if you decide to hire them. If a photographer won't agree to this, say goodbye and pat yourself on the back. Not only did you avoid possibly getting ripped off, but you've saved yourself a trip to his or her studio or home—when the answer would have been "No" anyway.

It wouldn't be advisable to shoot with any photographer who refuses to put things he or she quotes to you in writing. All the photographers with whom I've spoken said that they would have no problem at all putting in writing things they've quoted to actors or models.

Let me also remind you that just getting things in writing may not necessarily prevent you from getting ripped off, unless the photographer has referrals. Let's say you call a photographer and get his or her prices and replies in writing, but you don't bother to get referrals.

Many con artists use different names as they travel from city to city, so even if you have a name and other details on paper, it will not do you any good if they skip town with your money. On the other hand, if the photographer will give you the names of agents or casting directors who will vouch for his or her character and work, then you'll know that person is legitimate. Good photographers are known within their communities. If they're from another state they should still have a good reputation that can be verified.

Here are some case studies of actors and a model who didn't get things in writing and were subsequently inconvenienced.

SAN FRANCISCO PHOTOGRAPHER - ALLEN NOMURA

"One question that many new actors fail to ask the photographer is how much they will be charged for prints. I got a call from an actor who asked if I could make a print from another photographer's contact sheet. I told him I couldn't do it without the negative. Well, the actor wasn't aware that the other photographer was charging $50 per print, because he didn't ask prior to the shoot. Fifty dollars is pretty steep for prints."

Then there is the photographer who would quote one price for headshots over the phone and then after you've spent an hour or two doing the shoot and attempt to pay him, he will say that you haven't paid him enough. So you're stuck with two choices: you can either pay his price, which increased from his original quote of $40 to $150, or you can tell him to forget it, go to a different photographer and reshoot everything all over again. Since this is such an inconvenience, most actors will pay the price and, what's more, the photographer knew that they would. This is not just an isolated case; this photographer has tricked a lot of actors. So you can bet this photographer probably wouldn't want to put anything in writing and probably doesn't have legitimate referrals.

There was an ad in one of the trade papers that read: "Professional photographer seeks models for test sessions and fashion shows. Makeup/hair stylist included in price." A model who responded got to the shoot to find there was no makeup/hair stylist. Instead the photographer said that he was the stylist. Well, the resulting pictures were unprofessional because the photographer knew nothing about either hair or makeup. Needless to say, his ad was very misleading. (There were no fashion shows, either.) The photographer was building up his portfolio and trying to book fashion shows for the models he shot. The model took him to court because she had paid in full and he didn't want to return any of her money. Fortunately, the model won her case.

Every problem in these different situations could probably have been solved by getting everything in writing prior to the shoot. But many actors and models fail to do this and proceed only on a verbal agreement. Because the photographer seemed nice, or it seemed like too much trouble to get everything in writing. A verbal agreement is difficult to hold up in court. Few people win cases if they have no evidence.

MEETING THE PHOTOGRAPHER

Meetings with photographers should be at their studios. There was one scam in which the photographer would go to a person's house (making it convenient for the clients so they wouldn't need to go to her studio, which probably didn't exist), collect fees for a photo session, which would be scheduled for several weeks later, and then leave town with all the money.

Not all photographers who make house calls are running scams, but to be on the safe side, it is a good idea to see their studios. Not every photographer will have a regular staffed studio. Instead they save money by establishing a studio in their home and use a garage or an extra room for business space. This is perfectly acceptable, as long as they also have referrals.

Scrutinize portfolios carefully. After all, this represents their best work. Are the pictures focused and clear? Are the pictures spotless without floating white specks? Does the background upstage the model or actor? How is the lighting in the pictures?

A good idea would be to have the photographer show you the area in which you'll be shooting. Not only will you get a feel for the room, but you'll feel more comfortable on the day of the shoot if you have already visited it.

VERIFYING YOUR PHOTOGRAPHER'S LEGITIMACY

After you have found a photographer with whom you want to work, check out his or her referrals and background. If everything checks out, call and set up the date and time for the photo session. Schedule it so you have enough time to prepare properly for it.

Below is a list of contacts to call to verify the photographer's referrals or guidebooks (which can be found in the reference section of this book) to help find the phone numbers of referrals. For example, if the photographer gives you a casting director as a referral, you can locate the casting director's phone number by contacting agents, reviewing casting guides, Ross Reports, etc. (If you're an actor, you can skip the part about ad agencies, magazines and catalogs; they pertain only to models.)

* *AGENTS* - Try to find out from the photographer whether the agency is franchised. If he or she doesn't know, look through the list of franchised agencies in the reference section of this book. If the agency is not listed, try the phone book, casting directors and modeling and acting schools. Even the trade papers or phone directory assistance may be able to help.

* *CASTING DIRECTORS* - Agents, casting guides, Ross Reports; the union may even know.

* *AD AGENCIES* - Madison Avenue Handbook, Ross Reports and other guides.

* *MAGAZINES and CATALOGS* - Since magazines and catalogs have large staffs it would be best to find out from the photographer with whom he's worked and the location of the office. Magazines and catalogs often have several different offices. The number can then be found by checking a phone book or phone directory assistance.

It's important to get as much specific information from the photographer as possible, otherwise you may have difficulty tracking down his or her referrals. If you experience trouble verifying referrals, it's possible that he or she has given you false references—hoping that you wouldn't call to verify them.

Don't let any photographer talk you out of checking his or her referrals by saying that a magazine or other business won't be able to verify his or her employment. The bottom line is that if the photographer has legitimate referrals, there should be no reason why you can't verify these or at least that he or she has worked for them.

Even if the photographer has referrals, it doesn't necessarily mean that his or her background is clean. Most actors and models who are ripped off or dissatisfied with a photographer's work take him or her to small claims court or file a report with the Better Business Bureau. But some don't do anything at all.

There was an agency that had ripped off at least 200 actors and models in one city. During my research for this book, I went to the courthouse and discovered that only *15* actors and models had filed suit against the agency. This goes to show that most people either don't want to hassle with a lawsuit or they're too embarrassed to admit they were cheated.

Even if agents and casting directors think the photographer on your list is wonderful, a couple of actors or models may have taken him or her to court for something but didn't bother telling industry people. So you may want to dig a little deeper. (Who knows, if your acting or modeling career doesn't pan out, with all this experience in undercover work, you could probably become an investigator.) Here are some suggestions you can use:

* If you saw his or her ad in a trade paper or another publication, call to see if they've had any complaints.

* Check with the Better Business Bureau to see if there are any complaints against him or her. This will only be useful if he or she has been around your area for awhile and built a track record. If the photographer is from a different city, call that city's BBB. Better yet, call both.

* Check small claims court to see if he or she has ever been sued and what the case was about.

PAYING THE PHOTOGRAPHER

Each photographer has his or her own method of payment. Some will charge a nonrefundable deposit when you book the shoot to ensure that you'll show up. Then the deposit will be applied toward the cost of the session. Some will charge a deposit after the session, and you'll pay the balance when you receive your prints. But it wouldn't be a good idea to pay in full before you do the shoot. If you should decide to cancel your shoot, it could be a hassle to get all your money. If you pay in cash, either bring your own receipt book or ask for a receipt.

There was a scam in which a photographer had put an ad in a trade paper for his services; then he would ask for all the money up-front when you booked the shoot. Since he scheduled all the shoots for several weeks later, he was able to collect a lot of money and skip town before anyone caught on to what he was doing. The people I interviewed said that they hadn't bothered to ask for referrals, and I doubt if he had any to begin with.

There are some photographers who will recommend actors and models to different agencies, especially if they're new to the area and don't know who the legitimate agencies are. But watch out for photographers who try to charge you a *referral* fee for doing so. There was one photographer who would charge $50 to call his agency referral and recommend the actor or model, trying to get them an appointment with the agent. This is something you can do yourself without having to pay $50. Also, how do you know if the photographer actually calls the agency or even has an agency referral? He could just tell the actor or model that the agent isn't interested and pocket the money.

In case you need more incentives to avoid shooting with a photographer who isn't a referral, I have heard that there are some photographers who buy actor's and model's pictures from talented photographers and put together a portfolio of these pictures. So when you see their book you think they do excellent work (when they don't) and, impressed, you book a session and pay before the shoot. But when you get your pictures back, they look terrible. And since you probably wouldn't want to reshoot with that photographer, you end up going to a different photographer and spending more money and time.

Sure, you can take him or her to court, but you'll spend even more time and money, so most actors and models don't do this. These photographers who buy pictures from other photographers usually don't have the talent to be good at their craft, so they use other's work to build up a great, but phony, portfolio. Of course they don't shoot for any of the top agencies because they're not good.

A legitimate photographer spends a lot of time building a good reputation in the industry and isn't going to jeopardize that by swindling people out of their money.

THE DAY OF THE SHOOT

The most important thing is to allow yourself enough time to get there, especially if there are weather problems. It's better to get there a little bit early, rather than arrive at the last minute all stressed out.

If you're a bit nervous, don't worry, photographers understand and will do whatever it takes to relax you and make you feel comfortable. They might play soothing music or joke around. A bit of advice: drinking alcohol before or during the shoot to relax is not a good idea. You'll be too relaxed and tired, your eyes will be glassy and red-looking and you'll have a short concentration span. This also goes for drugs of any kind. If agents or industry people see any indication of drug or alcohol use in your pictures, they may reject you.

AFTER THE SHOOT

A couple of weeks will pass before you get back your proofs. Most photographers will mail them to you. When you get them, take a lighted magnifying glass (you can scrutinize easier with the light) and really look them over. Ideally you should have an agent assist you in the selection of photos. Models will have the help of an agent when it comes time to select the photos to be enlarged. Actors are usually on their own until they have an agent. However, you can still ask the opinion of the photographer, who is usually in tune with what agents and casting directors like, your acting teacher or even a casting director. You may even know an actor with an agent who would be willing to advise you.

But leave family members out of this decision unless they are also in the industry. They won't have the knowledge to know what the industry is looking for at the time.

It is great if the photographer includes a free print in his price, and you're satisfied with it. Sometimes the photo that you had enlarged will have shadows that you didn't see on the contact sheet. Since it can cost anywhere from $10 to $20 to have each shot enlarged, order them cautiously, one at a time.

COPYRIGHT LAW

At the shoot ask the photographer if there is a copyright symbol on the prints he will be giving you. If there is, you'll need to get a release letter from the photographer allowing you to get reprints of the picture. Not all printers will ask to see your release letter. However, a printer might tell you that he can't touch your pictures until he gets permission from the photographer. Then you would have to call the photographer, ask for a letter of release and return to the printer. What a hassle! So to be on the safe side, get a release from him if it's necessary, and ask him to mail it to you with your proofs or prints. In any case, you won't need the letter until you go to the printer.

PRINTERS

Once you have your print(s), your next task will be to get copies made at the printer. Reasonably priced printers can be found by asking your photographer, other actors and agents or by looking in the trade papers or phone book (under "Photo Printers"). You should try to stick to printers who deal mostly with actor's and model's pictures, because they are sometimes cheaper than other printers. If your photographer will print your pictures for you, and some do, you should still check with other printers to make sure you're getting the best possible deal.

When you're shopping around, get several quotes from various printers. If you live in a major city, try calling printers on the outskirts of your city. You could save considerable money. You may even be able to do all of it through the mail if it's very far from your home.

When getting price quotes you'll first need to know several things:

THE PHOTO'S FINISH

This is the coating on your pictures of which there are several to choose from:

* **Glossy** - This type of finish is popular with actors and is usually less expensive. Your pictures will have a shiny appearance.
* **Matte** - This finish is used mainly on composites. It has a grainy feel and a dull tone.
* **Gloss Tone** - Magazine ads have a gloss tone finish to them. Gloss tone can be used for headshots, but it scratches easy.
* **Pearl** - This is a combination of matte and glossy. A lot of printers have to make special orders for this finish, so if you select this finish, be sure to call in an advance order.

There are no industry rules as to *the* preferred finish, but most actors do prefer the glossy finish. If you're thinking of putting your picture in trade magazines or other publications, keep in mind that pearl, gloss tone and matte finishes don't copy as well as glossy.

THE BORDER

This is a white space or frame around the entire picture. You'll want to keep it thin, about 3/8", except at the bottom where it should be larger for your name.

The other two choices are:

* **Bleed Border** - There is no border at all on the picture.
* **Three-Sided Bleed** - The only white space on the photo is to accommodate your name. Until you have an agent, the only information on your picture should be your name and the name of the union to which you belong.

NAME IMPRINTING

* **Knock Out** - Your name is printed in black letters inside a small block of white space.
* **Overprint** - Your name is printed in black letters on the photo itself. Or you can have your name printed in white letters if you prefer.

TYPEFACE

This would be the design of the letters in your name. There are many different varieties to choose from, so you'll have to see what your printer has in stock before making a decision.

QUESTIONS TO ASK THE PRINTER

After you have answers for all the previous questions, you will be able to get a more-or-less accurate price quote from the printer. You should also ask:

* Will I be expected to leave a deposit or pay in full? If there is a deposit, how much is required, and when is it paid? Printers are different and some may ask for full payment up-front.

* Can I do business with you through the mail? If you're doing business from a distant city, this might be more convenient for you. For faster service, it's always better to go in person.

* Will you send my pictures to me? If so, who pays for the postage? (You could also have them shipped via UPS; this way they're insured and it's also faster. Of course you pay the shipping costs.) What happens if they're sent regular mail and the pictures arrive damaged or with some missing?

* How long will it take from the time I give you the print until I get my order from you?

* When I get my final pictures back what if there are flaws that weren't on the original test prints?

* What if my name isn't spelled correctly or appears to be crooked? You probably won't see your name on the test prints, so it's a good idea to ask this question.

* What is the cost of the copy run? When you're looking for an agent it's best to start with a small number of pictures. Then if your agent doesn't like them or you decide to leave acting, you won't be stuck with 300 useless pictures. Start with 100, and wait to see if your agent likes them or if you still enjoy acting, then have more run off. Remember also to get some photo postcards developed.

* What is the cost of the negatives? If you have the photographer's original negative, you'll be able to skip this usually small charge. If not, it costs approximately $10 to $20, and you own the negative. Another negative you'll also buy and keep is the negative used to make the name imprint.

* What is the cost for extra services? This would include test prints and wedges or cropping.

Before securing the services of a particular printer, make sure that you both agree on the price and the processing you want done to your pictures. The printer will usually supply you with an invoice that

100

outlines everything you've ordered. Look it over carefully to make sure the invoice includes everything you want before paying any money.

TEST PRINT

Most printers charge a small fee for a test print but it's well worth the cost. This is a sample of what your picture will look like (excluding your name), on your bulk order. Examine it very carefully. It's better to notice flaws on the test print than to get 100 or more flawed pictures back. (You can also order a test wedge, which is your picture in various light and dark shades.)

Your pictures should be ready in about two weeks. This is entirely up to the printer, however, and what his schedule will handle.

When you get your finished pictures, check every little detail once again. Did you get everything for which you paid that was specified in writing? Does your name appear straight and spelled correctly? If not, discuss any problems with the printer. He will want you to return for future business and to recommend his business. So he will usually be very helpful.

CHAPTER SIX

PHOTOGRAPHERS - MODELS

From San Francisco to New York, agents to whom I spoke told me that models should never attempt to put a portfolio or composite together without the guidance of an agency. They also said that many models come in for "open call" with elaborate portfolios and composites, and they were not impressed at all. Most of the time models don't get sent out any sooner on go-sees even if they already have professional pictures. Most agents like to groom the models themselves, so if models already have professional pictures, most of the time they've wasted their money and time.

Most agents also advise against getting a portfolio done to show the agencies that rejected you just how great you look. Unretouched snapshots are the only pictures models need prior to getting an agent. Most agents have been in business long enough to recognize from snapshots whether the model has potential or not—or is even right for their agency.

Agents are impressed by how you look and your personality, because that's what sells the clients. If you don't have the raw materials to start with, it will be hard to sell the clients whether or not you have hundreds of pictures.

PORTFOLIOS: WHY YOU DON'T NEED ONE UNTIL YOU HAVE AN AGENT

To help you to understand the situation on portfolios, let's take a trip into the agent's mind so you can understand his or her thoughts exactly.

The many clients who call modeling agencies include ad agencies, photographers, department stores, magazines, etc. The models whom each agency represent have a certain look and style. While one agency represents models with fresh, clean, innocent looks, another may represent exotic, sensuous types.

So let's say that you have an exotic, sensuous look, and you happen to go to the agency that handles this type of model, and hand your portfolio to the agent. Now the minute you walked in the agent's door they were sizing you up and, unfortunately, sometimes you've already been rejected before you even have a chance to say "hello." But instead, for this scenario, let's say you do have the right look and they are interested in representing you. But there are problems with the pictures in your portfolio. For one thing, the agent doesn't feel that you've tapped into your look and style, the layout is flawed, the photographer's technique is bad, the background upstages you, your clothes, makeup and hair don't flatter you, and the list goes on. So even though you went to a professional photographer to get this portfolio done, the agent doesn't like it. Now you have to get a new portfolio done, and spend more money and time when you should have just waited until you had an agent.

There are other reasons why agents want to help models put together their portfolios and composites. For one thing, most beginning models aren't familiar with how to arrange them properly according to each agency's style. They also don't know which photographers would be best for them. Each agency works with certain photographers, and the agents are familiar with whom you should be sent to get the best pictures.

Then there are some agencies that will send new models overseas to build up their portfolios (this does not apply to child models), whereas a new model would never have access to that. Agents also know what the clients like to see in pictures and what look each market is using. They're all different. For instance, the high fashion look in Europe is always one year ahead of the U.S., while the look on the East Coast is always months ahead of the West Coast.

I hope this gives you a better understanding of why agents don't recommend that models do their own portfolios or composites before getting an agent. Besides, a good portfolio mainly consists of tear sheets and pictures from tests, shot with many photographers from different cities and countries. It is not accomplished simply by shooting with one photographer who's charging you anywhere from $2,000 to $5,000 for it.

The reason most new models are convinced that they need to have a portfolio before they can even see an agent stems from the fact that they've received mixed messages from different people. Unfortunately it's all misleading. According to my observation, most of the time these people are just out to make a buck and have no interest whatsoever in your career.

For instance, there are many photographers who will try to convince models that, unless they have a portfolio, they will have difficulty getting an agent. Many ads to which I've responded in the paper or on the radio have turned out to be nothing but scams, in which they try to lure unsuspecting models into doing an expensive portfolio. While some modeling schools will include a portfolio as part of the tuition to increase the salability of the school.

People out to separate you from your money will tell you anything. It's really frustrating because you think you're doing the right thing by getting your portfolio done *before* seeing agents, and then the agency turns around and tells you that they can't use your pictures.

PICTURES MODELS USE

When you do get an agent, here are some tools that you and your agency will use to "sell" you to clients. Depending on your area, one or all of these items may be used.

Portfolio

A portfolio (also called a book) mainly consists of tear sheets (these are prints from actual jobs) and pictures done by testing with different photographers in various countries and cities. There's no set limit on how many pictures should be in a model's book; it's limited to just the best photos. So while one model may have five pictures, another may have 10, but they are always the best ones. Because of this, models are always getting new pictures done for their books.

A good book displays your different looks, styles and moods such as happiness, anger, surprise, etc. It shows how young or old, sophisticated or earthy you can look. Basically it expands your look, which in turn can get you a wider variety of go-sees and jobs.

Some agencies have empty portfolio cases imprinted with their logo that they will either sell or give to their new models. This might not be a bad idea if you're purchasing it at a reduced price. But shop around to compare prices and quality. An agency shouldn't tell you that you *have* to buy its portfolio case because it has their logo on it.

Even if they tell you that you have to buy your portfolio case through them, you might still want to shop around to compare prices and quality and if you find a better deal, bring it to your agency's attention and see if they'll match the lower price. Keep in mind that if the agency's logo is engraved into the portfolio case and you decide to switch agents, it may not look impressive if you show your book to potential agents with another agency's logo printed on it.

If you are buying your own portfolio case, be sure to look for a strong, durable one. Your book will be handled by lots of people. Look for a leather one if you can. You'll also need to find one that's big enough to hold your pictures, but not so big that it becomes a burden to carry.

Most models find that a size 9" by 12" does the job. Then all you'll need to do is to get one of the agency's stickers to put on your book, and you're set.

Composites

If a client calls an agency requesting to see some exotic, brunette models, but the client doesn't want to see all the models in person, the agency may send the models composites. This is a "mini-portfolio." On one side is a headshot, and on the other side are four to six smaller pictures, showing the model's versatility. In one picture you might be dressed in sophisticated evening wear and in another in jeans and a sweater.

Composites also contain your name, the agency that is representing you, your measurements and clothing size, along with many other items of information. Since these are considered your "calling card," you'll be taking them to your go-sees and auditions, and handing them out to clients, photographers and anyone else who is a potential employer.

Slides

Sometimes the client will request to see more pictures of certain models they're interested in before meeting them. So the agency may send slides. The agent may also, on request of the client, send color xeroxes of the slides. (These are enlarged versions of the pictures on the slides.)

Some agencies have their own equipment to make xeroxes, and it usually ends up being cheaper for the model than what photo labs charge. Agencies that don't own their own equipment take the slides to an outside photo lab. If you are going to pay the agency instead of the printer, sources have informed me that some agencies have been known to overcharge their models for these enlargements. Then the agent goes to the cheapest photo lab and has the work printed for much less, thereby giving the agency an extra profit.

Headsheet

Many agencies have a book containing small headshots of each model they represent. This is sent to clients as well as potential clients. Each picture has the model's name, height, weight, clothing sizes and sometimes the model's hourly and daily booking rate. If the model belongs to any unions, this information is also included.

The headsheet may also be broken down into different categories either by age or height. There are some agencies that don't charge their models to be in their headsheet book. But for the ones that do, the charge is minimal, and should *only* cover printing costs.

TESTING

When a model first signs with an agency many agents put the model on the testing board and send them to different photographers, who are sometimes new themselves. Like you, they will also be building up their books. Since you're both trying to accomplish the same thing while using your time equally, usually you just pay for the film and the prints that you select. More experienced photographers also do testing, but their fees vary. While some only charge the model for film and prints, others charge a flat rate for the entire shoot. Unless, of course, the photographer is testing new ideas for an upcoming shoot or for his or her own portfolio. Then the photographer will usually work only with an established model.

Besides building up your book, testing also increases your confidence in front of the camera and accustoms you to working with different photographers before the agency sends you to the bigger jobs—where hundreds or possibly thousands of dollars are involved.

It would be a good idea to use caution if a photographer recommends that you do lingerie shots for your portfolio unless your agent suggested you take these shots. One photographer with whom I spoke had this to say, "If a photographer recommends you do lingerie in a portfolio, you have to ask yourself, "Can I get work doing lingerie? Does my body warrant wearing lingerie?" If you feel the photographer is doing lingerie shots so he can get a peek at you, then don't do it. But if he's doing it because he feels you can get work, or you know you can get lingerie jobs, then you should do it. But you should speak to your agent about this first, because not everyone can model lingerie. It should also be tastefully done, and if it has the slightest indication of being close to some of the risque magazines, then you'll know what the photographer is all about and you should stay away from doing that."

If the photographer tells you that you'll get more bookings by including nude photos in your portfolio, *don't do it*. (See the "Pornography" section in Chapter 12.) In my opinion, he is either trying to get a look at your body or will sell your pictures to porno magazines. Which you wouldn't always know about because many times they use your body and replace it with another's face. Or the photographer may save your pictures until you make it big before selling them to a porno magazine. Then your modeling career may be damaged or destroyed. Keep your clothes on.

This also goes for any ads you may see in the trade papers or newspapers that ask for models to do nude work in motion pictures, videos or anything else. One wrong move like this and your modeling career could be over for good.

106

HOW TO FIND A LEGITIMATE MODELING PHOTOGRAPHER

Rather than repeat myself, you should read through Chapter 5 if you haven't already done so, as most of these things also apply to models, unless otherwise noted. However, in the section on printers, if you're going to be dealing with the printer directly instead of going through your agent, you should discuss with your agent how the printing should be done on your pictures, especially for composites. Each agency will probably have a certain way they want it done. Also, unless you're using photographers who have been referred by your agency, you should get referrals, check out their referrals and backgrounds, and ask for everything in writing, along with a signed copy of your agreement with the photographer *before* paying any money.

Here's what happened to one model who failed to get anything in writing. She had responded to an ad in the trade paper which said that a photographer needed models for a book he was building up. In exchange, the models would get *free* prints for their books.

She went down and did a photo session, and the photographer told her to call him in a couple of days because he would have the contact sheets by then. At that time she could pick out the prints she wanted to have enlarged. But when she called, his story had suddenly changed. Now he told her that he wasn't going to give her any free prints at all and that if she wanted the prints she would have to pay for them. In essence, he got free models for his book. Now if she had asked to get this business arrangement in writing, he probably wouldn't have agreed to test her, since he obviously was building his book up by using free models. She also told me that he wasn't a referral and that she didn't bother to check out his background because she didn't know how to go about this.

PICTURES CHILDREN NEED

Acting

Whether or not you should get a headshot of your child depends on the age of the child, and the extent of his or her involvement in acting. As a rule of thumb, unless your child has a lot of experience and training under his or her belt, you really don't need to run out and get a headshot before you get an agent. In addition, if the child is very young, his or her look will change, causing you to make many unnecessary trips to the photographer. The best thing to do would be to send agent's unretouched snapshots of your child consisting of a headshot, profile and full body shot. (For more on snapshots, see Chapter 3.) When you have an agent, he or she will be able to help you assess whether you should even invest in a headshot for your child.

Modeling

Just as with the adult models, most agents don't recommend investing in a portfolio or composite for your child before getting representation. All the agents want to see are unretouched snapshots to begin with, and then after getting representation, the agent will discuss with you what additional photos your child may need.

CHAPTER SEVEN

TRAINING-ACTORS

It's difficult enough to make it as a trained actor and without training you are going to find it even more diffficult. Yet many actors without ample training try to get an agent and then wonder why they keep getting rejected.

I think one of the reasons many actors don't take training seriously enough is not because they don't want to attend acting classes, but rather that they watch other actors in TV shows and movies, and think it looks easy—especially in commercials in which there are a lot of ordinary people. I can understand how someone sitting on the couch watching TV might think that they could sell toilet bowl cleaner just as well as the next actor. So some actors think that all they have to do is to get an agent, go to an audition and get a part in a movie, TV show or commercial. I hate to be the one to give you the bad news, but it usually doesn't work that way.

Sure, acting looks easy, but like anything else it results from good old-fashioned hard work. I was once on a TV set. At the time I was new to acting and had been under the impression that scenes were shot one time only. I was wrong; many scenes had to be shot over and over again. Some needed as many as five or 10 retakes, until the scene was perfected. Sometimes even when it was perfect, the director still wanted to film additional takes, in case he or she missed something.

So if you think you can just jump right into acting without training, you're going to be in for a big surprise. Let's explore the types of training you'll need as an actor.

TRAINING ACTORS NEED

The type of training you'll need depends on the kind of acting you want to get into. As an actor you'll want to be as versatile as possible, especially when you're starting, even if you only want to do commercials. Unless you don't mind keeping your regular job, you will need to act in a variety of situations to supplement your income. When you become well-known in the industry, you can afford to be selective.

Actors need to *continually* keep their skills sharpened. There will not ever be a time when an actor can say he's mastered acting. Even well-known actors sharpen their skills by appearing on Broadway or doing other stage work.

To keep as much fun in acting as possible, it is a good idea to vary your training. Training doesn't mean that you have to confine yourself to a weekly three hour acting workshop. It also doesn't mean that you have to continue just taking acting classes.

Many actors also get into directing or producing plays and student films. This is not a bad idea. Not only does it teach you new skills, which you could include on your resume (agents and casting directors like to see busy actors), but it lets you see things from the other side of the curtain, rather than always from the actor's point of view.

Another reason to vary your training is to allow yourself the opportunity to study with different teachers. Not every teacher will teach the same technique or have the same viewpoint. This will enable you to get as much feedback on your acting skills as possible. I've talked to some teachers who told me that they have had some students who stay in their scene study class forever. Finding a teacher with whom you feel comfortable is good, but staying with him or her until eternity can stunt your growth as an actor.

Another benefit to taking different classes is that it allows you to meet a wide variety of actors, and the more actors you know, the better it is for your career. By attending acting classes, you'll also find out if you like acting before investing your time and money in the wrong career.

Below is a list of the different types of classes along with a brief description of what you can expect to learn in each situation. (Of course each teacher will be different in what he or she has to offer.)

Commercials

Most teachers cover working with cue cards, products, videotape, improvisation for commercials and cold reading for commercial scripts. Videotapes and critiques of student's performances are also done.

General Acting

If you want to get into movies, TV, stage or industrials, this is one kind of training you'll need. General acting classes usually cover the exploration of relaxation through games, exercises and improvisation, as well as scene work, script analysis, monologues, cold reading, emotional recall and sense memory. Most teachers will also critique scene work by the students. General acting classes can also help if you want to get into soap opera work, but there are classes specifically

110

designed for that. It's just that some cities don't have specific soap opera classes. If this is the case, just stick to general acting classes.

Voice-Overs

Most voice-over classes cover delivery techniques, script analysis, examples of good and bad voice-over demo tapes, examination of the different areas of voice-over work, how to read commercial copy (usually done in a recording studio), and playback and critique of student's performances.

OTHER SOURCES OF TRAINING

Here are other areas of training you may want to explore. They can be beneficial to your acting career, as well as additional items to include in your resume.

Plays

If you lack experience, plays are an excellent way to beef up your resume. Plays put actors in direct contact with the same things they'll need on a production including discipline, working and cooperating with others, taking direction, commitment, stamina, patience and much more.

LOS ANGELES ACTOR AND TEACHER - ED HOOKS

"Plays are the best things actors can perform in. One play is worth about 10 classes. Some of my students have complained that they don't have the time to do plays, but I always encourage actors to try and arrange their schedules to accommodate them. Even if you don't want to be a stage actor, being on the stage is simply the best training there is. You are right there with the audience, and your rear end is on the line. It is immediate feedback and is more instructive than I can convey."

It should be pointed out that while each play is worth about 10 classes, you should not forget about taking classes altogether. It will be difficult to get auditions for commercials, voice-overs, movies, etc., without getting specific training for them. You won't learn how to hold props, slate your name, work with cue cards or the camera by performing only in plays.

Plays will also test your enthusiasm for acting. There will be rehearsals for which you won't be paid, and depending on how large your part is, you may have to be available to rehearse for many hours. This could be from three to six nights or days a week, and anywhere from one to three months. This could definitely cut into your weekend plans. But this is the same thing that will happen when you get a movie or TV job. Maybe it takes only a half hour to watch the TV show, but many times it takes a whole week just to tape it, with actors quite frequently working up to 12 hours a day.

On the bright side, plays can be great fun, and you'll meet lots of new and exciting people. It's also refreshing to hear the crowd's applause and excitement that are lacking in workshops.

Remember if you join *any* union, you may be prohibited from working in community theater. So don't close more doors than you must, especially if you need experience for your resume. It would be better to postpone joining any union until you've either gotten a job that's under a union's jurisdiction or you have enough plays for your resume. Casting directors are more impressed by the experience and training on your resume than your union membership, especially if it's a union that's easy to join, such as AFTRA.

Singing and Dance

Many movies, plays and commercials call for actors who can dance and/or sing, and if you can do both or at least one, you'll be better qualified for the audition. Part of being an actor is communicating with your body, so if you're not into dance, you may want to get into another type of body movement class such as stage combat, karate or gymnastics. You never know when one of these extra skills just might land you a union job and your SAG card.

Stage Combat

Stage combat can be fun to do and is a great workout. It can also teach you to think quickly on your feet, which is good for actors. Most stage combat classes will start with warm-ups and then move on to things like foot, point and blade work, choreographed moves and timing.

Voice

If people are always saying "What?" every time you speak or ask you to speak up, you might want to get into a voice/speech class. Especially when you're on stage, you need to speak in a loud voice and be heard clearly in the back rows. A bad speaking voice may also hinder your acting career if casting directors and other industry people can't understand what you're saying. Most voice/speech classes will cover things like vocal and breathing exercises, posture alignment, movement, diction and speech.

Improvisation

Improvisation can help you in all aspects of auditions, especially in commercials where many times you might have to pretend to be eating or doing something else. You may be at an audition and the casting director tells you "OK, you just came home from work and see that the living room window is broken and the front door is slightly ajar." Then it's up to you to try and hold a captive audience. Many actors freeze up when the casting director gives directions like these, because most actors are used to just coming in and reading a script.

Improvisation will assist you in overcoming this fear by helping you to become more creative and less self-conscious, which in turn can help you perform better at your auditions.

Improvisation classes teach you breathing, relaxation and focus exercises, movement with nonverbal scenes, games to increase awareness, concentration and creativity.

Another type of improvisation is mime and movement. These classes teach an actor mime illusions, commedia clowns, physical comedy, slow-motion acrobatics, stylized walks and conventional and ritualistic gestures.

Comedy

You're not going to have to tell jokes at your auditions, but this is another class that increases spontaneous creativity. Most comedy classes are designed to allow actors to present jokes and be videotaped, critiqued and receive feedback from the class. They also teach you how you can get a laugh (and double and triple your audience's laughter), how to deal with internal obstacles and exercises in assuming additional masks quickly.

Monologues

From what I've been told, monologues are not often used in the industry. But that doesn't mean that you shouldn't have one or two to recite at a moment's notice. For those of you who aren't familiar with what a monologue is, it is a scene played out by one person, done either with or without the help of props. There are classes that are specifically designed to train you to do monologues and how to find the best monologue for you. There are even some people who will write a personalized monologue for you.

Cold Reading

You will be doing *a lot* of cold readings at your auditions, so it would be a good idea to prepare properly for this by taking a cold reading workshop. A cold reading is a script that's given to actors at an audition without the actor having memorized or rehearsed the part.

Student Films

Lots of today's great directors and producers got their start by working on student films. You can find these by checking the trade papers, the bulletin boards of unions, different acting schools and college drama and film departments. If you are a member of SAG, you will only be allowed to do student film projects if the filmmaker or school has signed a student film letter agreement with SAG. (It is your responsibility if you're a SAG member to find this out.)

On most student films, a copy of the film and meals are provided. Some films may also provide payment for your time or expenses, but they shouldn't be asking for fees of any sort, such as charges to be in the movie or for registration. And from my viewpoint they shouldn't even ask for fees to cover the expense of making a copy of the film to give you. Most of the time you don't get paid to work on a student film, so the least they can do is provide a free copy of the film for you. If a copy is not provided, make sure you get one. Many times when you're interviewing with a casting director, they'll ask you if you've done any film so they can see your work. Well, here's the perfect opportunity to show them. You may have to keep after the producer or director of the student film to make you a copy or to let you make one, but it will be worth it.

Nonunion Films

Castings for these can be found in the same places as student films. If you're a union member, you won't be allowed to participate in a nonunion film. (You may want to check with your nearest union because this rule may vary from union to union.) Most of the time a copy, meals and expenses are provided and sometimes even a salary. If there is a salary involved, unless you are sent on the casting call by your agent you may want to check out the person in charge of the production, by asking for referrals and investigating their background if you get the part. If they don't have an agency or casting director to supply as referrals, try getting other referrals such as the union (even though it's nonunion), an acting teacher, school or some other industry person. If you have an agent, he or she can also give you an opinion on the legitimacy of the production.

If the filming will be taking place in another state or city that will require you to fly, make sure you get a round trip plane ticket, money for a hotel, transportation and food in *advance*. You don't want to arrive with a one-way plane ticket and no pocket money. Make sure they also provide a contract that spells out all the details including how and when you'll be getting paid. Remember also to get a signed copy of the contract.

When you do get a copy of your production, be sure it's copied onto a 3/4" tape (it's easier to edit) and edited to include only your scene. Agents and casting directors don't want to wait 30 minutes for you to come on. Ask around to find out who does professional editing and copy. Leave this to professionals.

NOTE: Many times there will be roles in films which require nudity. If you have an agent, be sure to discuss this with him or her before going to the audition. If you don't have an agent, it wouldn't be wise to do any roles that require nudity. (See the "Pornography" section in Chapter 12 for more on this.) At least don't do nudity until you have an agent and are able to discuss the matter with him or her.

There is lots of other nonunion work available such as industrials, educational films (such as for driver education classes), TV shows, music videos, commercials, even game shows. (You'd be amazed at how much extra money you can make by participating in game shows if you are good at it.) You can find all these jobs by looking in the same places as for the student films.

Acting Coaches

You can learn a lot in a class, but you have to compete with many other students. A private coach will give you undivided attention for an hour or so. Of course they are more expensive to hire than taking a class, but if you're having specific problems with auditions or another aspect of acting, a coach may be just what you need.

WHERE TEACHERS ADVERTISE

They advertise mainly in the trade papers. If your city doesn't have a trade paper, ask other actors, agents, acting schools and casting directors. The union may also be of help.

WHAT YOU DON'T KNOW ABOUT AGENCY CLASSES

First of all, you should only take a class if you feel that you are going to learn something, not because an agent feels you should take their training program. From what I understand, there are some agents who don't really have your best interests in mind when they recommend you take their classes. Their only concern is the amount of money they can make off you.

Sources have also revealed to me that most agency classes are twice as expensive as others. If you did a price comparison you might find that you could have taken the same class as the one you took through an agency, taught by the same teacher, for the same number of weeks and hours, but the nonagency class would have been $200 to $300 cheaper. The reason it's more expensive is because the extra money is profit for the agency.

Some agencies will try and persuade you to take their classes by saying that they can start sending you out on auditions or go-sees after you've had some training. Of course, it's always *their* training that they'll suggest. This is just like some agents who will tell you that you need photographs before they can send you out on auditions or go-sees and suggest you shoot with their photographers. From what I've heard, these agencies are usually taking kickbacks from this ploy. This situation has happened to me and other actors and models with whom I have spoken.

When I first got into acting and was looking for an agent, I sent out my picture, resume and cover letter to about 10 franchised agencies. Well, one by one, my submissions started coming back with rejection slips attached. Having this happen is frustrating, and you start to wonder if you'll ever get an agent. But, lo and behold, several days later, I got a call from an agent who said that she was interested in representing me and wanted to meet me. We set up an appointment for the following day.

When we met she said that I had potential to do well in commercials, but that I had no special training for that particular field. She said that she really couldn't send me out on any auditions until I did. Then she conveniently told me that a commercial workshop of theirs had just started the previous week and suggested I sign up. She added that after I completed the course I would be signed to a contract and sent out on auditions. (By the way, if an agency is franchised, they are not allowed to tell you in so many words that they will only represent you if you take their classes or use their photographer. If they do say this, report them to the union immediately.)

After being rejected by many agencies and finally being accepted by one, or at least I thought I was, I was thrilled to have an agent. Since I didn't know any better at the time, I signed up. After taking the course, I never heard from that agency again, nor did I want to. Because while I attended their workshop, there were many times when I tried asking the agent questions, she would always say that she was too busy at the moment and would speak to me later. But this never happened because she was *always* too busy. She sure hadn't been too busy to take my money, though. Of course, I never did see that contract. After I heard some negative things about this agency and the agent giving me the cold shoulder. At that point you couldn't have paid me to work with that agency.

One actress, who was in the class with me, said that when she had signed up for the class, she paid the agency a deposit. A couple of days before the class, the agency called and told her that she had to pay the balance of the tuition. She replied that she wouldn't have the money until the following week when she got paid. The agency told her that if she didn't pay, she would lose her deposit and the agency would put someone in her place. They said there were at least 50 other people waiting in line to take the same class and had the full tuition. So she ended up paying the balance because she didn't want to lose her deposit and her place in the class.

This agency was franchised, and if the union had known about what this agency was doing, it probably would have been in a lot of trouble.

I should point out that her receipt didn't say anything at all about the deposit being nonrefundable if she weren't able to pay the balance, nor did it state that the balance was due before the class began. You and I both know that the agency probably didn't have 50 students waiting to enroll in the class. Because if that were the case, why didn't this agent just tell the actress that her deposit would be returned, since after all, there were 50 other students waiting to enroll in this class with the full tuition? The bottom line is that this agency was just manipulating the actress into paying the balance due on the class.

The agencies that overcharge for their classes have a certain quota that they must fill for each class. If they don't fill the quota, then the class won't be profitable for the agency, or it may even lose money. So if there are 10 spaces to fill and only six actors or models have signed up for the class, where do you suppose they are going to find the other four students? More than likely the agency will go through some of the submissions sent to them and select the actors and models who have little or no training. Then they invite them in, tell them that they have a lot of potential to be an actor or model, but that they need training before they can be sent on go-sees or auditions, and then suggest that they take the agency's workshop.

Many actors and models fall for this scam all the time. If the actors or models were to tell the agent that they had no money to sign up for the class, the agent would probably just tell them to return when they did, and then would just move on to the other actors and models on their list until they found four other people with the cash. So it's very simple for agents to fill their classes, and with each agency receiving anywhere from five to 20 submissions every day, they have quite a bit from which to choose.

Being in a situation such as the one I encountered where you're sending your pictures out to many agencies and receiving nothing but rejection slips can really dampen your enthusiasm. Finally one agent does take an interest in you. So then when he or she suggests that you take the agency's classes, you feel somehow obligated to do so. A lot of actors and models don't want to come out and tell the agent that they don't want to take the agency's classes because they think that then the agent will not want to represent them.

But that's not the only reason: another reason has to do with the fact that most new actors and models aren't really familiar with the types of con games some of these agents play nor are they knowledgeable about how the industry really works. And when these agents see that naivete among actors and models, they think it's easy to persuade innocents into taking their classes and using their photographers.

If you do run into a situation in which an agency wants to represent you, but also suggests that you take their training classes, and you don't want to, here's my advice. First, I would thank them for pointing out the fact that more training is necessary, but explain that you already have some classes lined up and would rather not enroll in their class. One suggestion, though, if you tell them that you have classes lined up, they may ask with whom you'll be studying. So if you don't really have any teachers lined up, you may want to gather a couple of names of teachers in advance so you won't be unprepared if the question arises. Of course, some agencies may still try talking you into taking their classes by saying that their classes are more up-to-date with the industry technology than the teachers on your list, or that their training course would look more impressive on your resume than the teachers you have lined up.

The other suggestion is to ask for a list of agency approved teachers or schools besides their own. If you do choose this route keep in mind that it may not get you very far, because if they are trying to sell you their classes, why would they want to recommend other teachers or schools? But you might still try it.

It will be interesting to see how the agency responds after you tell them that you have your own classes lined up or ask for a list of agency approved classes or schools other than their own. But here's the key: if they are *not* honestly interested in representing you, then they will probably give you the cold shoulder or try to discourage you from going to classes other than their own. If the agency is franchised, there will only be so much that they can say to you without getting into trouble with the union if you happen to turn them in. So if the agency seems reluctant to go along with what you want to do, then they probably aren't really interested in representing you and are just out to take your money.

One thing that sometimes happens after you take an agency class is that they will suggest that since you've taken their training course, you now need pictures before they can send you out on auditions or go-sees. (Sometimes they'll even try to sell you additional training. Since you bought into their first approach of going to their workshop, you're now an easy target for more sales.) Of course, they'll recommend *their* photographer. Many times if you don't agree to use theirs they will say you can use your own photographer on one condition. The condition will usually be that if they don't like your pictures, the agency won't use them. Usually what happens is that you bring the pictures in for examination and the agent says he or she doesn't like them, even though you shot with a photographer whose work is well-respected in the industry. So you're stuck with either going to their photographer and possibly paying extra for the agency's kickback, or shooting with another photographer with the possibility of the agency not agreeing with your selection. (Like the situation with the classes, you can always ask for agency approved photographers besides their own if you don't want to use theirs.)

There was one actress with whom I spoke who had taken an agency class. After she took it, the agency told her it was time to get her pictures done, and suggested that she use their photographer. She already had a photographer lined up who she had used in the past and felt comfortable working with and didn't want to use someone new. The photographer she was using was respected in the industry for his work, but the agency still wanted her to use their photographer. She went against what they wanted and used her photographer anyway. When she got her pictures back and took them to the agency, the agent just tossed them aside and said that they would be looked at later. Several days later when the actress had not heard from the agency, she called to see what the status was on her pictures. The agent told her that he still hadn't found time to review them, but would do it in the next couple of days. After waiting another week without a word, she just decided to go to the agency and pick up her pictures. They still had not been looked at.

Now that you've heard the bad side, here's the good side. Most agency classes are taught by well-trained, knowledgeable teachers. Some of them are working actors or models themselves and can pass on a lot of helpful advice. I don't regret taking the agency class that was recommended. It was taught by a reputable teacher and I met some great actors. What I do regret is the fact that the agency raised my hopes by pretending that they really wanted to represent me, when in fact all they wanted was my money.

QUESTIONS TO ASK A TEACHER

* Do you have referrals?
* What are your prices?
* Do you ask for deposits? If so, how much and when does it have to be paid? (If they do, ask if you could get some, or all, of your deposit back if you give advance notice that you couldn't take the class.)
* Do you give a discount? (See "Paying the Teacher" in this Chapter.)
* Do you offer payment arrangements? (Ask this only if you can't come up with the full amount.)
* Is this a beginner, intermediate, or advanced class?
* How many students are in the class? (In an on-camera workshop, the maximum number of students for a three hour class should be 10, otherwise you won't get enough camera time, and you shouldn't have to pay to watch other people act. For that, you may as well see a movie.)
* Is videotape used in the class? If so, how much camera time is each student allowed?
* Do you allow auditing? Is it free or is there a charge? (If they don't allow auditing, ask if you would get your money back if you didn't like the class.)
* What will I learn in your class?
* When is the date or dates of the class? What are the hours?
* What is the address of the class?

The teacher should have agents or casting directors as referrals. When an agent or casting director is looking over your resume, it's important that you've studied with teachers they're familiar with or they may question your acting ability or even wonder if you made up the names up to make it appear as if you have more training than you really do. So instead of making them guess, it would be better to study with teachers that have been approved by an agency or casting director.

When I say that teachers should be agency or casting director approved, I mean that if you find a teacher on your own and ask for referrals, they should be able to give you the names of some agents or casting directors who can recommend them. This does not mean that you should take classes taught only by agents or casting directors.

Another reason to make sure that your teacher is agent or casting director approved is explained in one actor's story. He wasn't making any money acting, so he decided to venture out on his own and start teaching classes part-time. Well that's OK, but he was a new actor without any acting or teaching credits to his name, yet he was charging regular teachers' prices. This would be as if you were to study with one of your actor friends, except that you paid for it.

Good teachers, like photographers, are known within their commu-

120

nity. Even if they're teaching weekend workshops and come to your area only once or twice a month, they should still have referrals you can check out. So if the teacher with whom you're interested in studying doesn't have referrals, you're probably better off studying with someone who does.

There have been bogus teachers that open their doors only long enough to collect registration or other fees from students and then skip town, never to be heard from again. Many of these con artists go from town to town collecting thousands of dollars from unsuspecting actors and models. So it's very important to get referrals. I'm not saying that the teacher is a con artist if they don't have referrals, but how can you be sure that they're not without recommendations?

After you get the answers to your questions, and you've written them down, repeat them back to verify everything. Follow the same procedure for other teachers on your list.

CHOOSING A LEVEL: BEGINNER, INTERMEDIATE OR ADVANCED?

Starting a class at the wrong level for you can hinder or frustrate your growth as an actor. Obviously you would start at the beginning level of classes if you've never done any acting or if you're making a transition, say from stage to commercials. But let's say you got into acting for a short time and took a variety of classes, then decided to leave acting for awhile and pursue other interests. Now that you've decided to return to acting, you may not have to start at the beginner level again.

Or let's say you take a beginner commercial workshop and decide after taking the class that you really don't like the teacher or workshop. Then you decide to study with someone else. You may not necessarily have to start with the new teacher's beginner class. Or if you've done lots of stage work and haven't taken any acting classes, you may not have to start at the beginner levels either.

If you find yourself in this situation, the best way to determine your level is to ask the teacher you want to study with for his or her opinion. The teacher will probably have you do a cold reading or monologue. The teacher should give you an honest opinion and not reply that you should take his or her beginning class only to get more money from you. Because if you've taken another beginner commercial class and decided to study with a new teacher, you should probably start in an intermediate class, or you might feel frustrated in a new teacher's beginning class.

Whatever level you're in, it should be invigorating and challenging. If you're at a level that's not exciting, you will not stretch or grow as an

121

actor. It's like staying in the ninth grade when you should be promoted to tenth grade. So if the teacher tells you that you should start in their beginner class and you don't feel challenged, then talk it over with the teacher to see what is recommended.

BEFORE YOU MEET THE TEACHER

After you've talked to several different teachers, take some time to go over what each teacher is offering. Then ask yourself some of these questions: Did I get along better with some more than others? Do some allow auditing while others don't? Are the ones who don't allow auditing more lenient about refunding money if you're not satisfied with the class? Do some have more students than they should reasonably have?

Call back the teachers in whom you're interested (or keep searching) and make appointments to audit their classes if they allow it. As with the photographer, you should get your business arrangement in writing and signed with whomever you study. Ask the teachers you'll be meeting if they would be willing to put everything in writing if you decide to choose them. When someone refuses, end the conversation.

AUDITING CLASSES

If a teacher or school allows auditing, and most do, you should take advantage of it. Why? Because by doing it you'll get a feeling for the way the teacher handles the class. It is possible that you might get along great with the teacher on the phone, but don't enjoy the way he or she conducts classes. You'll also be able to judge how comfortable the environment is. I once audited a class in which practically everything was painted black, which made it a very uncomfortable place to be. Yet I had got along great with the teacher on the phone. Everything from the teacher to the actors and environment needs to feel good to you or else it could interfere with your acting ability.

Yet many actors pass up this opportunity to audit and pay for a class or school with which they are dissatisfied. Here's another reason: there was an actress who had called a well-known theater teacher for information on his classes. The man asked her if she had ever heard of a particular prestigious actor's studio to which he belonged. She said no. Then he became rude and asked her what kind of an actress she was if she'd never heard of the studio. (I guess she hurt his huge ego.) Well, she wisely ended the conversation right there.

Later, in a different acting class, she overheard a conversation between two actors who were discussing an audit one of them had just done on this same teacher's class. The one actor told the other about an actress in the class who was doing a scene that required her to

122

become very emotional. When she didn't express enough emotion, the teacher went up and started pushing her around and yelling at her to get her to become more emotional.

Now if you didn't audit this class, you wouldn't have discovered this teacher's unusual teaching style. So if the teacher allows auditing, take advantage of it. There are some teachers, however, who don't allow it.

SAN FRANCISCO TEACHER AND ACTOR - SCOTT DEVENNEY

"Some of the work that actors are involved in is extremely personal, particularly if they're studying on an ongoing basis with a specific teacher. And some of it requires the actor to dredge up a lot of emotion that they wouldn't normally show to the outside world. So in the course of discovering that, many times it's not controlled and can be very difficult to do when there's a stranger in the room. And after all, an auditor is a stranger. So some teachers, out of respect for their current students, simply don't allow it."

There could also be other reasons that they don't allow auditing, and that doesn't mean that the teacher or school is trying to hide anything. If you can't audit one or several classes on your list and you want to study with a particular teacher or school, ask for a list of former students. Call some of them and ask them what they thought of the class or school. Of course, you'll probably be given the names of students who will represent the teacher or school the best way, but you can still at least get some feedback.

When you audit classes, you should take a notepad and pen with you so you can take notes. This is important because if you're auditing several classes, you might not be able to recall specific details on the different teachers or schools later. When you're jotting down notes, here are some things to take notice of. Is the environment fun and challenging? Did some of the classes have more students than the number quoted to you over the phone? If there is video equipment, is each student allowed enough camera time? (In a three hour class each student should be allowed in front of the camera at least twice.) Are students allowed to ask questions and partake in the creative process? Does the class seem to be well-thought out, or does it seem as if the teacher just threw something together at the last minute?

One other thing you should note is the location of the building where the class is being held. If you will be taking public transportation to get there, and the class is a long way from the bus stop or train station, then you'll either have to take a taxi or have someone from the class pick you up. If you're a woman, you don't want to be walking the streets alone late at night. Some of these classes end at 10 p.m. or 11 p.m. This is another thing you may want to take into consideration.

There are, however, some teachers and schools who will charge you to audit their classes. Whether or not you feel the class or school warrants this is up to you. My belief is that if you're not participating in the class and merely watching others act, why should you have to pay? You're also doing them a service by considering the class or school. But, for the most part, audits will be free.

MAKING SURE YOUR TEACHER IS LEGITIMATE

After you have found a teacher with whom you want to study, what you should do next is check out his or her background a little. Follow the same procedure as in Chapter 5 under, "Verifying Your Photographer's Legitimacy." Of course substitute the proper wording and make sure you check out all referrals. Remember: just getting things in writing may not prevent you from being ripped off.

There was a teacher who placed an ad in the trade papers for his acting class. He would tell people who called that if they paid in full for the class, that they would receive $100 off the price of the class. A lot of actors bought into this scam, and before they figured out what was going on, this "teacher" had hit the road, disappearing with their money. Someone like this would probably not have any legitimate referrals. A con artist is certainly not going to hang around town stealing people's money while building up a good reputation at the same time.

There was another teacher who was conducting a workshop/sight-seeing trip in another state, and asking for a $500 advance deposit. The price included the flight, hotel, food, transportation and workshop. Many people signed up for this fictitious trip, and were taken. There are teachers who do arrange trips like this to other states, and it's OK, as long as they have referrals. But the actors who I spoke to didn't get any referrals on this particular teacher, and only went on the teacher's word.

PAYING THE TEACHER

There are many different ways that teachers will charge for the class. Some will charge students an advance registration fee to hold their place in the class. This fee is then applied to the balance, which is due usually on the first day of class. Charging an advance deposit also helps the teacher figure out how many students will be attending the class, so that he or she doesn't overbook.

There are other teachers who will give students a discount if they pay in full in advance for the class, and often you can save a good sum this way. But it should be a big enough discount to make it worthwhile. If it's just $10 off a $300 class, you might want to reconsider paying in advance. If you decide to cancel, it could be a hassle to get all your money back.

Some teachers will allow students to pay an initial deposit, and then make monthly payments during the time that classes are held.

However you elect to pay, just remember to make sure the teacher signs your business agreement and you've checked out his or her referrals and background *before* paying any money. Remember to get receipts. Actors undergo a lot of training, and it could add up to big tax write-offs for you.

WHAT CLASSES SHOULD CHILDREN TAKE

Most agents recommend that parents wait until they have found an agent for their child before enrolling them in any acting classes. Then they will recommend what type of training, if any, your child will need. Many children are very spontaneous and can really ham it up in front of a camera. But some classes, with their rigidly set programs, can hinder that natural ability.

Remember to keep an eye on some agents who don't have your child's best interest in mind and are only out to get your money. Parents are just as easy to con as adult actors and models. Agents like parents even better, because they know you have money, as opposed to a struggling young actor or model. So if the agent starts telling you how sweet and adorable your child is and how much money the child could make in acting or modeling, don't soak up their compliments too fast—or you may get suckered into paying for classes and pictures through that agency. If the agency isn't really interested in representing your child and is only interested in how much money they can get from you, then your child's career isn't really going to go anywhere.

Before securing representation, why not get your child into some of the following suggestions. Not only will it help build a resume, but you can discover whether your child wants to act before wasting your time looking for an agent or spending money on classes and pictures.

Plays would offer your child some great opportunities because they prepare your child for the same discipline that they will face on a movie or TV set, such as taking direction from other people. It might be easy for children to listen to their parents, but some of them have a difficult time taking direction from strangers. Cooperation is another thing they'll have to learn. Plays will also teach your child patience, commitment, perseverance and much more. You can find the local plays by contacting parks and recreation places, the chamber of commerce or even churches. Churches often put on plays especially around the holidays.

If your child has a hard time pronouncing words or being heard, you might want to consider a speech class. After all he or she could be the best darn little actor in the world, but if the casting directors or other industry people can't understand or hear the child, he or she may lose out on parts.

For the child that wants to get into modeling, the same things that apply to adult models will apply to children, as you'll read in the next chapter. Besides, your child may be too young to participate in or understand many things that models learn in modeling schools. An education in makeup, wardrobe coordination, diet, runway techniques, public speaking, etc., might be too advanced for children. Even if a modeling school offers courses specifically designed for children, get the opinion of an agent first as to whether your child should attend such a school.

CHAPTER EIGHT

TRAINING-MODELS

Many of today's top models never went to a modeling school and they are making top dollars off their looks. But for some reason each year thousands of models flock to modeling schools to learn this trade before getting the opinion of an agency. And later they find out that the tuition spent on a school could have been better utilized by keeping it in the bank and collecting interest.

IS MODELING SCHOOL NECESSARY?

Models do not need training to interest an agent. Does this sound foreign to you? If it does, join the crowd because most beginning models believe that not only do they need to have a portfolio to interest an agent but a modeling diploma as well.

My theory is that there are three main reasons that many new models think they need to go to a modeling school in order to be a model. The first reason they attend a school is because they feel that by doing so, it will increase their chances of getting an agent.

As you've read so far throughout this book, there are some main ingredients a model *must* possess before they can interest an agent. A school cannot make you taller or change your facial or body features. You could attend a million schools, and not one of these schools would ever be able to give you these items. So attending a school to increase your chances of getting an agent, without having the main ingredients first, is like trying to drive your car without gasoline. You and the car won't get very far.

The second reason has to do with society. Society has pretty much planted into everyone's mind that before you can make a career out of anything, you need to go to school to train for it first. So naturally some models fall right into that mindset and attend a school.

The final reason is that many new models getting into this profession don't really know where to begin. So they turn to the hype of the radio or newspaper ads suggesting that the proper way to get into modeling is to attend a modeling school first. So that is exactly what

127

many of them do.

Before you decide to attend a modeling school, you should first seek the advice of an agent. Why? Because in my opinion there aren't many modeling schools (which are in the business to make money) that will give you an honest opinion of your potential. But on the other hand, an agent (at an agency that doesn't have a school attached to it) will be in a much better position to tell you the honest truth. After all, an agency that is only making money from the commissions they receive from models who work has no incentive to lie to you.

PATRICIA CHAMOUN - LOOK AGENCY

"Models don't have to go to modeling school to get into modeling. There are some great looking girls and guys who have graduated from different modeling schools, but the chances are that if those same models had walked into an agency *before* they had gone to the school, they would have been snatched up, and they wouldn't have had to shell out all that money."

PAUL NELSON - CITY MODELS

"Not all models need training. They should first seek the opinion of an agency before spending money. Besides, a lot of what a model learns can't really be taught in a school and is better learned on the job."

THE PROS AND CONS OF MODELING SCHOOLS

For some of my readers who may need more incentive to get an opinion from an agent first, let's look a little further into the world of modeling schools and the pros and cons of going to one. We'll start with the cons first. (No, I'm not referring to con artists.)

There are many things that a model cannot learn in a modeling school that are best learned on the job or through working with an agency. For instance, many modeling schools include, as part of their curriculum, putting a portfolio together. You've read throughout this book that a model needs *only* unretouched snapshots to make an entrance into a modeling agency. Getting a portfolio done through a school is no different than going to a photographer and getting one done.

Most agents to whom I spoke said that they really don't have their models use a portfolio done through a modeling school. When most of these agents, decide to represent a model, they start them from scratch, which means relearning many things the models were taught in a school. This is one of the reasons why *free* training in such things as diet, makeup, grooming and wardrobe is offered by some agencies.

If a model needs more intensive training, the agency may have the model spend time with a private tutor, someone who has experience in the industry.

The cost of a tutor can range anywhere from $50 to $100 (or more) per hour depending on your area, and who's teaching you: the tutor will give his or her undivided attention for a lot less money and time than a school. (I should also tell you that I've heard from sources that some agencies take kickbacks by booking you with a private tutor.)

Here are some other things that most modeling schools frequently participate in—and an inside look into each:

Graduation Day

Each year, after models have finished their training, many schools hold a graduation ceremony for them. Every model is allowed to participate. The graduation is supposed to draw lots of industry people such as agents, casting directors and photographers. However, many of the agents with whom I spoke said that they very rarely attend modeling school graduations because often it's a waste of time. Most modeling schools take just about anybody who walks through the door with money. Since most schools make the majority of their money from tuition, they can't afford to turn models down. Some agents don't attend because many of the graduates will never be high fashion models, and never should have been told that they could be in the first place.

Another downfall at some graduations are the other people who attend. A couple of the models I interviewed who had participated in a school's graduation said that just about anybody is allowed to attend. This means it is a big night out for the con artists. These models had been under the impression that only industry people and the model's family and friends would be invited.

Since the date and time of some graduations are advertised in the classified section of the newspaper, it also makes one wonder if some of these schools even send invitations to industry people or if they just advertise it in the newspapers, and hope that the right people notice.

With questionable people attending some of these graduations, many of the models are approached by people who really aren't interested in their careers and are more interested in getting a date with the model. Or they may offer to help advance their careers only if the models are willing to pay the price.

I suspect one of the reasons that some modeling schools advertise in the newspapers is to sell lots of tickets, which range in price from $45 to $100. But this is also easy access for the con artists. Many times there's also dancing and mingling after the show.

Most industry people will not mix business and pleasure with potential talent. It's just not good business ethics. Instead, most industry people will go up to the models they are interested in, hand them a business card and tell them to call their office during business hours to set up an appointment to discuss their career. Then they will leave. So most of the people left to dance with the models probably wouldn't be able to advance the models careers *properly*.

I do want to point out however, that not all the models who had participated in a modeling school graduation had a bad experience with con artists. Some of the models said that they weren't approached by anybody, including industry people, and felt as if they had just wasted their money.

Competitions

Another thing some schools participate in is the modeling competitions held in New York. The expense for this is paid by the model, which can range from $1,000 to $2,000, for air fare, hotel, tips, food, transportation, wardrobe and many other little odds and ends. Many New York agents do attend, because it's practically in their backyard.

But is it worth all that money? Some of the models I interviewed didn't think so. Some of these models spent a great deal of time preparing for this event, including flying to the location to participate, only to be told that they really don't have the potential to be a model or that they should have spent their money on something else—like acting lessons. Again, if more modeling schools were to take the time to discourage models who don't have potential and redirect them into something more constructive, many of these models wouldn't be wasting their time and money on a career that will never manifest.

MISLEADING RADIO AND NEWSPAPER ADS

There are some ads that you'll hear on the radio or read in the newspaper that are just enticements for schools. Frequently the ad will say that a free photo session and an honest evaluation, are waiting for eager models. Many people have told me that what usually ends up happening is that you go there and get your free photo session. Then when the school gets the photos back, you and one of the school directors evaluate them. They pump up your ego by telling you that you have lots of potential and that you'll making a great deal of money modeling in New York or traveling to places like Europe and Japan. You end up feeling great that someone thinks you have a chance at modeling, and you buy into their hype and lies and fork over the money for the tuition.

If the model is under 18, the parent usually accompanies the model and gets suckered right into the school's hype because the parents are beaming with pride and joy that someone else thinks highly of their child. What parent doesn't want to be told that their child is talented and beautiful or handsome? So the parents also get conned into paying for an expensive modeling school.

I am not condemning or recommending modeling schools, and if an agent suggests that you go to a modeling school, there are many advantages to attending one.

Many schools have, in their curriculum, courses about building your image, wardrobe coordination, public speaking, interviewing skills, modeling etiquette, diet and nutrition, runway techniques and much more. With a young model who is rough around the edges in these areas, it is advantageous for the agency to send them to school rather than hiring a private tutor. (In the next chapter there is information on finding a legitimate modeling school.) In the meantime, the model would also be working with the agency by building up their book and going out on go-sees.

But again, get the opinion of an agent first. You may not need to attend a modeling school, and the money that you would have wasted on tuition could be spent on other things.

As one agent summed it all up: "Many schools aren't in the business to sell modeling, they are in the business to sell dreams. A lot of models who come to our agency have come from various schools after they have graduated complete with a portfolio and graduation certificate. They should have never in a million years been told that they could make a living off modeling, because they won't. And it's sad, because somebody sold these people a dream that is never going to materialize. I know it sounds harsh, but it's very true."

LEARN TO MODEL BY MAIL

"For only $59.95, you to can enter a rewarding and glamorous career in modeling." This is a video designed to teach you the same things you'd learn in a modeling school. One of these ads even gave out graduation certificates, which they said almost guarantees you an appointment with any agency.

One ad which aimed to increase the salability of its video pointed out that, by using a video instead of going to a school, you would pay less money and could watch it in the comfort of your own home. How convenient! You can play the tape whenever you want (which means you won't have to miss Tuesday night's TV shows to drive an hour to sit through a three hour class), and replay the video repeatedly in case you missed something or weren't paying attention. There's one point they didn't mention and that is: what if you had questions to ask on material that the video didn't cover? At least in a school environment you would have opportunities to ask questions of a teacher.

Still another ad mentioned that several top models had succeeded by following a video train-at-home course. (It's a good thing that doctors and lawyers don't have train-at-home courses or else we'd be in trouble.) Even if top models had purchased videos such as these, they are now successful because of their salable look, not because of the video. But by saying so in an ad, it is hoped that the ad will entice you into buying the tape. Because after all, if these models can watch the video and become successful, so can you, right?

Another ad mentioned in their sales hook that videos such as theirs were being sold by top modeling agencies all over the country for $200, while theirs cost only $59.99. That's interesting, because none of the top agencies I spoke to sells videos like these, and isn't aware of other agencies selling them.

You can probably see just how easy it is for these companies to persuade models into buying these videos by the things they say in their advertisements. The companies selling them probably make thousands of dollars each year off the videos.

Incidentally, if you do know of an agency that sells videos teaching you how to act or model, and if you decide to buy one it would be like going to their school, even if they don't have one. (By the way, none of the agencies with whom I spoke recommends taking a video model course. They especially thought it was funny when I told them about the "graduation certificates.")

CHAPTER NINE

SCHOOLS

When you are looking for an acting or modeling school, you should look for one that's state licensed. A school that isn't licensed may be fraudulent. The school could also be legitimate, but isn't aware that it needs to be licensed. Yet why take your chances? Some of the actors and models I've interviewed went to unlicensed schools that turned out to be nothing more than fly-by-night schools, which took their money and ran.

Even if you already know how to determine whether a school is state licensed, you should still look over this chapter. Other things such as refunds, deposits and much more will be discussed about which you may be unclear.

Unlike some states that don't have licensing regulations for talent agencies, there are licensing regulations for schools in each state. (This is what I was told. However, in case this isn't true and you are in a state that doesn't license schools, you can find out which are the reputable schools in your area by asking agents, casting directors, the union and other actors and models.) The things discussed in this chapter apply *only to California*, and may vary in each state, but this will give you a good idea of what to expect.

REQUIREMENTS NEEDED TO GET LICENSED

A school needs two licenses: one for administrators and instructors, and one for the school itself. The license for the administrators and instructors is called a "Certificate of Authorization for Service" (COAFS). To get this license they must first fill out a form which asks for everything from their name to the driver's license numbers of the applicants.

They also have to provide the names of four people who can act as character references. They do not have to secure a bond; to protect students, the Department of Education has what is called a "Student Tuition Recovery Fund" (STRF). This is designed to reimburse students for prepaid, but unused, tuition if the school in which the student is enrolled suffers a financial collapse and untimely closure. The students who are excluded from STRF include those:

* Who enroll in courses that are free.
* Who pay all fees after instruction has been completed.
* Whose tuition is totally financed by a rehabilitation program, scholarship or other sponsor.
* Who are not residents of California.

It is important for all students to keep a copy of any enrollment agreement, contract or application to document enrollment, tuition receipts or cancelled checks to document the total amount of tuition paid and records that will show the percentage of the course which has been completed. Such records would substantiate a claim for reimbursement from the STRF. *Claims must be filed within 60 days following the school's closure.*

Fingerprint cards are not required to get a COAFS license, but the Department of Education does check for any previous arrests or criminal activity. Each person applying for this license is also required to pay for a three year license, which costs $50. The fee to license the school is $1,005.

There is one other thing an instructor must pass before getting a COAFS license. To insure that students are getting qualified instructors, an instructor must meet at least one of the following qualifications:

* Possession of a bachelor's degree in the field in which he or she is to teach, from an institution listed as an institution of higher learning by the United States Department of Education or a comparable institution of a foreign country, or the equivalent of a bachelor's degree or an advanced degree from any such institution.
* Possession of a valid adult or secondary school teaching credential or certificate from this or a state authorizing the holder to teach in the particular field of instruction in which he or she is to teach at the school applying for approval.
* Five years of successful experience in the profession, trade, industry or technical occupation in the field in which he or she is to teach.
* Five years of a combination of such experience and education at a postsecondary level.
* Possession of a license to teach issued by an appropriate state licensing board or federal agency for the field in which he or she is to teach.
* In the opinion of the Superintendent of Public Instruction, the instructor has adequate and appropriate experience and education, and demonstrates his or her ability to properly instruct in a particular course or subject.

This is another reason to attend schools that are licensed, because at least then you know you are getting good, qualified teachers.

The license they need for the school is called a "Postsecondary

License." There are certain minimum standards with which the school must comply to retain this license. These include:

* The quality and content of each course or program of instruction, training or study are adequate so that each student is able to achieve the stated course or program objective.

* In the school there is adequate space, equipment, instructional material and instructor personnel to provide the necessary training to attain the object of the particular course.

* Every instructor and administrator holds an applicable and valid Certificate of Authorization for Service issued by the Superintendent in the specified competence area in which the individual will serve.

* The school maintains written records of the student's previous education and training, with recognition where applicable.

* A copy of the course outline, schedule of tuition, fees and other charges, regulations pertaining to tardiness, absence, grading policy and rules of operation and conduct are given to students upon enrollment.

* The school maintains adequate records to show attendance, progress and grades.

* The school complies with all local city, county, municipal, state and federal regulations such as fire, building and sanitation codes.

* The school does not exceed an enrollment which its facilities and equipment can reasonably handle.

There are reasons why a school isn't granted a license. Some of these include if the owner or any of the owners, members of the board of directors, officers, administrators, or instructors of the school has pled guilty to, or has been found guilty of any crime other than a minor traffic offense, or has entered a plea of "nolo contendere" to a charge, or has committed unscrupulous acts, made material misrepresentations, committed fraud or is otherwise unfit to engage in the business of private, postsecondary education.

As you can see, it is important to attend licensed schools, because unlicensed schools may be unstable, or perhaps an unlicensed school applied for a license but was turned down because of a crime committed by an applicant. (This does not apply if the schools in your area don't need to be licensed.)

RULES AND REGULATIONS OF SCHOOLS

After a school gets its license, it also has certain rules and regulations to comply with. If it doesn't, it could lose its license or have it suspended. If the Department of Education has looked into a student's claim and thinks that the school has violated a rule, the school may have to reimburse the student for any tuition or fees that were collected. Schools are not allowed to:

* Make or cause to be made, any statement or representation, either oral, written or visual, in connection with the offering or publicizing of a course, if such a person, firm, association, partnership or corporation knows, or reasonably should have known, the statement or representation to be false, deceptive, inaccurate or misleading. (In other words, if you see an advertisement for an acting school that says "Actors who attend our school get work," or an advertisement for a modeling school that states, "Ten models took our course and now they are signed to top agencies and making big bucks," or "Earn while you learn," then these schools should be able to back up those claims. Otherwise, the ads could be considered deceptive and misleading.)

* Promise or guarantee employment.

* Advertise concerning job availability, degree of skill and length of time required to learn a trade or skill, unless the information is accurate and in no way misleading.

* Solicit students for enrollment by causing any advertisement to be published in "Help Wanted" columns in any magazine, newspaper or publication, or use "blind" advertising which fails to identify the school.

HOW TO FIND A LEGITIMATE ACTING OR MODELING SCHOOL

Now that we've discussed the fact that you should look for a licensed school, here are some suggestions for going about it:

1) The first thing is to start compiling a list of schools you may want to attend. Schools can be found by looking in the phone book and trade papers.

2) The next step is to find out if the schools on your list are licensed. You can probably get a list of licensed schools for your area by contacting the appropriate Department of Education for which there is a list of phone numbers for each state in the reference section of this book. At the same time you may also want to ask for a list of rules and regulations for licensed schools. Each state's Department will probably vary in the way they handle your request so if they don't have lists of schools to give out, then just wait until you find a school that you want to attend and then follow the procedure under "How to Check Out A School's Background" in this chapter.

If you were able to get a list from the Department of Education, check to see if the schools you are interested in are currently licensed. If some of them are not on the list, then call the Department to determine their status. These schools may have just filed and haven't been added to the list yet. If you see that a school's license has expired, check with the Department to see if they've renewed it.

When you find a licensed school or schools that you're interested in possibly attending, give them a call and set up an appointment to visit their facilities. If they allow auditing of courses, take advantage of it. (For more on Auditing, see Chapter 7.)

When you visit the school, you should ask for a tour of the facility so that you can become familiar with the surroundings as well as meet the staff and teachers. Even though you won't be studying with the staff and some of the teachers, you should still get a feel for the school's environment and people, especially since you'll probably be comparing schools.

When you visit a school, ask for a copy of the school catalog. The catalog should list most of the material below (but some of it may be included in their contract instead):

* Names of the school administrators, including active owners and titles.

* Names of the instructors and their qualifications.

* The operating dates and hours and also the vacation and holiday periods during which the school is closed.

* A brief description of the physical facilities, including parking areas, classrooms, library, sanitary facilities, etc.

* The maximum occupancy level of the facility.

* Course information including course title, description and length of the course, the maximum number of students who may attend the course at any one time and hours of the class(es).

* Course charges and fees. A school is allowed to charge a registration fee that under certain conditions need not be refunded to the student. The maximum up-front charge the school is allowed to collect is limited to an amount between $25 or 15 percent of the actual amount charged for tuition, not to exceed $100. A school may not have other fees, such as for application, library, student body requirements, identification cards, audition for entrance, etc.

* Enrollment requirements that state when a student may enroll and include information on late enrollment, such as "daily," "beginning of each term," "two weeks prior to the start of the class(es)," and so on.

* Attendance policy including absence, tardiness, interruption for unsatisfactory attendance, class cuts, make-up work or leaves of absence.

* Progress and grading system.

* Student conduct and conditions for dismissal as a result of unsatisfactory conduct.

* Placement assistance provided by the school. NOTE: placement assistance is the proper phrase. The average person will understand that he or she will obtain only minimal help toward finding a job (or representation with a talent agency) with such wording. "Placement service" or "employment service" are improper descriptions, since the

137

average person will assume a guarantee of employment.

* Records retention. Enrollees are advised and cautioned that California state law requires schools to maintain school and student records for a five year period only.

CONTRACTS

Besides picking up a school catalog when you go to visit a school, you should also get one of their contracts, take it home, look it over and make sure you understand everything on it before signing it. If they are licensed, there are certain things that must be listed on it, including:

* The name, address and telephone number of the school.

* The first page should include the sentence: "Any questions or problems concerning this school which have not been satisfactorily answered or resolved by the school should be directed to the Superintendent of Public Instruction, State Department of Education, Sacramento, California 94244-2720."

* On the same page on which the student's signature is required, the school must cite the total financial obligation, in numbers or letters, that the student will incur upon enrollment in the school (as shown below):

1. Tuition $ _____
2. Registration fee $ _____
3. Materials Fee $ _____
4. Textbook(s) $ _____
5. Total cost $ _____

Under no circumstances is the school allowed to have any hidden charges that are revealed halfway through the course. So if you've signed up for a particular course, and you are told that it's going to cost $1,500 and then in the middle of the course, they tell you that there are three books you must purchase, remember: they are not allowed to do that.

* Refund policy. A school has two different refund policies from which it can choose from when submitting its school catalog to the Department of Education for approval. (Or the school can make up one.) Here are the two policies they can choose from:

I Refund Policy for Tuition and Other Fees:

This school has and maintains a policy for refunding the unused portion of tuition, fees and other charges in the event the student fails to enter the course, or withdraws, or is discontinued at any time prior to the completion of the course for which enrolled. The policy also

138

provides that the amount charged to the person for tuition, fees and other charges for a portion of the course does not exceed the approximate pro rata portion of the total charges for tuition, fees and other charges that the length of the completed portion of the course bears to its total length. (The student is obligated to pay only for educational materials obtained and services rendered.)

II Refund Policy for Tuition and Other Fees:

A.*Cancellation*. A student may terminate enrollment in person or by mailing such notice as certified mail. The effective date of cancellation is the date postmarked. Any refunds due will be made by the school within 30 days.

B. *Materials*. Once purchased, books and other materials are the property of the student. This school does not accept returns and makes no refunds for materials.

C.*Three-Day Full Refund*. An enrollee may cancel enrollment within three working days following enrollment and receive a refund of all money paid, including registration and materials fees, provided no classes have been attended.

D.*Cancellation After Three Days*. The school is entitled to keep the registration fee, but will refund all other tuition money paid if cancellation occurs after the three-day full refund, but prior to the date the enrollee is scheduled to begin classes.

E. *Tuition Refund After Classes Begin*. Cancelling enrollment after classes are scheduled to begin, whether or not the enrollee is in attendance, will permit the following tuition refunds:

Percent of "Attendance Time"	Amount of Refund
Up to 10%	90%
10% - 25%	75%
25% - 50%	50%
Over 50%	No refund

The school's refund policy must also be fully, clearly and conspicuously included on each contract of enrollment.

Other requirements

In the event that a school allows student installment payments for the cost of the educational services for which the contract provides, then the contract shall include the following notice to be placed conspicuously on the face of the contract: "Any Holder Of This Consumer Credit Contract Is Subject To All Claims And Defenses Which

The Debtor Could Assert Against The Seller Of Goods Or Services Obtained Pursuant Hereto Or With The Proceeds Hereof. Recovery Hereunder By The Debtor Shall Not Exceed Amounts Paid By The Debtor Hereunder."

HOW TO CHECK OUT A SCHOOL'S BACKGROUND

After you've had a chance to look over several schools, taking a look at their facilities and comparing prices for what each is offering, you should do some background checking on the school you wish to go to before paying money and signing contracts.

The first thing you should do is contact the appropriate Department of Education to find out if the school has a clean record, and to check and see if they are licensed if you weren't sent a list. Even if you saw an ad somewhere that claimed that the school is state licensed, you should still check on the status of its license. The Department may have a lot of complaints on file and is getting ready to close the school down.

To finish your background check on a school, just follow the same procedures as outlined in the previous chapters. A great place to check is definitely small claims court. When I went to the courthouses, I dug up a lot on some of these schools. For example, I found several cases of licensed schools that didn't want to refund money, even though the school had 30 days in which to refund it.

There was another case in which a student was told her class would start in two weeks, which turned into four weeks because the school kept putting the student off while it tried to get other students to fill up its quota. So it might be worthwhile to check the courthouses before selecting a school. Because unless students complain to the Department of Education, the Department would never really know about these court cases.

CHAPTER TEN

THE OTHER SIDE OF YOUR CAREER

There are some people whom you should hire right away, some whom you may need later on and some you may never need. But if you are a model, you won't need to hire a personal manager or publicist unless you get into acting.

ATTORNEY

As your career takes off and you start hiring people like a personal manager or you become a big actor or model and gain more clout, you may need the guidance of an attorney to help review all your contracts. (No one said being at the top of the mountain would be easy, right?) It's a bad move to wait to find an attorney when you need one immediately, because then you may get stuck with one you really don't like. So start looking around as soon as possible.

There's only one type of attorney you should look for, and that's an entertainment attorney. Look in the phone book or ask other industry people for recommendations.

CERTIFIED PUBLIC ACCOUNTANT (CPA)

A CPA will be like your best friend all year round, and especially at tax time. Models and actors spend a lot of money for all sorts of odds and ends, which can add up to substantial write-offs. When you do hire a CPA, have him review receipts that you should save. An actress friend of mine habitually threw away all her receipts because she didn't know any better. She was quite mad when she discovered that much of what she discarded could have been written off at tax time.

141

CPAs will cost more money than a franchise tax return service, but their expertise could get you back not only their fee but much more on your tax returns. Again you need one who is entertainment oriented, so ask around.

BUSINESS MANAGER

This person will be another one of your best friends, although you won't need him or her until you have money to invest. In the meantime, you might still shop around to find someone you like and get acquainted. After all, they will be handling your hard-earned money, so be choosey.

A good business manager is, plain and simple, in the business of investing money. He or she can also arrange loans and put together your financial statement and portfolio. You want someone who is reputable and has experience, so it would be good to seek referrals from reliable sources. Watch out for fraudulent investors who promise to take a small amount of your money and turn it into a $1,000,000 overnight. So deal only with referrals. This is your hard-earned money, and you don't want someone running off with it.

PUBLICIST

When your career starts to take off, you'll need a publicist. But if you hire one sooner, you'll be wasting money. If you're new, who or what would they publicize? That you played Goldielocks in the community theater? You're sure to have tons of movie personnel running to your side. Most publicists won't even meet you until you have established a career that's worth publicizing. Again, hire only professionals who have been referred to you through people in the industry.

CAREER CONSULTANTS

If your career isn't going anywhere, or if you are having difficulty getting an agent, a career consultant may be able to put you on the right track. Many of them are former actors and/or models themselves who are quite knowledgeable about the industry. Some of them also provide private coaching on audition and interview techniques, help with resume and cover letter writing and much more.

Since anyone can put an ad in the newspaper or trade papers claiming to be a career consultant (and charge a hefty hourly fee), tread carefully and get referrals. If he or she gives advice on the acting and/ or modeling industry, they should either still be in the business or just recently out. If the consultant left acting or modeling 10 years ago, the information they give you will likely be outdated. How can that possibly help you?

IMAGE CONSULTANTS

Does your appearance need an overhaul? An image consultant may be just what you need. They can be expensive, as much as $100 or more an hour, but their services can be of great value and help to your career. Image consultants guide you with decisions on your hair including the right shade and style, and makeup (including the best colors either to bring out or enhance your present features). They can assist you in wardrobe coordination to help you find great fashions to emphasize your assets. They will even go shopping with you to help you pick out that wardrobe and accessories.

PERSONAL MANAGERS

Their job is to manage and consult with an actor regarding his or her professional career. When you start getting a lot of different movie or TV offers, a manager can advise an actor on which parts to accept. But they also do much more than that—they basically follow right behind you and help you make all kinds of decisions, from which banks to invest your money to the best publicist for your career.

Personal managers can't get work for you, but what they can do is to keep an eye open for auditions by looking over the breakdown service or other services and nudging your agent a little.

One of the differences between an agent and a personal manager is that the agent represents hundreds of actors whereas a manager will handle only a small number of actors. They also take more of a personal interest in your career, whereas the agent mainly responds to casting calls and books actors, among other things.

When you are first starting out in acting, an established personal manager, like the publicist, won't even look at you. You don't have a name yet, and if you think that by hiring a manager your career will take off, you've been looking at the wrong one (see Chapter 12). Getting a personal manager also depends on the market you're in. In Los Angeles, you'll definitely need one when the times comes, but in a smaller market, their services won't be of great value, because there really isn't enough activity.

It's easy for anyone to be a personal manager. A manager doesn't need to be licensed by the Department of Labor or franchised with the union, he or she can take any percentage amount (some of the better ones take up to 15 percent or more) and basically do whatever they want—within limits. Most agents don't believe you need a personal manager, likewise, most personal managers don't feel you need an agent. It's an argument that has been going on in the industry for a long time. I think it has a lot to do with the fact that an agent telling an actor he should do one thing while the manager says he shouldn't, can create conflicts.

Personal managers can also make big mistakes in your career, such as advising you against taking a particular role in a movie because they feel you've been typecast and should be doing other roles. So you turn down the job and then are out of work for several months, even years. No matter whom you hire to work for you, you are ultimately in charge of your career. You should *always* rely on your own gut feelings and instincts no matter what anyone says.

Since anyone can call himself or herself a personal manager, here's what you should look for when it comes time to hire one. The first thing you should seek is a personal manager who doesn't charge you up-front for anything such as fees for registration, interviews, auditions and so on. The only money they, like agents, are entitled to is a commission from the work you've done, unless specified otherwise in a contract. You also want to find a manager who has clout, so look for someone who has been in the business for a couple years, represents at least one or two well-known celebrities and has no more than 10 to 15 clients.

Your best bet to find a legitimate personal manager is to check with other industry people. By the time you're ready to hire a personal manager, you will have lots of acquaintances in the industry who also have personal managers.

Before you sign any contract with a personal manager, make sure you take the contract to your attorney to have him or her fine-tooth comb it for you. I've heard some bad stories of people locking themselves into undesirable contracts with managers.

CHAPTER ELEVEN

CASTING DIRECTORS

Casting directors come from all walks of life. Many have previously been actors, secretaries to casting executives, talent agents, photographers or wives of industry people. But they all have one thing in common: to find the best talent. Which brings us to:

HOW CASTING DIRECTORS FIND TALENT

There are two times that a casting director looks for talent. When they're casting something or when they're just generally looking for new faces. When casting directors are looking, there are many places they can find talent. These include:

Theater

Many casting directors scout theaters all over the country looking for talent (this is becoming rare, because the industry now has showcases where casting directors can at least get paid for their time). Theater includes Equity and 99-seat equity waiver shows and community theater.

Many great actors have been signed to an agent or caught the interest of a casting director on the strength of his or her part in a play. If you're going to invite a casting director to a play you'll be in see Chapter 2 under "Theater." Remember, you don't want to invite a casting director to a play where the cast and crew are rusty, or your part is small, or if you're not ready to show your acting talent to the world.

If you invite a casting director to a play you'll be performing in, and your acting skill is below average, here's what could happen. Let's say your agent gets a casting call from the same casting director who attended your bad performance, and the agent wants to send you on the audition. Usually the casting director will either have the agents call in the names of the actors who will be attending the audition, or the agents will submit pictures and resumes so the casting director can pick whom they want to audition.

145

Casting directors usually have pretty good memories, so if this person hears your name or sees your picture and remembers you as the below-average actor, it may ruin your chance to audition for that part. This may not happen and you may be called in anyway (especially if it has been some time since they saw you act). But rather than take any chances, wait until you're skilled enough as an actor to start inviting industry people to your shows. This includes showcases, summer stock and even workshops.

Showcases

A showcase is a prepared scene acted out by two actors in front of an audience of casting directors, agents, and sometimes producers, directors and personal managers. This is not a bad way to be seen. You have a guarantee that industry people will be in the audience watching, you have control over who your scene partner will be and you don't need to worry about the rest of the crew being bad because it's just you and another actor. Unlike being in a play, it doesn't take many months to rehearse and set up. Sounds good, doesn't it? Well here's the bad news, from what I've been told you have to pay to perform at a showcase. Then to top it off, all the industry people who attend get *paid* to watch you perform, while you get no money at all for your time.

I don't see where the fairness is. Some of these industry people have said that they have to take time out of their busy schedules to attend (while this is true, these showcases are usually held at night so I'd like to know what busy schedule we're talking about) with the possibility of not finding any competent actors.

On the other hand, do you think actors just walk into the showcase with the script in hand and miraculously give a great audition without practicing? Of course not. These actors put in a lot of hard work, which includes finding the right scene and clothes, and then they rehearse, rehearse and rehearse till they get it right. Often when actors arrive at the showcase, they sometimes have to wait until five or six other actors have performed before they can do theirs.

Someone told me about reading in a newspaper of a casting director who had made $20,000 in one year just from going to showcases and watching actors perform. Now what do you think is going to happen two or three years down the line (possibly sooner) as casting directors and other industry people get wind of this? This applies even more so with the agents and casting directors because you have to get through them first before you can get to the directors and producers.

Do you think they will want to live off just one salary when they could be making so much more from going to showcases? Of course not, they will want a piece of the action, too. Especially when each industry person who shows up gets paid, for an average showcase, anywhere from $100 to $200 to watch around 10 to 20 actors showcase their scenes.

What I feel may happen is that there will come a time when agents and casting directors will not attend your plays and just tell you that they will be happy to see you at a showcase they'll be attending on a particular date. After all, why should these people go to a play for which they won't get paid, when they can go to a showcase and at least get paid for their time. That way, even if they don't find any good actors, they really don't waste their time.

Sure, actors do need to be seen by agents and casting directors, or else their careers don't go too far, but why should they have to *pay* to audition? I've spoken to actors who have participated in lots of showcases, but they didn't feel that it helped their careers all that much. A couple of them got an audition a *year* later because their agents had submitted them for the roles, and the casting director remembered them.

Even though a couple of actors did get an audition a year later, it was probably due to the fact that they fit the image the casting director was looking for, and not because of some scene they did at a showcase. It doesn't matter how good an actor you are, if you don't fit the casting call, you won't get called in. (Of course, there are always exceptions to the rule, especially in the entertainment industry.)

I think it really should be the other way around: the industry people should have to pay the actors for the privilege of watching them perform. (Actually no one should get paid for their time, but if money is going to change hands, then it should be the actors who get paid.) Paying for auditions will continue to go on as long as actors continue to *patronize* them.

My philosophy is that showcases should not be a place where industry people use their names and clout to influence actors into paying for an audition which should ultimately be free. I'm not the only one who feels this way; there are plenty of other actors who agree.

If you feel the same about this situation as I do, it would be better to stay away from showcases until you feel better about paying for an audition. Otherwise some of that resentment and anger will probably pour over into your scene, and I don't think you'd feel comfortable after the showcase shaking hands with the same people who are getting paid for their appearance at the showcase.

If you do attend a showcase, make sure to bring lots of headshots, resumes and even photo calling cards to hand out. After the showcase, avoid asking if you did well (you didn't attend a class, you gave a performance). This just shows you lack confidence in yourself. What if they come back at you with "Well, how do you think you did?" then what would you say? "Oh I was wonderful?" Instead, look confident, turn on the energy, shake hands and thank them for coming.

If refreshments are provided after the show, don't pig out; get out and mingle. You can always go home and eat, but you aren't always going to get the opportunity to have all these industry people in one place at one time.

Always remember to follow-up by dropping them a line in the mail every couple of weeks to remind them they saw you in such performance and to keep you in mind for future auditions or interviews.

If you're a member in good standing of AFTRA or SAG, the union offers free showcases and your audience would consist of agents, casting directors and other industry people.

Seminars and Workshops

Take a glance through a couple of trade papers, and you'll usually find at least one or two seminars or workshops given by casting directors or agents that teach you everything from how to get an agent to handling cold readings. This is another paid audition but at least the casting directors and agents are working for their money, unlike the showcases where they're just sitting watching actors perform.

But what you must bear in mind is the fact that you should only attend a seminar or workshop (even showcases) attended by a casting director because you *want* to, and not in the hope of getting cast in something. Many actors make this mistake, and they usually end up feeling frustrated and let down.

I think a lot of actors are under the impression that all they have to do is go to one of these workshops, seminars or showcases, impress the casting director, and they'll get cast in a movie or TV show because the casting director thought they were spectacular. Well, it doesn't work that way. I'm not saying that would never happen, because if they were casting for a part in a movie and were impressed by your audition, and you fit the part, who knows what could happen? Anything's possible in this business.

But I will say this: if you don't live in the Los Angeles area, and you attend a workshop or seminar given by a Los Angeles casting director, you can almost bet that the chances of getting cast in something are extremely slim. Why should they cast you when there are thousands of highly talented actors with their SAG cards in Los Angeles from whom to pick?

A casting director is not going to go to all the trouble to have you flown to Los Angeles (regardless of whether you're paying) unless you are a highly skilled actor with a SAG card and a good, promotable look—and you also fit a part that they are casting. Remember there are thousands of very talented actors in Los Angeles, so unless you stand out, it will be highly unlikely that they would have you go to Los Angeles for an audition.

Anyone can put an ad in a newspaper or trade paper claiming to be an out-of-town casting director. Unless it's a free seminar or workshop, ask for referrals. The main referrals they'll probably give you, if they're legitimate, are agents, since they work closely together. When you get to know the industry better and recognize who's who, getting referrals really won't be necessary.

One good idea before taking any workshops taught by casting directors or agents is to make sure you audit the class first. One actress with whom I spoke said that she was glad she audited one casting director's class before deciding to take it because she said that the casting director wasn't really doing anything worthwhile. For one thing, this person did not give feedback to the students who were doing cold readings, he allowed the classmates to do it. This is ridiculous. Most people take a class to learn from the teacher, not the students. You could have stayed at home with several of your actor friends and critiqued one another instead of shelling out all that money for this class.

The actress said it was apparent that this casting director was only out for money and couldn't care less about teaching any students. This is why it's always good to audit so you can see the teacher in action.

There are some casting directors who are very interested in passing on their knowledge to students, but then there are some who are only profit oriented and unconcerned about whether you learn anything or not.

Guide Books

There are books that you should be listed in depending on your area. The "Academy Players Directory" is for actors in Los Angeles. In New York, there is the "Players Guide." For actors in the South and Southwest, the "Whitmark Directory" is your guide. (Addresses for these are located in the reference section of this book.) To find out which, if any, guidebooks are used in your area, you can ask your agent or call the local union. (These particular guidebooks are not the same as talent books described in the next chapter.)

Auditions

Another way they find talent is through auditions. These can sometimes be as frightening as going to the dentist to get a root canal. When I first started out in acting, I thought that the more auditions you went to, the less nervous you would feel. It never happened. Even other actors who have been in the business for years said that they still feel anxious before each audition, although their feelings were a little more controlled. Finally it made sense to me. Each time you go on an audition, you go to a new place, meet new people and read from a new script for a new commercial, TV show, etc. And just like with anything else in life, whenever you experience something new and unknown, it's foreign and it can be frightening.

Just as when you begin a new job, you're nervous because you don't really know what to expect on the first day or what they will expect of you. But after you've been there for several weeks, it becomes more of the same old routine because you've gotten used to the job and your co-workers. It would probably be the same with auditions: if actors were allowed to audition repeatedly for the same part in front of the same people and in the same room. Unfortunately, it doesn't work that way.

To give you an idea of what happens at an audition, here's an inside peek into a commercial audition:

When you first get to the casting studio, you will usually find a sign in sheet. (If it is a union job, this sheet is required to be there because if you're held longer than an hour for an audition, you're supposed to get paid for it.) This sheet will ask for your name, the agent's name and phone number, your social security number, the time you were told to arrive, the time you actually arrived and any unions to which you belong. It also lists numbers one through four, so if this is your first audition, you'd circle number one. For auditions after your second, you're supposed to get paid.

Your audition will usually be scheduled for a certain time, but always try to get there early to look over the script. If your audition is at 10:00 a.m. and you arrive at 9:15 a.m., don't sign in right away unless you plan to audition earlier than scheduled. Instead get the script and look it over, then at 9:50 a.m., sign in. (Of course, this all depends on the audition. On some casting calls you're not allowed to arrive too early, or they may want you to sign in as soon as you arrive. This is why it's a good idea to clear this issue with your agent.)

When you pick up the script, look to see if there's a storyboard provided. (This will look like a cartoon strip depicting the actual sequences of how the commercial will be shot, including the dialogue. It is not a requirment for every commercial audition, but if there is one, it's usually taped close to the sign in sheet.)

It is highly recommended that you utilize your time well at an audition. You're there to get a job not to exchange makeup tips or sports information with other actors. This will not only throw off your concentration, but it can be annoying to the other actors who are trying to look over their scripts. If someone starts up a conversation with you, be polite and tell them that you'd rather study your script and talk after the audition.

You're not confined to the waiting room, however, so it is OK to go outside or to another room to loosen up and read your script aloud. (This is a good idea, because you'll be more relaxed when you go in to do the audition. Speaking aloud also helps to eliminate the possibility of your vocal cords tensing up when you need them the most.) Don't wander too far, though, because if your name is called and you're not there, they may think you didn't show up, and you may not get to audition.

When it's your turn you will be ushered into a room where there are one or more people. Each type of audition is different in terms of whom you can expect to be there, especially on the first audition. I've been to auditions where the casting director was the only person there and on other ones where practically everyone involved in the production was present. But every person in that room plays a part in the casting process or they wouldn't be there.

For a first commercial audition usually just the casting director will be present. For callbacks the client, ad agency, director and the casting director are usually present.

Besides the people in the room, you'll also see a video camera, a cue card conspicuously placed somewhere (if it's a union job and the commercial has a script, there has to be a cue card), and sometimes the background is provided as well.

I once went on a potato chip commercial, and they had a little barnyard scene complete with hay on the ground. A lot of times the client wants to see exactly what you'll look like in the commercial, so instead of having you do the audition with a plain backdrop, they sometimes provide the background to get the full effect.

Introductions will be made if there are other people present besides the casting director. Next, you'll be given some direction and possibly other instructions such as where to stand. Then you'll be asked to slate (industry jargon) your name. This is not the time to start giggling or acting cute. Just look straight into the camera, smile and say something like, "Hi. My name is: _____." After a pause, the casting director will say "Action." You're usually allowed only one take, but sometimes two or three takes are permissible.

You'll never be pressured into starting your lines until you're ready. It's not as if the casting director has a stop watch, and is telling you: "On your mark, get set, go!" You have as much time as you need to prepare yourself once inside the audition room, so if you need to take several deep breaths, go right ahead. It can be intimidating, because everyone is watching and waiting, but one of the reasons many actors goof at auditions is because they don't give themselves enough time to collect their thoughts. Don't take 20 minutes, but one minute isn't going to hurt, and if it helps you do better at the audition, you will have a better chance at landing the job.

If the audition calls for you to hold a prop, hold it close to your face when you are referring to it in the script, then drop it to your side when you're not. But don't wave the product around as you speak or hold it

151

you're not. But don't wave the product around as you speak or hold it outstretched from your body. This video will be viewed by people who will be making decisions on whom to callback, and they will want to see the product (including the name of the product), not an outstretched arm, or the product being waved around.

After you've finished your scene, you're free to leave. (Remember to sign out.) Don't hang around trying to get an interview with the casting director or see if you're going to get called back. Go home and call your agent to tell him or her how everything went. Unless you totally bombed, refrain from reporting every little detail.

One thing that you may want to make a habit of is sending thank you notes to your agent and the casting director saying that you had a great time at the audition. Thank the agent for sending you on the audition and whatever else you may want to add. Remember to include a photo postcard of yourself whenever you send notes to casting directors; they remember faces more than names.

One piece of advice: rather than sitting around waiting to see if you get a callback, it would be better to go and do something constructive to help get your mind off it. Go audition for a play, rehearse with a new scene partner or do some publicity for your career.

Callbacks

If you are chosen for a callback, it could be anywhere from a couple of days to a week (depending on the project) before you hear from your agent. There is no magic formula for getting called back, except that you are what the client, director or producer was looking for.

If you don't receive a callback, there could be several reasons why. First of all, we will assume that your picture and resume don't need overhauling because you wouldn't have been at the audition if they weren't good enough.

When your agent sends you on an audition, it's not because the agent is sitting at a desk randomly pulling straws—and you got lucky. You are sent because you fit the casting call that the agent got from the casting director. This is why we can rule out your resume and picture as being the culprit. So what's left then?

There are fifty million other reasons. The problem could lie with your acting ability. It's possible that just because you've taken 10 different acting workshops, you might not be a skilled actor. Every actor is different; while one actor needs only a small amount of training to do well, another may need more extensive training.

The other problem could lie with genetics. Many times you are matched husband and wife, mother and daughter, and so on. If the role of the mother has been cast, and you're up for the role of the daughter, but you don't "genetically" match, this could be a reason you didn't get called back.

Some other reasons why you aren't called back could be that they didn't like your nose or thought your teeth weren't white enough. Maybe they thought they wanted a blonde, blue-eyed actor, but changed their mind to a brunette, green-eyed actor, and the list goes on. So don't despair if you aren't called back. The best actors in the world sometimes don't get callbacks. In the meantime, just keep becoming a better actor. Don't sit around trying to analyze why you didn't get called back. It will just drain your energy. The best thing to do is to move forward and don't examine the past. Eventually you will get where you want to in your acting career. Patience and perseverance are musts in this industry, and if you don't have these virtues, this business will teach them to you.

Now that we've taken care of that, let's move on to what actually happens at a callback.

The script that you'll receive should be the same, but you might want to check with your agent. When you go to the callback, duplicate everything you wore to the first one because it's hard to tell why they called you back.

Anything could happen at this audition, so be prepared. They may end up having you switch roles. You might have originally read for the supermarket clerk, but maybe they want to see what you would be like reading for the part of the customer, so they'll ask you to switch roles. After the audition, thank everybody, and then call your agent when you get home to say how it went and also to find out when you should expect to hear whether you got the part.

If you didn't get the part, again it could be one of a million reasons, so just move on.

DO'S AND DON'TS FOR AUDITIONS

Do

* Leave all personal problems at home, especially if the audition is for a commercial. They want lively, happy people.

* Give your body and vocal cords a workout. Try exercising and practicing some tongue twisters.

* Get plenty of sleep the night before, so you can be alive and vibrant at your audition.

* Dress for the part. If your agent tells you to wear green pants and a red blouse, don't come in wearing a blue outfit in an attempt to be different. Your agent wants you to get that part just as much as you do, because if you do, then you both receive money.

* Ask questions. If you're at the audition and you don't understand the pronunciation of a word, don't feel as if you'll be labeled stupid if

153

you ask for help. If you don't and you pronounce the client's product wrong, you'll look even more foolish.

* Wait out in the lobby if you're the parent of a child actor.

* Bring a headshot and resume to every audition, even if your agent has already submitted one to the casting director.

* Apply makeup before going to the audition because there may not be enough time to do it when you get there. But bring along your makeup kit, in case you need to freshen up a bit.

Don't

* Bring your boyfriend, girlfriend or anyone else to the audition, unless you're under 18. Then you are allowed to bring your parent or guardian.

* Call the casting director. If you have questions about what you should wear to an audition or when callbacks will be, ask your agent unless you were told otherwise.

* Be rude, obnoxious or inconsiderate to anyone, including your fellow actors.

* Wear jewelry of any kind, unless it's been specified by your agent. You want the people who will be doing the hiring to concentrate on you not your jewelry.

* Wear black or white. These colors don't look good on camera. Instead choose colors in the medium-to-light range. Also avoid any loud or splashy colors and prints that can upstage you.

* Lie to the casting director, producer or director about anything. If they ask if you can ride a horse bareback and you can't, be honest and tell them so. If they want you badly enough, they may just tell you to get a couple of riding lessons. In any case, lying can get you into trouble.

There are many states where it is illegal for a minor to sell cigarettes or alcohol, so don't tell them that you're 21 when you're only 20 if they ask your age. When it comes time to do the shoot and they find out, you will be replaced.

QUESTIONS TO ASK YOUR AGENT BEFORE AN AUDITION

Agents usually call you for an audition when you least expect it. They will talk at incredible speeds when they relay the information to you while you try to write it all down. Then you get off the phone and discover that you forgot to ask several questions, so you call back and ask. Several hours later you remember a couple more questions, but by then it's too late to call. So to clear up this confusion, here is a list of questions to ask. Always have enough copies made so you don't have to write on the original. It's a good idea to repeat the answers back to

154

the agent. A misunderstanding could cause problems.

* What should I wear?

* Who should I see when I get to the audition? (Usually you'll see the casting director, but you should get a name.)

* What is the name, address and phone number of the casting studio? (If driving, get directions and parking information.)

* What is the time of the audition?

* How early can I arrive at the studio to look over the script? (You might also want to ask the time you should sign in, in case you want to get to the audition early to look over your script.)

* If your audition is at a studio in Los Angeles, ask if there will be a drive-on pass for you at the gate.

* Who will I be reading with? (You want to find out if you'll be reading with another actor, by yourself, with the casting director or someone else.)

* Does the audition call for a cold read, monologue or improvisation? (For most auditions expect to do a cold reading. This is why it's good to enroll in some cold reading workshops.)

* Should I call you when I finish the audition?

* Will there be callbacks? If so, when will they be?

* If you're under 18, be sure and ask your agent if a parent or guardian should accompany you.

GETTING AN INTERVIEW WITH A CASTING DIRECTOR

The purpose of an interview with a casting director is to display your "wares," such as your personality, acting ability, look and voice for future use. When you're not busy with auditions, acting classes or other things related to acting, you should be trying to meet casting directors. You will find out quickly enough that trying to get an interview with a casting director is like trying to win a contest. But like anything in life, it can be done with lots of determination and patience.

Before arming yourself with a bunch of pictures and resumes, you need to do some prior planning. First of all, depending on where you live, dropping off your submissions can be questionable. Take Los Angeles, for example, where many casting directors are on studio lots. Unless you can get past the guards, you won't be able to get in. But it has been done before, so let's not label it impossible.

The other problem in Los Angeles is that most casting directors really don't like actors dropping off their submissions, so unless you live in that area, it would be safe to assume that making rounds is an accepted practice in your town. But even if you're in Los Angeles, do you think that aggressive actors just sit back and let this get in their way? No way, and it's not all the casting directors who are opposed to this. One of the reasons they don't like it is because some actors don't use common sense.

One casting director had this to say: "One of the reasons why we really don't like actors dropping by is because some of them hang around while we're on the phone, trying to get an interview. I mean they can see that we're really busy, and yet it doesn't seem to faze them at all. They need to use common sense, to just drop off the pictures and resumes, and then leave. I mean if we want to talk, we'll talk, but rarely will an actor ever come into a casting director's office and see him or her just sitting there twiddling their thumbs, waiting to interview actors."

So Rule Number One is, "Don't Wear Out Your Welcome." Put yourself in their shoes: you wouldn't want people trying to get an interview with you while you are on the phone or otherwise extremely busy. This is probably the reason that some of these casting directors are on guarded lots; it's actually a good idea. So just drop off your pictures and resumes and leave.

But before you can drop anything off, you'll need to gather the names and addresses of casting offices. For a large area such as Los Angeles, there are guidebooks such as "The CD Directory." For other areas, similar books are available at your local bookstore or ask your agent for guidebook suggestions. If your area is too small to justify having one, you could just have your agent give you the names, addresses and phone numbers of local casting directors.

Just mailing or handing casting directors your submission may not yield you an interview. You might have to do a little more prodding such as dropping them a note every now and then to remind them of your existence. However, *do not* call; if they are interested they will get in touch with either you or your agent.

Another thing some actors do is to send cards for Christmas and birthdays. Your main goal is to keep your face and name planted in their minds. I've known some actors to send notepads or pen holders with the casting director's name engraved on them so that these things become a reminder of the actor's existence each time they're used.

But you should never try to buy someones attention. You should do things because you want to do them not because you expect something in return. Casting directors should not be regarded just as stepping-stones in your career. This may be true, but treat them as people and don't try to sugar coat them. Phoniness can be spotted a mile away. Sending flowers to a casting director is great if you do it out of friendship, but if you do it because you really don't want to and just want to keep your name in front of them, then it's not a sincere gesture.

THE INTERVIEW

Finally, your hard work and determination has paid off, but it's still

156

not over quite yet. Now you need to show them what you can do. They wouldn't have called you in if they didn't feel as if you had something.

Many actors tend to panic at the thought of interviewing with a casting director. It's not all that bad, if you will just remember a couple of things. First, you're not applying for a job, so don't treat this as that type of interview. Second, be yourself and not somebody you're not or somebody you think they want to see. They want to see the real you.

One other tip: when you interview with any industry person you should never have to model lingerie, swimwear, or do anything else out of the ordinary, unless you're at an audition, and your agent has specifically stated that you will need to wear such items. I have heard about one casting director who asked actresses to model skimpy lingerie in his office, just so he could get his thrills for the day.

Another thing that you should never have to do is audition (or interview) for an industry person in his or her apartment, house or hotel room (unless you were specifically sent there by your agent). Auditions happen during business hours and in an appropriate business environment.

One actress told me the story of a well-known director who would hold auditions at his home at night and then try to persuade actresses to have sex with him. This is completely unprofessional behavior, and if you ever run into a situation like this or the one above, just get up and walk out. It is highly unlikely that your career will be advanced by sleeping around with industry people. Be sure to call your agent and report that person. If it is your agent who is doing this and he or she is franchised and/or licensed, report him or her to the union, the Department of Labor or some other law enforcement agency immediately.

What to wear to the interview

Don't run out and buy a new outfit for the interview. Not only is it unnecessary, but we all know that a new outfit can make us feel awkward because we're not used to wearing it. You will need to concentrate more on the interview than on your outfit. It doesn't really matter what you wear, just so long as it's professional, neat and clean. However, stay away from skimpy or revealing clothes. Dressing this way will not get you cast any quicker. Even jeans are OK, as long as they're not faded, ripped or have patches all over them. And watch the amount of jewelry and makeup.

What you should take

You should take the two items that are necessities in an actor's life: a headshot and resume. Some actors (and I think this is a good idea) always have a surplus supply of extra photos, resumes, photo post-cards and sometimes even extra clothing stashed away in the trunk of their car. You never know if you'll run out the door one day and forget to bring these to an audition or interview. Or let's say you're at a party and you happen to bump into a couple of industry people. This would be a perfect time to hand out some of your calling cards, but since you didn't bring any, what are you going to do? Run home? So rather than be unprepared, keep some in your trunk. If you have a modeling portfolio, leave it at home unless you were asked to bring it.

Another thing you should take is any videotape you have of yourself. This includes student and nonunion films, industrials, TV shows, movies and commercials. Getting copy for some of these, especially an unreleased movie, may be difficult. You may want to enlist the help of your agent.

San Francisco teacher and actor Scott DeVenney explains how to go about getting a copy for a commercial you've done. "On the day that you're working, find someone who has the authority to release a copy, such as the executive producer or ad agency representative, get their card and extract from them a promise that you can get a copy of the commercial from them. Then once the commercial has been shot, follow-up immediately with a letter saying something like, "I had a great time working with you. Thank you for assuring me that I could get a copy of the work that I did. Please let me know when it's available. I will be happy to pay for any reproduction costs." If you don't hear from them, follow-up with a phone call and tell the person, "Sorry to bother you, but I really would like a copy of this. Of course I'd be happy to pay the cost of having it reproduced and shipped to me. Just let me know what the cost is."

"I've even heard that some actors go so far as to send a check for $50, made out to the ad agency and sent to the person's attention saying, "Thank you so much for your kind offer to get me a copy of the latest commercial I did for you. Enclosed is a check for $50 to cover reproduction costs and handling. If it's not enough, please let me know." That's sort of a final desperate attempt. If all else fails, you can always pirate it off the air when it's broadcast. Find someone who has a 3/4" betacam or high-quality equipment of some kind, and get a schedule from the ad agency of when and where the commercial will be aired. Then set up your recorder and just tape it off the air. It's usually best to take it off of a cable feed because regular over-the-air broadcast is sometimes not clean enough."

When you arrive

Be sure you arrive on time. Many casting directors get very upset if you're late, even if you have a good excuse. Leave plenty of time to get there and find the casting office. Even if you take public transportation, it would be better to take the train scheduled before the one that would get you there on time. You never know if the train will fall behind schedule.

If the casting director is on the phone when you get there, don't stand there and stare. This is rude and annoying. (You don't want to start your interview on the wrong foot, do you?) Instead, find a chair where you can read a magazine or do something else to keep yourself occupied in the meantime.

There are some things you shouldn't take to the interview (or audition) such as food, drinks, gum or candy. If you smoke, it would be a good idea not to light up unless they do. If the casting director is a nonsmoker and you light up, it will be awkward for both of you. Even if they light up, you should still ask if they don't mind. (Better yet, refrain from smoking. The interview isn't going to last that long.) If they offer you a cup of coffee, and you drink it, fine, but sitting there slurping a soda, eating a sandwich or snapping gum while talking to the casting director won't go over too well. You're trying to leave a good impression, not a bad one.

QUESTIONS CASTING DIRECTORS ASK

Expect to be asked questions: no interview would be complete without them. To help you out a little, below are some of the popular questions, along with a brief example of how to answer them.

What have you done recently?

This means what work you've done such as plays, movies, commercials, etc. So refrain from talking about your job as a waiter or anything that isn't related to show business. It would be like going to an interview for a computer programmer and talking about all the plays and acting classes that you've done. The interviewer will figure that your mind is more on acting than it is on being the best computer programmer. They would much rather hear that you've been taking workshops and seminars on computers. It's the same thing with casting directors; you want them to believe that all you think about and do all day is act. So pretend that you don't even have another job and just keep the conversation related to acting.

If you haven't done any recent work, it would be better to say you've been auditioning for plays, taking acting classes or something related to acting rather than saying that you haven't done anything. Don't look like a couch potato.

Tell me a little about yourself

This has always been an awkward request because it's not specific. "Tell me a little about yourself," can mean many things. Maybe they want to know about your personality or about your good and bad habits, or even your childhood. The question is too general. And yet this question seems to be asked at just about every interview, including nonentertainment interviews.

But be prepared for the question; it can catch you off guard if you're not ready for it. The key here is to be interesting: talk about your hobbies such as sky diving or rock climbing. (But don't make up something just to sound interesting.) You never know whether the casting director also enjoys rock climbing and would want to discuss it with you.

Why do you want to be an actor?

Answering this by saying that you want to be rich and famous is definitely the wrong answer. Saying something like you love challenges and meeting new people, or that you've had a burning desire to act and express yourself since childhood, would be a much better choice.

Let's talk about your resume

This subject will probably come up sometime during your interview. Each casting director is different, some will go over your resume with a fine-tooth comb asking something about every credit while others will just hit one or two credits.

Don't say anything negative about your resume. If they ask you about a credit, and it was only a small part when you should have been cast in the lead role, don't reply by telling them so or answering with hostility. And don't do the opposite and make the small part you had sound like the lead role either.

How old are you?

Remember: do not lie about your age, there are certain things that minors can't sell, and the casting director would certainly not want you to audition for them. If you are not a minor it's still not a good idea to lie about your age. Why would you want to anyway? So if they ask, just tell them the truth. Besides, if you make up an age, you will be stuck with it; you can't be 25 for one audition and 30 on the next; it doesn't work that way.

OTHER TIPS FOR INTERVIEWS

Always be prepared to do a monologue, in case they ask. They may just have you do a cold reading with them. If this happens, make sure that you take some time to look over the script. You won't lose any points if you do, and trying to wing it isn't going to help.

Also, don't expect the interview to be smooth sailing. What I mean is, it's not like a job interview where you walk in, fill out an application, get asked some questions by the personnel department, then go home and wait for a decision to be made. You need to take control of the interview. Instead of waiting for the casting director to come up with all the innovative questions, take the initiative yourself rather than just sitting there. You're not going to have two hours, so you really need to lay it on them. But don't be overwhelming.

Listen to what the casting director is saying. Most of us are so caught up in what we're going to say next that we lose track of what the other person is saying. It is very annoying when someone doesn't listen to you. How many times have you been out with someone having lunch or coffee, and while you are talking to them, he or she is looking around the restaurant or staring out the window. Or they keep interrupting you in midsentence. It's very irritating, because you don't feel as if the other person is interested in what you have to say.

So when you're talking to the casting director, listen to what he or she has to say. If there's a lot of action going on around you, block it out and concentrate on the person you're speaking to. Listening and paying attention will create one of the best impressions you can leave.

AFTER THE INTERVIEW

Inevitably the interview will end, but it is up to you to keep the fire going. One of the first things you should do is send a thank you note. After all, casting directors are extremely busy, so a nice thank you note will be appreciated. Say something like "Thanks for taking the time out of your busy schedule to meet with me. Hope we can work together sometime in the future." Then just keep doing your follow-up.

Follow-up is the key to this business. There are many actors, and unless you keep your face and name constantly plastered all over your area, not only by sending out your pictures and resume, but also by participating in plays, nonunion work (until you join the union) and so on, you will have a difficult time getting known. At times you may feel that your follow-up isn't paying off. But the day will come when your timing will be perfect, and your photo will arrive the same day that the casting director is looking for your type.

One more thing before closing this chapter: casting directors do not get paid *anything* by actors (this is not referring to showcase, workshop and seminar fees), not even a commission from your work. So if someone tries to charge you to be in a movie or tries to get you to trade sex for a part in a movie, he or she is not a professional casting director. Most casting directors in this business are extremely professional, and they will not try to take advantage of you. So just beware.

CHAPTER TWELVE

OTHER SCAMS TO WATCH OUT FOR

Flip through the performing arts or modeling section in the classified ads of practically any newspaper or other publication, and you're
bound to see at least one or two ads seeking new faces for acting or
modeling. Or the ad will state "Actors/Models: no experience necessary; training and photos are available." When I was doing research for
this book, I responded to many of these ads and also talked to other
actors and models who had responded to different ads.

Most of these ads turned out to be nothing but profits for the
business, with little or no gain for the actor or model. One of the main
problems most new actors and models have is that they have a burning
desire to get into the business but very little understanding of how it
actually works. This is how many of them are taken advantage of. So
I hope as you read some of the descriptions of these scams you'll make
cautious decisions when you do come across an ad whether in a
newspaper, trade paper or elsewhere.

PERSONAL MANAGEMENT SERVICES

This service is not at all like the other kind of personal manager,
who will represent you only if you have a career to manage, *and* will
not charge you fees for classes or photo services. This particular
service, on the other hand will take on anybody as long as they have the
money.

Their advertisements usually say something similar to "Models/
Actors: all ages, no experience necessary; training and photos are
available."

163

Usually when you see an ad that says *No experience necessary; training and photos are available*, it's a setup to sell you their training and photo services. Of course you pay a much higher fee than if you were to find your own photographer and classes.

The main job for this type of personal management service is to develop and prepare actors and models for the business by offering classes, portfolio development and headshot and resume preparation. But these are all things you can do or find on your own without having to pay an arm and a leg.

Especially for models: just as you've read in the previous chapters, you don't need a portfolio or training to get an agent. Remember: all new models need are simple, unretouched snapshots of themselves, and that's it. They don't need an elaborate portfolio, training or even a resume, to interest an agent, just the unaltered snapshots.

It would not be advantageous for an actor to go through a program like this either because you're paying for things you can do or find on your own for less money than what these services charge. To top it off, you usually have to pay a hefty fee even to join this type of management program.

A personal manager who takes a commission only off the work his clients get, is certainly not going to waste his time representing an actor unless the manager feels confident he has a sure thing on his hands.

In my opinion these personal management services are a waste of time and money. Not only are you paying more for their services, but many of the people operating such services haven't been in the entertainment business long enough to guide you properly. Furthermore, even though some ads claim to give an honest opinion of your potential, you would almost certainly not get it because their only concern is how much money they can make off you. They don't care if you make a career in acting or modeling.

TALENT AGENCIES

Guaranteed exposure for actors and models, claimed the ad. This type of ad almost guarantees response from unsuspecting actors and models. It promises that not only will you get the exposure that you need to get into this business, but you're even guaranteed that you'll be seen by people in the industry. Not a bad idea—but where are the underlying messages?

An actor who responded to the ad explained that the "guaranteed exposure" meant that, if you joined the agency, you would be performing instead of sitting around waiting for phone calls for jobs. The work could be at weddings, fund raisers, movies, TV shows and other events. It just depended on the type of skills you possessed.

The actor was told that he would get auditions from three times a week to three times a month, depending on how much talent he had. So unless the actor was also a disc jockey, stripper, clown or had other talent, the only work that he would be getting would be as an "extra" in movies and TV shows.

To join this agency, there was a $400 membership fee that was good for three months. After that you could either renew it, or if you were getting lots of work, they would keep you free of charge. So if you are an actor and can only do extra work, you would be paying $400 to do work that requires no skill—and is fairly easy to get on your own.

Models were also encouraged to apply, but most of the work for them was for nude and lingerie work in calendars, videos and parties. This really isn't a good deal for a model because as you'll read in this chapter under "pornography," if you're a serious model, you should steer clear of any work requiring nudity.

I should also mention that this agency was closed down because not only were they unlicensed but they were charging registration fees as well. If the actors and models who had been signed with this agency had inquired whether the agency was licensed prior to paying the $400 they might have avoided getting ripped off.

This agency was making money not only from hefty registration fees but also from commissions. So the agency would probably take on everyone who applied and had the registration money, because it would be no gamble on its part, and they would profit $400 from each person.

But what would probably happen if you asked them to put this guarantee in writing, is that they would either turn you down or discourage you from trying to get it in writing unless they felt they could definitely get you work.

In my opinion no legitimate operation can guarantee you anything in the acting or modeling business. The industry is unpredictable and most of your success depends on talent, luck, good timing, charisma and much more. So to make *guarantees* is misleading and deceptive.

Since it is so hard to get any guarantees in this business this is what enables these talent agencies to get more people to respond to their ad, and in turn they can collect more registration fees. If they are selling classes or photo services, it is easier for them to persuade you into purchasing these services by saying that in order for them to fulfill their "guarantee" you will need the tools to get work.

You should never have to pay to join an agency. Think of it this way: by paying an agency there's really no incentive on their part to get you work, and even if they happen to do it, they make just a little bit more money. With an ad saying that you're guaranteed exposure, and the agency is telling you that you'll be working instead of sitting around waiting for calls as opposed to the average agency. Who wouldn't want to join?

TALENT SCOUTS

There are legitimate talent scouts who work for some of the top modeling agencies. There are some who even work for agents handling actors, but usually it's the agents themselves who do the actual scouting.

But then there is the other type of talent scout. These scouts do not work either for or with agencies, although many of them claim to have inside ties with top agencies. By telling you this, they hope you'll buy into what they are selling.

This one particular scout service was selling photo services not classes. What they would do, for $2,000, is have a makeup/hair stylist fix you up, then bring in a photographer who takes numerous pictures that they have made into composites. These are inserted into a folder with the agency's name on it, and a cover letter telling potential modeling agencies who you are and that you are looking for representation.

They would send this package to all their agency contacts in the United States and overseas. If one of the agencies was interested in representing you, the scout service would take five percent from the agent's commission for each job you did.

But let's look logically at it: if you were an agent, would you want to share your commission with a scout service? Unless the model was an absolute knockout and would thus bring in lots of money for the agency, probably not. When you think about it, the chances of this talent scout finding an agent for you are slim.

In addition, you could gather your own list of agency contacts and send out your own snapshots. You don't need to spend $2,000 to do it. Most of it's pure profit for the scout service, anyway.

There is one problem with overseas contacts. If a European agency wants to sign you, would you know how to get around in a foreign country? This includes speaking a foreign language, exchanging currency and understanding foreign transportation services. Even their customs are different than in the United States. Most foreign agencies won't deal with an overseas model anyway unless the model has a U.S. agency behind him or her.

With the claim that they had overseas contacts, the scout service was made to look as if they had more going for them. Most models want to go abroad to model. Therefore it's a big enticement to attract models to buy into their program and spend the $2,000 for their photo services.

And how would you even know if they are honest and are truly sending your pictures to all their contacts? For all you know they could just throw your pictures away, and pretend to be actively looking for representation for you. I once asked one of these scout services for a list of the contacts to whom they were supposedly going to send my pictures. They told me it was confidential and couldn't do it because they didn't want models to use the scout service's name to get representation on their own.

I don't believe they had the contacts they claimed to have. Sure, maybe a model could mail snapshots and state in a cover letter that so-and-so scout service recommended sending in the snapshots. But it wouldn't make a difference if the model used the service as a recommendation. The bottom line is: it doesn't matter which scout service you use, if you don't have the potential to be a model, you will have difficulty getting representation.

Another company had an ad in the newspaper that read, "Modeling: new faces needed, all ages, $1,500 to $2,000 a month." Now doesn't this sound like a job is being offered for models to make anywhere from $1,500 to $2,000 a month? But when an actor responded to the ad there was no job. Instead, for $300 a talent scout arranges *one* appointment for you with an agent who signs talent exclusively.

This scout had 10 agents with whom he worked, and if you got signed to one of them, he would take five percent off the agent's commission from each job you did (like the scout above). If he wasn't able to get an appointment for you with one of his contacts, he would refund the money, which was guaranteed in the contract.

When the actor asked if he could take the contract home to look it over thoroughly, the scout said that the actor would have to sign it first. The actor replied that if he signed it, he would then be binding himself to it and agreeing to pay the scout $300. The scout just said that he didn't let anything leave his office without a signature.

You should *never* sign a contract without looking it over thoroughly and possibly having an attorney read it. I suspect one of the reasons he discouraged people from taking it home to review is so that they wouldn't be talked out of paying the $300 for his services by someone else.

If you read between the lines, this scout was saying that for $300 he will get you an appointment, not signed, but an *appointment* only. So if an agent agrees to see you but doesn't sign you, the talent scout still keeps all the money. He may even be paying the agent a small fee, to interview you so that he can keep the money.

Even if the deal were turned around, and this scout did get you signed to an agent for $300, for that price, the agent could still be paid to sign you but put you in a back file where you would be forgotten.

Again, why pay to have someone do something for you that you can do for yourself and for less money? All this person would do is to send your pictures to different agents and then phone them to try and set up appointments. That's very simple, and not worth $300.

Many models and actors go to a scout service in the hope that the service can get representation for them. The actor or model may have spent months trying to get an agent, only to be repeatedly turned down. So they think that since the scout service has contacts and more clout, they have a better chance. But to repeat for the thousandth time, if you don't have what it takes to be either an actor or model, you will find it difficult to get representation, regardless of the number of contacts or prestige the scout service seems to have.

This particular scout claims to send your pictures out to 10 agencies, and yet I heard through sources that he was sending the pictures out to only one. This is why I wonder how you can be certain that your pictures are actually being sent to the amount of contacts that they claim. At least if you gathered your own list of agencies, and sent your photos to them yourself, you would at least have a guarantee (and peace of mind) that the photos were mailed.

By the way, if you are ever approached in a bar, nightclub or any other nonprofessional situation by anyone representing himself or herself as a talent scout, casting director or other industry person who promises to advance your career, be careful. The best solution is to take the person's business card, get referrals and tell them that you'll contact them—not the other way around.

Under no circumstances should you go anywhere with the person. Several years ago a man who said he was a photographer would approach young women in shopping malls, nightclubs and other nonbusiness locations. He would persuade the women to leave with him, then he would kidnap, rape and kill them. So first make sure that everyone you meet this way is legitimate by getting referrals and checking them out. Then you can meet them during business hours at their office or studio.

TALENT BOOKS

These are books that display one to four pictures in color or black and white, and range in price from $150 to $20,000.

The book is then distributed to thousands of producers, directors, ad agencies, photographers, casting directors and agents all over the world. If someone is interested in you, they merely call the company to inquire about you. The company will then contact the actor or model with this information, and then it is up to you to contact the person yourself.

This doesn't sound like a bad arrangement, but let's examine some of the problems. The biggest problem has to do with who receives the book and what you're actually receiving for your money.

Big time, well-known producers and directors are not going to be flipping through these books because they have casting directors to find talent for them. So the only producers and directors who most probably will look at these books are the ones who are casting for low-budget or nonunion work. Usually they will either need extras or actors who will work for free or a negligible amount of money. This is the kind of work you can find on your own, and it won't cost you a pretty penny, either.

Let's move now to the ad agencies and photographers. We can well rule out ad agencies right away, because most of them won't deal with a model or an actor unless he or she is represented by an agent. You may get a fair shake, though, with photographers. But if you're a model you won't be needing a photographer until you have an agency to work with. Actors can find their own photographers for a lot less than what these companies charge.

Moving right along to casting directors: in most areas, especially Los Angeles, it will be difficult to get big-time casting directors to audition you if you don't have an agent. And most talent in these books are without an agent. This is one of the main reasons most casting directors don't look through them. So forget the majority of the casting directors.

The only person left is the agent, who is usually about the only industry person who will see a new actor or model without representation. But the problem is that most of the agents I spoke to said that they rarely, if ever, have the time or patience to look through these books.

Here's what one agent had to say: "I personally think being in these books is a waste of money, and the price of getting into one or the name of the company doesn't impress me or other agents at all. Besides, we do not find our talent by looking through some book, we're too busy. We find our actors through mail submissions and our models through open calls. And it doesn't cost you thousands of dollars to do that."

One actress I interviewed admitted that she had responded to one of these ads offering a free, honest evaluation. They gave her the rundown on how talented she was and how she would do really well in this business—the same things you hear from many of these scams, along with other compliments. Then they tried selling their training program by saying that even though she has talent, it still needed to be developed. They sold her a $5,000 ad by saying that if she bought a smaller ad she wouldn't be seen by as many industry people and should at least get her money's worth. Then added that they didn't give everyone the opportunity for such choice space, just those with the most potential. (Of course they left out the most important part and that is that whoever had the money got the choice space, not because they have potential.)

When she told them that she couldn't come up with that kind of cash, they told her to take out a loan or borrow it because, after all, it was for her career. One person told me that one company even suggested that she take out a second mortgage on her home. It just goes to show that they don't care how you get the money, just so long as you have it.

The actress told me that she decided to find out just how many people actually get work or agents from a book like this before paying any money. She asked the woman to supply her with a list of people who had been in the book, so she could call them to ask if they'd gotten work or an agent. The woman told her that the phone numbers were confidential and weren't given out even to people inquiring about talent.

When she asked the woman to contact some of the actors and models and ask them to contact her, the woman agreed to do it. But she never heard back from either the company or any actors or models.

Another thing you have to ask yourself is this: even if you do happen to get an agent or work by being in one of these books, don't you think you could have done the same thing on your own without spending a

170

large amount of money?

If you don't live in the major acting or modeling cities and are trying to boost your chances of getting seen by a big-time agent by being in one of these books, you need to ask yourself why? If an agent did happen to like your picture and wanted to represent you, you would have to move to that city. Most of you would not be able to just drop everything and move suddenly, nor would most of you even have the money to move. If you think an agent is going to advance you some money to move because he or she thinks you're fabulous, you might be sadly mistaken.

Let's just speculate that you actually do get a job by being in one of these books. Would you know how to negotiate your own salary? Would you understand how to read contracts? You surely aren't going to work on a verbal agreement, are you? Do you know how to bill clients and make sure they pay? There are many other little odd details about which an agent (if you had one, which you probably don't at this point) would be knowledgeable.

There was an actor who actually did get an audition from being in one of these books. Since he wasn't familiar with the type of questions to ask a casting director prior to an audition, when he arrived, he discovered that he was dressed completely wrong for the part. This is something an agent would advise you about prior to an audition. He didn't get the part, and was out the money for the trip.

Which brings me to another point. Since some of these books are sent all over the world, if you got a call from someone in Japan interested in seeing you, you would have to call Japan at your own expense, and pay for the flight, transportation, room, etc., for the trip out of your own pocket. Unless you received a well-paying job from it, your money and time would be wasted.

Plus, anyone can inquire about you, and these companies are probably not going to do any kind of background checking on the people who make inquires. That's left up to you. So there's a good chance that many unsuspecting, starry-eyed actors and models get ripped off by some photographers or other industry people who respond to their pictures. In the midst of the excitement that someone has finally taken an interest in them, actors and models lose all sight of reality and get conned into doing a portfolio, going to an agency's school or being ripped off in some other way.

It's up to you whether or not you feel it would be worth the money to be in one of these books. I'm sure people do get agents and work from being in these books, but it's still something you can do on your own practically for free—except for some miscellaneous expenses like postage, phone calls and gas. Instead of spending up to $20,000 for an ad, that money could be used more productively for your acting or modeling career. Because even if you plunk down $5,000 for an ad in one of these books and happen to get an agent, you're still going to have to fork out more money for costs involved in your acting or modeling career.

FASHION SHOWS

Not all fashion shows you do will have problems. I've done lots of shows in which I've worked with honest people and had absolutely no problems. But then there's always one or two in the bunch that can ruin it.

There was a man who put on fashion shows at various nightclubs and offered to pay models $50 a show. But one model was told that she would make the $50 *after* she did the first five shows without pay. He said all the models did this for practice and so he could see if he wanted to hire them permanently. She did the shows for free.

However, the man apparently changed his mind and told her that he had altered his policy and that now she would have to do 10 shows for free before he would pay her. So she just cut her losses and left.

Another model was smarter. Before she agreed to do any of his shows for free, she asked him to put it in writing. He refused, saying that he didn't put anything in writing. In other words, this man had unpaid models working for him all the time. After awhile, the models either left or kept working hoping someday to get paid. Then he gets a whole new batch of models and starts all over.

I encountered a similar situation with a woman who also did fashion shows at nightclubs. I did a show for her which was her final show at that particular club. The show was very disorganized—to the point where no model received payment after the show because she was trying to collect money from customers who had bought outfits that evening. Since it was late, she said that she would pay everyone the next day.

I called her the following day, and she told me that she wasn't going to pay me because she and I had spent an hour going over the walk routine that was used in the show. In short, she felt that we had essentially traded services.

I explained that I never agreed to trade services and she had taught me only specific steps that she wanted the models to use in her show.

172

Since these weren't regular runway steps that I could have used in other shows, they were of no use to me. After threatening her with legal action, she finally paid me.

You should be getting paid for every show you do. As you've read, many of these people try to avoid paying by having you do the first show, or five shows, for free before they pay you. This is a decision you'll have to make, but don't expect to ever get paid in these types of situations. If you decide to work for someone who's offering fashion shows, you may want to get everything in writing. If they won't do it, then go ahead and work for them only if you *don't* expect to get paid.

It's OK if they want to barter services, if you're in agreement with it. But I would even get bartering in writing, as they could try to get you to do more than one show for free by saying that you agreed to it.

MOVIE SCAMS

There was an ad in one of the trade papers to which actors responded. For $2,000, this company would guarantee you a union job, so that you could get your SAG card. This scam didn't get very far because a couple of smart actors caught on and turned them in to the union.

There was a casting director who placed ads in newspapers looking for actors to audition for parts in his upcoming movie. Anybody could be in the movie, but they had to pay to get a role, and the bigger the role, the higher the price. This guy was going from town to town placing ads in newspapers and convincing people to pay up to $1,000 to be in his movie. To this day he has still not been caught. Last I heard, he was in Nevada pulling the same scam.

You never have to pay to be in a movie. If anyone tries to say that you are investing in the movie and will not only get a part, but a cut of the profits as well, they are pulling your leg with a scam. Or they might say that the money is a donation to be sent to starving children in Africa or any other of the 50,000 ways that these con artists try to extract money from eager, starry-eyed, unsuspecting actors and models.

PORNOGRAPHY

Models

Any model who does any type of pornographic work will substantially damage his or her career. Products—whether cosmetics or clothes—do not want a model who's done porno to represent them. It would ruin their advertising image. If you need extra money, it would be best to do something that leaves your clothes on. You'll feel better, and your career won't be ruined.

You will also have difficulty finding an agent if you have done any type of porno work. In fact, you may not ever get an agent except a porno agent. So if that's where you want to aim your career, go ahead and do it.

Keep in mind that if you do any nude pictures, they may come back to haunt you. Most photographers keep negatives. If you think that you'll do a couple pictures for some extra cash to pay for your modeling career, think again. If you happen to become famous, you can bet the photographer will retrieve those negatives from his file, dust them off and sell them to a porno magazine. Then you are in for a big surprise. Sure, you could probably sue the photographer and maybe even the magazine, but the damage will already have been done, not only to your career but to your image. (Besides, what would your family think?)

There was a male model who wanted to be on the cover of a magazine so bad, he didn't care which one, just so long as it was a magazine cover. So he went ahead and posed for the cover of a gay magazine. He was a heterosexual, but by appearing on that cover he lost many subsequent jobs because no one wanted a homosexual image associated with their product. So it would be best to stay away from any covers that are not fashion oriented.

Actors

Doing pornography will not damage an actor's career as much as it will a model's livelihood, but it won't help it, either. One rule you should keep in mind is this: "Once you take off your clothes in a movie, you'll always be taking them off." Think of it this way: most movies today are rated "R," and most "R" movies have nudity in them. Sex sells movies. It's not the only thing that sells a movie, but some movies wouldn't sell as well without those steamy sex scenes.

In this industry you are typecast according to categories, so if you've done porno, whenever a role comes up that calls for nudity, and you also fit the casting call, you'll be sent. In the beginning you are going to take any audition that comes along. Then you'll be known as the actor or actress who does nude scenes, and it may take a long time to break out of that mold once you are typecast.

PORNO AGENCIES DISGUISED AS MODELING AGENCIES

Even if you are an actor you should still read this section because there are lots of actors who get caught up in the porno scene.

At first it can be hard to spot porno agencies because they advertise among the regular modeling agencies. A new model just getting into the business would have to do some investigating to determine if it's a regular or a porno agency. You won't be able to go through your list of licensed agencies because if the porno agency takes a commission, they would need to be licensed as a talent agency, in California at least.

But there are other signs to watch for. Some of the porno agencies upon meeting you will ask that you remove all your clothes so they can not only take a look at your body, but see if you are inhibited in any way. Other agencies work in a more progressive way, first by starting the model posing in skimpy lingerie. If the model doesn't protest, they'll move on to sexually suggestive photos with a man or woman, until finally they've got the model doing hard-core pornography.

Each agency will operate in its own way, but somewhere down the line they will either ask you to disrobe completely, or to do some type of nude or seminude photos for them. Even if they don't ask you to do nude or seminude pictures, keep in mind that there are agencies that don't deal in "porno movies," but that lean toward that particular market by dealing with risque magazines. A reputable agency will not ask you to do sexually explicit poses in skimpy lingerie or bathing suits or any type of pornography. Many agencies will have you model lingerie and swimwear for different catalogs and magazines, but there is a big difference between doing poses for a department store catalog and those that you would see in a risque magazine.

Porno agencies will never force the model to do anything he or she doesn't want to do. But then they will start dropping the fact that a fairly attractive porno actor or actress can make *$1,000 or more per day—and it's tax free.* Most models and actors will find this hard to pass up because they think they'll do it for a short while, just enough to pay for their career expenses, then get out of it and into their "real" career. This rarely happens because many times the money becomes so enticing that these people get immersed in doing porno.

There is often drug and alcohol use as well, and once they've hit that point there's no turning back. The drugs, alcohol and money are too powerful. Often they do the drugs and alcohol to help them deal with the porno, and they do the porno because it pays well and enables them to buy more drugs and alcohol. This is when they will start riding on a carousel which they won't, if ever, come off for a long time.

There are many talented people who could have succeeded in acting or modeling but are now caught up in porno and ruined their careers. Some of these people get into porno by accident and some are forced into it, such as the model or actor who gets on a plane or bus headed for California or New York hoping to make it big. What they didn't realize is that it's going to cost a lot more money and time than they've estimated. So they get into porno, or even prostitution, to make money not only for their career but to live on. but what happens then is that they rarely ever get out of it.

Also watch out for escort services that advertise not only under "escort services" but under "modeling agencies" in the phone book. These are pretty easy to spot. They'll usually include the name of the company along with "escort" or "massage" after it. If you do happen to visit one of these places by accident, the only modeling work they'll usually have for you is in beds. So stay away from them, unless you want to make a career out of prostitution.

While still on the subject of pornography, I should mention one other thing. If you are trying to find additional modeling work whether or not you have an agent, you should stay away from the sleazy magazines and underground publications. Many of them will advertise for models for fashion shows and other modeling work that is frequently in other countries such as Japan along with colorful enticements like round trip airfare, limousines, expensive dinners and gifts. This is just a way of luring naive models into the world of pornography or prostitution. If you look logically at this, what type of legitimate modeling work are you going to find in a sleazy magazine?

Finally, you should be cautious about many of the companies that do lingerie shows. Many times these shows are fronts for prostitution. Not all lingeries shows are connected to prostitution, but there are a few that eventually are arrested for it. You can tell the good shows from the bad because the bad shows will tell you that the average model who does their shows can easily make an extra $200 or $300 per night by entertaining some of the clients who attend the show. I'm not talking about dinner and a movie. They will never come out and tell you that you have to sleep with the clients because in most states, prostitution is illegal. So they say it in a more subtle manner.

PHOTOGRAPHERS

In the summer be careful of photographers who hang around beaches and offer to take pictures of you for a fee. They'll usually ask for the fee up-front and tell you that you'll be contacted as soon as the pictures are done. Many times there is no film in the camera and so you are out the money that they've asked for up-front. If you are approached by a photographer while at the beach, ask for a business card and referrals, and then check them out. If they turn out to be legitimate, then set up an appointment to shoot with them. But you really don't know who you're dealing with when they approach you on the beach or anywhere else for that matter.

This also goes for some photographers who attend fashion shows, modeling competitions and other types of shows. They will approach you after the show and say that they work for a well-known magazine and offer to do your portfolio or shoot some pictures of you. Most legitimate photographers don't attend such shows, so if you do get approached, ask for a business card and referrals. If they have told you they work or have worked for a magazine, find out with whom at the magazine you can verify their employment. If the photographer can't tell you, he or she is bluffing.

There are other scams in which a photographer will use a well-known photographer's name or say that they worked in that person's studio, to either get more models and actors to shoot with them or just to rip people off. The photographer isn't going to use just anybody's name, because if they did they wouldn't get much response to their ad. So they will use a well-known photographers name.

Fortunately, this is very easy to check out. For one thing most well-known photographers rarely need to advertise because they already have established clients. But let's say you see an advertisement saying that so-and-so is doing testing or portfolios. To investigate whether it's the real photographer or an imposter, the first thing you'll want to do is find the well-known photographer's phone number. (You can't very well use the ad's phone number because the phone would be answered under the well-known photographer's name, and at this point you don't know if it's a real or phony ad.) This can be done by asking agents, checking different books like the "Madison Avenue Handbook" along with others listed in the reference section of this book, inquiring of other photographers and even from telephone information. Then call for verification.

If a photographer is claiming to have worked in a well-known photographer's studio, get the number and call to see if it's true. He or she might be lying to get people to believe he or she has more connections. Be sure to get the number yourself. The photographer could very easily give you the number of a friend who's covering for him or her.

MAIL SCAMS

There are fraudulent personal management services, casting directors and other industry people who buy lists of children's names from hospitals, school photographers and others.

Then parents will receive a letter from them saying that their child could be making thousands of dollars doing commercials or modeling. It's usually a long, elaborate sales pitch that ends with them saying that they'd like to send a representative to your home for further discussion. When the sales representative arrives they will con you into buying expensive pictures and training for your child. Then they take your money and you will never hear from them again.

VIDEO AND CABLE SCAMS

There was a person who charged $500 to tape you doing a monologue or acting scene that would go onto a laser disk. This disk would then be sent to all casting directors, agents and other industry people. Think logically here: how many industry people own laser-disk equipment?

There was a similar scam that used a local cable station to carry out. Someone would charge an expensive fee to tape you on video doing your acting scene, which would be shown on this cable station during the day. How many industry people do you think sit and watch daytime TV? These people do not find talent by watching cable TV, especially during the day. They are extremely busy. Most of the industry people with whom I spoke said that they usually don't even have time to eat lunch. The only person who benefited from this scam was the con artist.

FREE SEMINARS

Many times you'll come across ads offering free seminars. Very rarely is anything free without some strings attached to it. If you see an ad for a free seminar, by all means go, but keep your eyes and ears open for *strings*. If it would end up costing lots of money, then the *free*

178

part of the seminar was just an enticement to attract people to the seminar. I'm not saying that all free seminars are this way, because I have attended several that were very informative and there was nothing they were trying to sell. But be alert.

OPEN CALL

Frequently you'll see the advertisement of an agency looking for models to work either locally or internationally. Their ads will usually say something like: "Models: looking for new faces to work in New York, Los Angeles, Paris and Milan" or "Models for open call, no experience necessary."

When you respond, they will give you the same old song-and-dance routine by telling you that you have lots of potential, but that it needs to be developed. Then you are supposed to take their training and sometimes even get pictures done through them. Not all open calls are like this—some agencies are actually looking for real talent with no strings attached. But if you do go to an open call, be on the lookout for something like this.

I responded to one of these ads just to see what it was all about. The agency I went to had two offices. The first office had been known to sell classes and pictures to everyone who walked through their doors. The open call was for their second office. I went down there and went through all the regular procedures of filling out an application and waiting.

When I was called in, I asked if I would have to go through any training program or get my pictures done through them, and they told me *no*. They said that the office was an agency without any of those things. All they wanted to do was to videotape me cold reading a piece of commercial copy. After that, I was told to call back the following day to find out if I had been accepted into the agency. Of course I didn't call because I was not looking for representation.

I did not hear from them until three months later. There was a message on my phone machine that the agency had called and wanted to speak to me. When I called them, the name of the agency had been slightly altered. This is when I started suspecting something.

The man who got on the line was someone with whom I had never had contact. He told me that the man who had originally interviewed me was no longer with the agency, but that he and his present partner had reviewed everyone's videotape, and the reason he was calling was that they felt I had a lot of potential to do commercials. He explained

179

that he wanted me to come down to the agency to discuss the marketing plan the agency had for me.

I asked him if I would need to take any of their training courses, and he told me that even though I had potential, it needed to be developed. (I knew this was coming sooner or later.) I also asked him if I would need to get pictures done through them, and he said *yes* that I would need such marketing tools to be sent on auditions.

Then I decided to be clever and I told him that I would be willing to get training and pictures, but that I wouldn't do it through his agency. I asked him which classes and photographers, besides their own, he could recommend. He said that they were not a referral service and did not give out such information. (Obviously, because this agency has been known to rip people off.) So I asked him if the reason they didn't give referrals is because they were taking kickbacks, and he didn't know what to say. It was actually quite funny. That's when I ended the conversation. I just wanted to call this agency back because I couldn't imagine why they called me *three months* after my visit to their agency.

My guess is that this agency decided to expand its training and photography center into two agencies. Then they reviewed all the previous applicants, called them up, told them what great potential they had and invited them to come down to the agency to discuss a marketing plan which also included going through the agency's training and photo services. If I had so much potential, why did they wait three months to call?

CON ARTISTS AT WORK

One thing that most con artists have in common is that they are *very* adept at using psychological and manipulative tricks to get people to buy whatever they are selling. To illustrate this; the next two situations will be explained in detail to show you exactly how they operate.

I found an ad for an acting school which said that a small amount of students would be selected for a one month course to be taught by an established producer. It said that many aspects of modeling and acting would be taught. The tuition for this school was $435.

I responded to the California address and received a packet of information from another state—not California. (My curiosity was aroused: why was I sent a packet from another state and not from California?)

The letter in the packet started off by saying that this producer had worked with many "top stars," and had even discovered a few. (In other words, by enrolling in his school you might be discovered by this producer.) The rest of the letter discussed how difficult it was to get into acting and modeling and that the small amount of people accepted would be guests in his home for the one month course.

The letter closed by saying that if I were interested, I should enclose a $20 application fee (which he probably doesn't give back if you're not accepted into the school).

To a beginner's eye, his resume would look quite impressive, but not to a trained one. There were two sections on his resume that I didn't even need to research.

The first section of his credits covered about half the page, and were totally unrelated to teaching, acting or modeling. I suspect he listed this information to make his resume look bigger.

In another part he said he was listed in several Hollywood books. For a fee anyone can get listed, so it means nothing. Many actors and models just starting out would think these books are prestigious and you need to be pretty important to be listed in there. But it's just not true.

Further down on his resume, he listed the names of movies that he had worked on *without* screen credits. Nobody in the industry, except extras, would work on a movie without getting some kind of mention in the credits. Even catering services are mentioned. More than likely he did absolutely nothing on those movies, but put them down to make it look more impressive.

When I got into the meat of his resume, it was even more interesting. He claimed to have worked on a couple movies doing script negotiations and producing. But when this was checked, no one had ever heard of this man. Yet this man claims to have been in the entertainment industry for over a quarter of a century.

While I was researching his credits, I got another letter from the producer. He had sent me a copy of a new form letter along with an explanation that it was different from the one I had originally received.

The new one was slightly altered and said that the producer was going back to the industry after being retired for many years to make a couple of new movies. This was a manipulative move on his part. By saying that he was going to be making some new movies, he wanted me to believe that if I attended his school, I would have a good chance at being in one of his movies, especially since the producer was going to be teaching the class.

Posing as a potential student, I filled out the application form saying that I was 5'9", with blonde hair and blue eyes, (to show him that I had potential as a model). I attached a letter asking him to send me a current client list so that I could see what other students thought of the course. I also asked why he taught students in his home instead of teaching in a regular classroom. The last thing I asked was if he was registered with the Department of Education.

I received a rude reply back from him. In regard to the client list, he said that he didn't have one because this course was being offered as a special one-time offer only. (That would be true if he was running from town to town with this scam. And by ripping people off he would have no happy former students.) He said that commercial property can't be rented for only one month and that was why he was teaching in his home. (He must live in an unusual state if it doesn't allow residents to rent office space monthly.) He said that he wasn't registered with the Department of Education because the state he was in doesn't require it. (This is probably why he conducts his school there.)

Then he blasted my application and said that even though I had listed my best academic subjects as math and English, I had misspelled Los Angeles. (I did that purposely to make him think I was dumb and naive.) He said that if my other subjects were worse, then there was the question about my ability to learn.

He also said that I had failed to list any of my favorite movies or TV commercials. Big deal.

Then he said that my letter to him was argumentative and had revealed a lot of ignorance, but since it had been mailed from Oakland, Calif., that explained it.

He topped off his clever letter by saying that I didn't have a telephone as normal people do. (I certainly didn't want to hear from him.) He said that, judging by the way I filled out my application, I not only didn't qualify for his school, but also wouldn't qualify for anything else that would be acceptable to civilized people. Then he thanked me for my amusing letter. If anyone is amusing it's him.

Any *legitimate* teacher certainly wouldn't have written such a rude, defensive letter. They would have just politely answered the questions and that would have been that. In my letter I asked questions that most new actors and models would most likely not know enough to ask. So he probably thought I was an investigator of some sort and tried to discourage me.

Before I finish this first situation, there is one other thing I want to point out. He said in his cover letter that if I were one of the lucky students accepted, I would be trained morning, noon and night, seven days a week for one month. Now, the average acting weekend workshop runs about six hours a day for two days and costs about $300. Yet this person is going to teach you almost 24 hours a day for one month for only $435. Since there was no mention of additional fees for room and board, it must mean that the $435 would also cover that. Not a bad deal, if it were true. But it probably wasn't.

My theory is that he probably accepts everyone who applies, telling each one that he or she was one of the lucky people chosen. Who wouldn't feel they had a lot of potential and talent after being chosen by the producer himself to attend his school? And you would probably end up paying the $435 tuition, which is what he wants you to do. He collects all the money, telling everyone that the school will be starting in a couple of months, thereby giving him more time to keep taking money from other people, before skipping town.

For the second situation, I interviewed several different models and actors who had been defrauded of their money by this agency.

This agency had an ad in the paper saying that they were a *licensed and bonded* talent agency looking for actors and models of all ages and heights. No experience or training was necessary. Anyone who was interested was invited to attend the open call held at a hotel.

The actors and models who showed up were asked to fill out a questionnaire. One of the questions was whether they had a portfolio. After each person filled out the questionnaire he or she was to go and talk to one of the agents who reviewed the questionnaire and talked to them briefly. Then there was a break while the agents made some decisions. When the break was over the agents announced the names of people whom they wanted to return for a second interview. (What they had done was simply exclude anyone who already had a portfolio.)

At the second interview, the models and actors were interviewed by someone who made the final decision as to whom they wanted to represent. At the interview they were told about two requirements that the agency would need to promote them: a portfolio and the agency book. They were put together in a package deal that cost $1,500. The price included everything from a professional photographer to the portfolio case.

The agency book was a book that would be sent all across the United States to the agency's clients which included photographers, ad agencies and casting directors to pursue commercial work such as print work, TV commercials and major motion pictures. For actors this would only be extra and nonunion work, because this agency wasn't franchised.

The talent was told that they could use their own photographers but that they would be saving money if they went with the agency's

183

package deal, because the agency was producing in mass quantity and would therefore be getting excellent discounts. This was a little trick that they used with the talent; they told them that they could use their own photographer so that it would not seen to be a scam.

Obviously, the way this agency was making money was by selling portfolio package deals. Well, if you decided to hire everyone on your own, they wouldn't get any money. But then they turned around and used psychology on the talent by saying that if they went through the agency, they'd save a great deal of money on everything. Most new actors and models aren't familiar with which photographers they should use. Since this agency was offering a package deal—complete with everything—all they would have to do is pay and show up to do the shoot. They thought it was a good deal and went for it. That's exactly what the agency wanted them to do.

The talent was also told that the agency would be offering a *free* 16 week seminar program that would tell models and actors all about the business, how to land jobs and much more. This short training course normally costs a lot of money, but they were offering it for free. (I guess they thought it was the least they could do, since they were ripping people off.) This was another one of their sales incentives. This agency had designed its sales package so well that it would have been difficult to turn down. Most agencies don't offer free classes, so by also offering a free training program, it sounded like a deal you couldn't pass up.

There were two other things that were discussed at the interview. If you bought into the deal, they then discussed how you were going to pay for it. It had to be paid for in full prior to the shoot and there were two choices for payment. They could either pay it all up-front, or in weekly installments each time they attended the seminar. Most people wouldn't have been able to come up with $1,500 at once, and would have refused the deal, which the agency anticipated. That's why they offered the payment plan.

Then they were told all about the agency: that they had booking offices in New York, New Jersey and Los Angeles, with one to open soon in San Francisco as well. They had other branches of their agency located in Florida, Pennsylvania, Arizona and Washington. They really praised their agency and made you believe that you would be getting lots of work because they were so extensive.

Then the talent was told to leave and that they would receive a call if the agency wanted to represent them. The only people who were called back were the people who were interested and could afford to buy into their program. That's why at the first interview they rejected anyone who already had a portfolio. The purpose of the second interview was to see who could be conned into buying into their program. These were the people who were accepted into the agency.

Another way that actors and models were easily conned is that whoever got accepted into the agency had to go through two separate interviews. So it made people feel special to be accepted, as if the agency believed in you enough to pick you out of all those other actors and models. This was all part of the manipulation they used on the talent.

The talent who were called back had to come down and sign contracts. One of the contracts said that the talent had to adhere to the weekly payment plan (if they had chosen this route) established at registration, and that any money received by the agency would be forfeited if the talent canceled or was expelled from the agency. The thing for which you could be expelled were missing the seminars and failure to adhere to the weekly payment plan. They had trapped you as soon as you signed those contracts because if you didn't keep paying you would lose your investment. One of the reasons they held those seminars was to collect the weekly payments from you and if you didn't attend the weekly seminar you would be kicked out, thereby losing your money.

Midway through the seminar, the agency told the talent that they could be promoted far more extensively if they also had composites done, which would cost $435. The agency had a particular way they wanted these composites done, including having them liquid laminated. Again, this was something that the talent could get done anywhere, but the agency said it had a special offer going on for the same price as the composites.

These were two other ways to squeeze more money from the talent. Liquid lamination is rarely, if ever, used in either the acting or modeling business because it is so expensive. One model I interviewed said that she had called around and found the going rate to have 500 composites laminated was about $1,000. This agency was obviously familiar with the local prices and had lowered their price considerably so you would accept their deal. Since they told the talent that the composites had to be laminated, what choice did they have?

Now the composites didn't have to be done, but the agency had said that they could do better promotion with them, which would result in more work. Who would turn down something like that? The composites didn't need to be paid off right away, but they wouldn't be able to start booking you a lot of appointments unless the agency had them printed. Of course they couldn't be printed unless the agency had the money. This was Catch 22. They didn't want to overburden people to come up with a lot of money at once, so they eased up a little. But there was an incentive on the actor's and model's part because by getting the composites paid off and done meant that they would get many more bookings.

The seminar ended in nine weeks instead of the original 16 weeks. When it was over the agency set up appointments with everyone for photo sessions. They were also told that any remaining balance left on the package deal had to be paid off before the shoot, and this was also to insure confirmation of the photo session since the photographer was flying in from New Jersey and they didn't want him wasting his time if no one showed up for the shoot. This agency had planned it so that the amount of seminar classes would exactly match the weekly payment plan, and the package deal would be paid off by the last seminar. With the seminar ending in nine weeks, the talent had to come up with the balance at an earlier date.

There are many reasons they could have done this. One theory is that they exaggerated the length of the seminar to make it look like a better deal than nine weeks. They also could have just run out of things to teach actors and models. These people were investing more time into devising ways to deceive talent than in teaching.

The photo session that took place was like any other professional session, complete with hair/makeup stylist and a photographer's assistant for sets and props.

After the sessions, the talent was told that they would be able to view the contact sheets and slides two weeks later. It actually was eight weeks later. The maximum time for this should have been the two weeks they quoted.

At the viewing they were to select pictures from the slides and contact sheets to be enlarged. It was $30 each or four for $100—which is much too expensive. At the most it should have cost $10 for each enlargement. If the agency were developing the pictures themselves, it would have cost the agency even less.

The talent was then told that it would take six to eight weeks for the pictures to be enlarged. This turned into 14 weeks when it should have been only two weeks.

When the talent finally got to pick up their pictures, they only received one fourth of their order. They were told that the rest was back ordered and should arrive in eight weeks.

They had been told that the agency's printer was in New Jersey, and

186

that the delay was caused by all the orders the agency was doing and the amount of time it took to send them through the mail.

In the meantime, the talent was told that the remaining balance on the composites had to be paid off if they wanted to be included in the Fall/Winter edition of the agency book. This was just a quick way to get the rest of the money from the people. Since the initial investment that the actors and models made on the package deal also paid for the agency book, if they didn't get into the book, they would have wasted some of their investment. They were to receive their composites and agency book in 12 weeks.

To keep the models and actors believing in the agency, they had the talent come in to fill out some forms that explained their booking procedures and when to call the bookers. They were told that as soon as the rest of the pictures and composites arrived that they would be sent on go-sees.

In five months, the talent finally received the agency book. They were told that the rest of the pictures and composites were still delayed and would arrive in eight weeks. But in the meantime, the agency would start sending the book to different clients to try and book go-sees for them.

When the eight weeks passed, the talent started calling the agency and were told that it would be four more weeks until the pictures would arrive.

This waiting game went on for several more months until people started filing lawsuits in small claims court for which the agency never showed up. Finally, when it got too hot for them, they closed all the offices in every state and fled, with thousands of dollars from talent in many states.

Scams like this don't happen very often, but when they do, it can be difficult to unravel. The first red flag on this agency is the fact that its newspaper ad said they were *licensed and bonded*. This was not true. The Department of Labor had confiscated it several months earlier. (This is why it's always important to verify with the Department that an agency is licensed instead of just taking the agency's word for it.)

This agency may have said this in its ad because they didn't want anyone to check with the Department to see if they were licensed and possibly turn them in. So by coming right out and saying it, there was need to call and check. Since most new actors and models aren't familiar with licensing, it also made the agency sound legitimate.

The agency even told potential talent to check their clean record with the Better Business Bureau. Anyone new to an area however, would undoubtedly have a clean record as they wouldn't have been in the area long enough to dirty it. The BBB that should have been called was in New Jersey. That's where their corporate office was, and was the office that had been around longer.

I heard through sources that this agency had been around for many years. If that's true, it would have been even easier for them to con people into their program. But even if that were the case, an agency that would try to sell you a package deal like that would be a scam. Most legitimate agencies have models expand their portfolios through tests with different photographers, not by doing it through a $1,500 package deal.

One way that people could have avoided getting ripped off in this scam would have been to hire all services on their own. The only way the agency was making money off this scam was by selling this package deal, among other things. Whoever insisted on hiring everyone on their own wouldn't have been accepted into the agency. The talent also could have avoided them altogether if they had checked on their licensing status (provided the agency was in a state that licensed talent agencies.)

This agency was able to fuel this scam by continually buying time with the actors and models. Notice how they kept pushing up the dates on everything? They had only a small amount of pictures printed to lead talent to believe that they were eventually going to receive all their photos. If the agency hadn't shown them anything after they had paid all that money, they might have started getting suspicious and start to sue. Since they wanted to string this scam out as long as possible while they sold new actors and models on package deals, they had to show the talent something to keep them believing in the agency's good faith.

The sad part about this whole scam is that these people are still free and possibly running the same scam in another town and state. Since they supposedly had many offices, they must have ripped off thousands of dollars. If you ever come across a similar type of scam, report it immediately to the appropriate law enforcement agency in your area. These people should be caught and punished.

CONTESTS

Watch out for talent search contests that advertise in publications such as newspapers, TV Guide and radio. One contest I looked into was a baby model search that was looking for children under the age of 5 to win fame and fortune along with a $5,000 U.S. Savings Bond. They probably got a great response because every parent wants fame and fortune for their children.

The ad didn't ask the parent to send in a photo of their child because the competition included a professional photo shoot. It just asked for the child's name, age, address and phone number.

Pretending to be a mother with a child I responded to the ad and received a response several days later. This company wanted a $45 registration fee. This was to cover the costs of the photo shoot which was scheduled for the following month, along with other costs such as the U.S. Savings Bond, meeting space, etc.

I wasn't able to speak directly to anyone who had actually experienced this situation, but my guess is several things could have happened. This company may have just been going from town to town collecting these $45 registration fees and scheduling photo shoots for a month down the line. Then when the parents and children show up they find that the place is deserted.

The other possibility is that there actually was a photo shoot, but they might have used an inexperienced photographer instead of the professional fashion photographer they were claiming to employ. They could have that person go through all the motions of a photo shoot, with only one oversight. There would be no film in the camera!

Even if there was film in the camera, they could have tried conning the parents into doing an expensive portfolio for their child, saying that the child was very photogenic and that this company could get the child an agent, but that the child would first need a portfolio.

One thing I should point out is that this company was also offering a $100 scholarship to a modeling school. Why would a child under age 5 need to go to modeling school? There's no way they need to be learning about makeup, wardrobe coordination, diet or grooming. That in itself should be a red flag indicating a possible scam.

One of the questions you always need to ask yourself, especially if it involves money, is: why is someone doing something? What is their motive for doing it? What are they getting out of it? In this situation for instance: why was this company even having a baby model search contest? I could understand if it were a modeling agency putting it on or a department store trying to find the best looking child to model their fall lineup, but there was no apparent reason for this contest, except for some con artists separating parents from their money.

The other contests in which you need to proceed with caution are the ones that are given by a talent agency. Even though many times you don't win, they have your name, address and phone number on file. Then several days after the contest, you receive a call from the agency. They will tell you that they saw you in the contest and want to represent you because they believe you have a lot of potential.

But then they persuade the actor or model into doing photos or attending classes through the agency for them to be represented. Many people fall for this scam because they feel thrilled that the agency picked them out of all the other contestants to be represented and it makes them feel special.

Another scam for a talent search contest advertised in the newspaper for actors and models of all ages, heights, weights and nationalities. First of all this company wanted a $100 registration fee to just participate in the contest. Then they told all the contestants that the agency had access to jobs paying at least $500 or more per hour, but that they would need portfolios (for models) or headshots (for actors) and classes beforehand. The total price for the classes and pictures was $2,000. (By the way, the contest was canceled.)

I spoke to a couple of actors and models that went through this scam and they said that after they paid the $2,000, the talent agency told everyone that their pictures and resumes would be shown to industry people. In order for the agency to do this, the talent would be charged an additional $100 for each person who viewed the pictures and resumes. The agency justified this charge by saying that it was for their time, phone calls, gas and other expenses. They also said that in order for them even to see industry people, the agency had to pay these people to get appointments with them.

That in itself should have made one suspicious. Industry people *do not* get paid to view your submissions. The only money they get if they're entitled to it is their commission for jobs that you've done. So for this agency to say that the talent would be charged for expenses and for them to even see industry people was an obvious lie on their part. I can only imagine how many innocent actors and models kept on paying into this scam hoping to get well-paying jobs.

Look logically at this situation: if you pay someone for his time, would you really know if he is showing your pictures and resumes around? For all you know he could just say that no one is interested in you at the moment and sit there counting his profits. He might even tell you that several major industry people have expressed interest in you just to keep you happy.

PHONE SCAMS

Beware of anyone calling you at home who represents themselves as an agent, photographer, producer, casting director or other industry person and then tries to sell you a portfolio or some other service. Many of these people get lists of actors and models from photographers, modeling schools and other outlets, then get on the phone with some long, enticing sales pitch. They may even say they saw you in a play, modeling show or competition, or that they saw your picture in a photographer's portfolio and feel you have a lot of potential to be a highly paid model or actor. For a fee they'll want to represent you, get you an agent, etc.

Industry people *do not* get on the phone and solicit talent. You've read throughout this book how industry people find their talent and it certainly isn't through phone solicitations.

Another type of scam that just recently emerged has to do with the 900 phone number. There was an ad I happened to come across one day in the newspaper and it said to call this 900 phone number to learn how to get started in the acting and modeling business. It said that you would also learn how to find work and contacts safely and affordably. The key word in this ad was that you could find work and contacts *affordably*.

As I've mentioned before and will say again: you should never have to pay to get work or contacts. You also don't learn about the industry by calling some 900 phone number. This company was probably racking in several hundred dollars a day because each day there would be a new message. If the average person called and stayed on the line for several minutes, it could really add up.

Out of curiosity I did call, but they really didn't give out any information on how to break into the industry. Most of their messages referred you to different photographers, agents (most of whom were not licensed and should have been) and casting directors who were charging fees for one thing or another. The message also said that if you mentioned this company when you visited any of the industry people mentioned you would receive a discount. If this company were taking kickbacks, along with the money they were receiving from each phone call, it would bring in some nice profits for them. I can only imagine what other money-making schemes they conjured up to include in their daily phone message that I'm sure many actors and models bought into.

My advice is don't waste your money on any scam. Con artists are only interested in *one* thing, and that is how much money they can make off you. They are not interested in advancing your career nor would they even have the connections to do so if they wanted to. It can definitely be tempting if you've spent many agonizing months either trying to get an agent or trying to get acting or modeling work, to pay someone who is promising you work or an agent. But I can tell you from experience that it won't get you anywhere, except possibly in a courtroom, which is where many victims of scams wind up. Keep in the back of your mind that many times you will *never* see the money that you paid into a scam. It's not worth it, you're better off taking that money and investing it into a car or leaving it in the bank to collect interest.

CONCLUSION

Now that we're at the end of our journey together, I hope that this book has shown you not only how to get into the business properly, but has also opened your eyes to the different scams that go on in the industry. I hope it has armed you with enough knowledge so that you can make better decisions and avoid getting ripped off.

Many potential actors and models want to be in the entertainment business and get lots of recognition and wealth, and if you're willing to work real hard at it, eventually it will come to you. But always look before you leap into anything. Like the old saying goes, "If it sounds too good to be true, it probably is."

Before closing, I will leave you with one more piece of advice told to me by an agent. "Actors and models need to be more cautious when they start out in the business and check things out thoroughly. Many of them tend to just jump in and pay for the first thing that comes along. When con artists play upon the hopes and dreams of these people, they fall for it. You won't be a movie star or model overnight by paying someone; it doesn't work that way. Everything you do in life takes hard and persistent work. You're not going to get rich overnight. Most of today's actors and models got to where they are because of their discipline and dedication to make it. They didn't get there overnight or by paying someone."

This business, like any other, is constantly changing and growing, as such this book will be revised and updated accordingly. I'd really love to hear from you for these future editions. Tell me what sections were helpful (including if any of them helped you avoid getting ripped off), along with what confuses you. If you have any suggestions for improvement, or if you've been ripped off in any way, please write to me and tell me what happened. Your story may be used in future editions. (Of course, your name will not be printed.)

Also, feel free to write me if you have any questions on anything in this book or if you just have a question in general about the business (including scams). If you would like a reply, please enclose a *self-addressed, stamped envelope.* The address is P.O. Box 919, Newark, CA 94560.

You can also order additional copies of this book. Just send a check or money order for $19.95 plus $2.00 for shipping (Calif., residents add $1.45 sales tax) made payable to Mystique Publishers. Send to address above.

I wish you much luck and success in your venture to become an actor or model!

APPENDIX

Sept 29, 1990

Joe Petterson
Blue Light Model Agency
23344 Blue Lake Rd.
New City, CA 89000

Dear Mr Petterson,

    I am seeking modeling representation and have enclosed my snapshots and resume (if you have one) for your consideration.

    I am 19 years old, 5'9" and weigh 115 lbs; my hair color is brown and I have blue eyes. I wear a size 8 in clothes and an 8 in shoes. My measurements are 32"-22"-32". (Boys and men: state your suit size instead. If you are still in school it would be a good idea to mention it. If you have any special skills, training or experience, include this as well.)

    If you would like to set up an appointment so that we can meet, you can reach me at (111) 222-2222. If you feel I am not right for your agency, please return my snapshots in the enclosed SASE I have provided.

    Thank you for your time and consideration. I look forward to hearing from you.

Sincerely,

Jolene Conners

Sample of a model's cover letter

194

Sept 29, 1990

Chris Cole
Blue Light Agency
21534 Hacienda Rd., #433
New City, CA 98807

Dear Mrs Cole,

I am an actor seeking representation and have enclosed my picture and resume for your consideration.

Please feel free to call me at (111) 222-2222 so that we can set up an appointment to meet. If you feel I am not right for your agency, please return my picture and resume in the enclosed SASE I have provided.

Thank you for your time and consideration. I look forward to hearing from you.

Sincerely,

Jolene Conners

Sample of an actor's cover letter

CHRISTI COLE
P.O. BOX 223
New City, CA 98807
(111) 222-2222

VITAL STATISTICS

Height: 5'9"   Age: 19
Weight: 120 lbs.   Clothes size: 8
Hair: Brown   Shoe size: 8
Measurements: 32"-22"-32"   Eyes: Blue
(Men and boys include your suit size instead.)

RUNWAY AND PRINTWORK

Charmanes Bridal Shop   Fall/Winter Show
Cable TV Channel 8   Sportswear
Sun Magazine   Swimwear
Lotus Restaurant   Evening Gowns

TRAINING

Modeling: New City Model and Charm School

Dance: Ballet and Modern: New City School of Dance

SPECIAL SKILLS

Roller skating, fishing, ice skating, tennis, horseback riding, international chef and surfing.

Sample of a model's resume

CHRISTI COLE
SAG - AFTRA - AEA

Height: 5'9"   BLUE LIGHT AGENCY   Hair: Brown
Weight: 120 lbs.   21534 Hacienda Rd., #433   Eyes: Blue
                             New City, CA 98807
                               (111) 222-2222

FILM

Partners In Dirt	Gallery Owner	Off The Wall Production
The Days Go By	Lisa Joe	Moonbeam Production
Go Take A Hike	Shoplifter	Up Stream Films

TELEVISION

Get Off It	Store Clerk	B & B Productions
The Old And Weak	Marrianne	Wheelchair Int'l
All My Garbage	Shooting Victim	Bag It Productions

THEATRE

Don't Kill The TV	Phoebe Smith	New City Repertory
Dark Side Of the Sun	Joanie Coats	New City Repertory
East Side Story	Dancer	New City Repertory

COMMERCIALS

List And Tape Furnished Upon Request.

TRAINING

Acting: New City School of Acting (two years)
Commercials: Scott DeVenney, Joe Brown, Judy Kite
Improvisation: Pat Tusk (one year)
Stage Combat: John Lancaster (one year)
Dance, Jazz & Ballet: New City School of Dance (three years)

SPECIAL SKILLS

Roller skating, International Chef, Swimming, Ice Skating, Tennis,
Weight Lifting, Horseback Riding and Aerobics.

Sample of a Los Angeles acting resume

REFERENCE

All reference material can be found through the appropriate addresses or through your local bookstore. You may want to confirm all prices and mailing addresses as they may have changed by the time this book is published.

TRADE PAPERS

DRAMA-LOGUE
P.O. Box 38771
Los Angeles, CA 90038-0771
(213) 464-5079

Subscription rates are $45 for 52 weeks; $26 for 26 weeks or $1.50 (in So. CA) for one issue and $2.50 (if you're outside of So. CA).

The information listed in this paper is mainly for the Southern California area, although it has from time to time had information for the San Francisco area.

It contains casting information for nonunion and union work, student films, Equity and Equity waiver plays, classes, photographers, acting coaches, answering services and much more.

BACKSTAGE
P.O. Box 2078
Mahopac, NY 10541
(914) 628-7771

Subscription rates are $50.00 for one year or $1.50 (in NY) for one issue and $2.00 (outside NY).

This paper is geared toward the New York area. It contains castings for nonunion and union, students films, stage club acts for singers and dancers, Equity and Equity waiver castings, classes, photographers, resume and answering services, articles on industry people and so much more.

SHOW BUSINESS
1501 Broadway, 29th Floor
New York, NY 10036
(212) 354-7600

198

Subscription rates are $25 for six months; $40 for one year and $65 for two years. Or $1.25 (in NY) for one issue and $1.50 (outside NY).

It contains up-to-the-minute production news of theater, film, TV, industrial shows, Off-Broadway and complete casting news. Future productions are listed before premieres. It also contains reviews of shows, addresses and phone numbers of producers, talent agencies and casting auditions. This information is mainly geared for the New York area.

VARIETY
1400 N. Cahuenga Blvd. (daily)
Hollywood, CA 90028
(213) 469-1141

154 W. 46th St. (weekly)
New York, NY 10036
(212) 582-2700

Subscription rate is $75 per year or $1.50 per issue.

Not much casting information in this paper. It mainly talks about the industry such as data on the grosses of movies, television deals, plays, etc. It also talks about which executives have moved to which offices and so on. The weekly editions also contains national casting information not found in the daily.

HOLLYWOOD REPORTER
6715 Sunset Blvd.
Hollywood, CA 90028
(213) 464-7411

Subscription rate is 75 cents for a single issue or $60 for a six month subscription.

This paper features industry news, listings of TV and film productions including the casting directors, but not much casting information. This is mainly a gossip paper and is geared toward the Hollywood area.

CALLBOARD
2940 16th St., #102
San Francisco, CA 94103
(415) 621-0427

Subscription rate is $27 for one year or $3.00 for a single issue.

It contains castings for Equity and Equity waiver plays, lots of classes, photography, services and ongoing plays. Members also receive discounts on theater tickets, other publications and public programs. They also have an audition hotline which only members can call to find out about other castings in addition to the paper.

THEATRE DIRECTORY

This directory is something else offered by Callboard. It gives you detailed, updated information on more than 130 theater companies, performance and rehearsal facilities, opportunities for playwrights, training programs, publicists, producers, agents and casting directors, touring resources, and much more. It also includes articles, essays and helpful hints. The cost is $11.50 for Callboard members or $14.50 for nonmembers.

It also has a Talent Index where for $30 or $40 (for nonmembers) your photo, name, agency phone number, or your own and any union affiliations will appear in a 3 5/16" by 2 3/16" box.

THEATRICAL INDEX
Price Berkley
888 8th Avenue
New York, NY 10019

This is a weekly listing of play productions and includes what's opening, what's on, what's in previews or rehearsal and what has been announced or projected for the future. The producer, playwright director and casting director for each show is named. Sometimes there is a brief outline of the play and a description of the roles that are available. Also included is Off-Broadway information.

Theatrical Index can be found by either contacting the above address or it's also posted on the bulletin board of the Equity lounge at 165 W. 46th St., New York, NY 10036.

There is also a Theatrical Calendar that's similar to Theatrical Index, except that this listing is published twice each month. It also contains information on Off-Broadway, Off-Off Broadway and all current and projected Broadway productions. For subscription information on this, write to 171 W. 57th St., New York, NY 10019.

DIRECTORIES

GEOGRAPHIC CASTING GUIDE
P.O. Box 46423
Los Angeles, CA 90046

There are separate New York and Los Angeles versions of this guide. It contains lists of franchised agents, casting directors offices, production studios, TV stations, ad agencies, union theater companies and current TV series descriptions.

REGIONAL THEATRE DIRECTORY
P.O. Box 519
Dorset, VT 05251

This directory lists 200 Equity and non-Equity dinner theaters in the United States. It also gives information on the producers who do the hiring in the theaters.

CD DIRECTORY
Breakdown Service
8242 W. Third St.
Los Angeles, CA 90048
(213) 276-9166

This directory is especially useful for locating casting directors in the Los Angeles area including addresses and phone numbers. It costs around $35 a year, and they send you updates every two weeks.

THE WORKING ACTORS GUIDE

This is *the* directory for actors as it contains listings and comments on entertainment attorneys, publicists, personal managers, production houses, theaters and much, much more.

MADISON AVENUE HANDBOOK
17 E. 48th St.
New York, NY 10017
(212) 688-7940

This is considered the *bible* for models because it's comprehensive, easy-to-use and accurate. There are names, addresses and phone numbers of photographers, TV producers, fashion houses and firms using models for film, video and magazines.

Besides New York, other major cities are covered such as Los Angeles, San Francisco, Chicago, Detroit, Florida, Texas and even Canada.

THE NEW YORK CITY MODEL AGENCY DIRECTORY

This is another useful guide for models in the New York City area. This directory breaks down the NYC model agencies allowing a page per agency, giving the name, address, phone number, types of modeling the agency handles (fashion, print, runway or commercial), basic physical requirements and policy on interviews, whether pictures are required beforehand and if they have special interests such as petites, plus sizes or ethnic types.

TEST PHOTOGRAPHERS IN NEW YORK CITY

This directory is carefully researched with mailings and phone numbers of photographers in New York who take tests for aspiring models and what the conditions are. This book can be used when you get an agent.

ROSS REPORTS
Television Index, Inc.
40-29 27th St.
Long Island City, NY 11101
(718) 937-3990

Subscription rate is $17.10 for six months or $32.10 for one year.

The East Coast guide includes: New York ad agencies, independent casting directors, producers of TV commercials, talent and literary agents, lists of unions, network studios and offices, network-program packagers, dramatic serials and prime time programs.

The West Coast guide also includes: network prime time programs, casting people, program packagers and production facilities.

THE AUDITION BOOK

This is an excellent guidebook for auditions, and if you're an actor you will be going on *alot* of them. This book is a complete guide to different audition techniques for the working actor. It provides step-by-step guidelines on auditioning for stage, TV shows, commercials, corporate films and features, along with "changing hats" for each of them. This book can be found through your local drama bookstore. Or you can mail $16 (includes postage) to Ed Hooks, 2510 Lyric Ave., Los Angeles, CA 90027.

FILM ASSOCIATION

SAN FRANCISCO INTERNATIONAL FILM FESTIVAL (SFIFF)
1560 Filmore St.
San Francisco, CA 94115
(415) 567-4641

Membership fees are as follows:

Associate: $35 per individual or $60 per couple

Your membership includes unlimited free member screenings of new and classic films. Up to 20 percent off the admission price of most public exhibitions and educational programs presented by SFIFF. Advance mailings on all upcoming events, including the annual festival. Also discount admissions to festival events and selected theaters.

Patron: $100 per individual or $150 per couple

You get all the associated benefits, plus invitations to special screenings and invitations to private parties in honor of special guests and celebrities during the annual festival.

Chairman's Circle: $250 per individual or $500 per couple

Includes all Associate and Patron benefits, plus special invitations to private film related events throughout the year.

TALENT BOOKS

ACADEMY PLAYERS DIRECTORY
8949 Wilshire Blvd., 6th Floor
Beverly Hills, CA 90211-1972
(213) 273-2033

This is *the* guidebook for the acting industry. To be listed you either need to be signed with a franchised agency or a member of the union. It costs $45 for a one year listing or $15 to be listed in one issue. It includes a 1 1/2" by 2" black-and-white headshot of you with your name, your agency's name and phone number or your phone number. There's a listing for every category including ethnic and disabled actors.

PLAYERS GUIDE
165 W. 46th St., #1305
New York, NY 10036
(212) 869-3570

This is another guidebook for the serious actor to be listed. In order to qualify you need to be a member of Equity, AFTRA or SAG. The cost for one picture and information such as your name, agency's name, address and phone number and any stage, screen, radio or TV credits you want listed is $65. Two pictures and information for a single category is $80.

The category listings include leading women and men, young leading women and men, character women and men and girls and boys through teens. There is also a section for directors, choreographers and stage managers.

WHITMARK DIRECTORY
P.O. Box 26009
Dallas, TX 75226
(214) 871-8901

If you live in the South or Southwest, this is the guidebook to be listed in. Since Texas is a right-to-work state you don't have to be in a union or have an agent to be listed. The fee is $65 for one photograph and $35 if you want two printed. There are four categories to be listed under: Men, Women, Teens or Children. This book is distributed to

1,800 agency approved casting directors and corporations. You also get a free listing in the Whitmark's new talent data base and a subscription to the Whitmark magazine.

SCREEN EXTRAS GUILD

LOS ANGELES
3629 W. Cahuenga Bl. West
Los Angeles, CA 90068
(213) 851-4301

SAN DIEGO
3045 Rosencrans St., #308
San Diego, CA 92110
(619) 222-6059

SAN FRANCISCO
100 Bush St.
San Francisco, CA 94104
(415) 391-7510

MIAMI
1190 NE 125th St., #130
Miami, FL 33161
(305) 891-9714

CASTING OFFICES FOR EXTRA WORK (No Fee)

Intercontinental Casting Inc.
8489 W. 3rd St., #1008
Los Angeles, CA 90027
(213) 651-4365

Central Casting
2600 W. Olive St.
Burbank, CA 91601
(818) 569-5200

L.A. Casting
2000 W. Magnolia Bl. #209
Burbank, CA 91601
(818) 766-2296

Disc Casting
3601 W. Olive St.
Burbank, CA 91601
(818) 841-0687

Cast & Crew
4201 W. Burbank Bl.
Burbank, CA 91601
(818) 848-0906

Producers Casting Agency
P.O. Box 1527
Pacific Palisades, CA 90027
(213) 459-0229

UNION CREDIT OFFICES

The AFTRA Federal Credit Union
260 Madison Ave., 7th floor (at 38th St.) New York, NY 10016

The Actors Federal Credit Union (for Equity and SAG.) 165 West 46th St., New York, NY 10036

The AFTRA-SAG Federal Credit Union
6922 Hollywood Bl. #304
Hollywood, CA 90028

SCREEN ACTORS GUILD BRANCH OFFICES

National Headquarters
7065 Hollywood Bl.
Hollywood, CA 90028
(213) 465-4600

ARIZONA
5150 N. 16th St., #C-255
Phoenix, AZ 85016
(602) 279-9975

ATLANTA
1627 Peachtree St., NE #210
Atlanta, GA 30309
(404) 897-1335

BOSTON
11 Beacon St., #512
Boston, MA 02108
(617) 742-2688

CHICAGO
307 N. Michigan Ave.
Chicago, IL 60601
(312) 372-8081

*CLEVELAND
1367 E. 6th St., #229
Complex
Cleveland, OH 44114
(216) 579-9305

DALLAS
Two Dallas Communications
6309 N. O'Connor Rd., #111-LB 25
Irving, TX 75039-3510
(214) 869-9400

**DENVER
950 S. Cherry St., #502
Denver, CO 80222
(303) 757-6226

DETROIT
28690 Southfield Road
Lathrup Village, MI 48076
(313) 559-9540

FLORIDA
2299 Douglas Road, Suite W.
Miami, FL 33145
(305) 444-7677

HAWAII
949 Kapiolani Bl., #105
Honolulu, HI 96814
(808) 538-6122

HOUSTON
2650 Fountainview #325
Houston, TX 77057
(713) 972-1806

MINNEAPOLIS/ST PAUL
15 S. 9th St., #400
Minneapolis, MN 55404
(612) 371-9120

NASHVILLE
1108 17th Ave South
Nashville, TN 37212
(615) 327-2958

PHILADELPHIA
230 S. Broad St., 10th Floor
Philadelphia, PA 19102
(215) 545-3150

SAN DIEGO
3045 Rosecrans Ave., #308
San Diego, CA 92110
(619) 222-3996

*SEATTLE
601 Valley St., #200
Seattle, WA 98109
(206) 282-2506

NEW YORK
1515 Broadway, 44th Floor
New York, NY 10036
(212) 944-1030

*ST LOUIS
906 Olive St., #1006
St. Louis, MO 63101
(314) 231-8410

SAN FRANCISCO
100 Bush St., 16th Floor
San Francisco, CA 94104
(415) 391-7510

*AFTRA offices which also handle SAG business for their areas.
**Denver is a regional office which also covers Nevada, New Mexico and Utah.

THE AMERICAN FEDERATION OF TELEVISION AND RADIO ARTISTS

6922 Hollywood Bl.
New York, NY 10016
(212) 265-7700

260 Madison Ave.
Hollywood, CA 90028
(213) 461-8111

ACTORS EQUITY ASSOCIATION

6430 Sunset Bl.
Los Angeles, CA 90028
(213) 462-2334

165 West 46th Street
New York, NY 10036
(212) 869-8530

203 N. Wabash Ave.
Chicago, IL 60601
(312) 641-0393

100 Bush Street
San Francisco, CA 94104
(415) 391-7510

SAG TALENT AGENTS

The abbreviations following the agent's telephone number indicate the type of representation offered by the agency: (T) Theatrical/Television; (C) Commercials; (FS) Full Service; (Y) Young Performers; (A) Adults

HOLLYWOOD

All agents listed below have Los Angeles addresses and (213) area codes unless otherwise noted. BH-Beverly Hills, NH-North Hollywood.

A Special Talent Agency: 6253 Hollywood Bl., #830 (90028) 467-7068 (FS-A)

A Total Acting Experience: 14621 Titus St., #100, Panorama City (91402) (818) 901-1044 (FS-YA)

Aaron, Sally: 5301 Laurel Canyon #116, NH (91607) (818) 980-6719

Abrams Artists & Assoc.: 9200 Sunset Bl., #625 (90069) 859-0625 (FS-A)

Abrams-Rubaloff & Lawrence: 8075 W. 3rd (90048) 935-1700 (FS-YA)

Aces, A Talent Agency: 6565 Sunset Bl., #300 (90028) 465-8270 (C-A)

Actors Group Agency: 8730 Sunset #220 (90069) 657-7113 (T-A)

Agency The: 10351 Santa Monica Bl., #211 (90025) 551-3000 (T-A)

Agency for Performing Arts: 9000 Sunset Bl., #315 (90069) 273-0744 (FS-A)

Aimee Entertainment: 13743 Victory Bl., Van Nuys (91401) (818) 994-9354

Agency II Model & Talent: 6525 Sunset #303 (90028) 962-7016

All Talent Agency: 2437 E. Washington, Pasadena (91104) (818) 797-8202 (FS-YA)

Alvarado, Carlos: 8820 Sunset Bl. (90069) 652-0272

Amaral Agency, Pat: 10000 Riverside Dr., #11, Toluca Lake (91602) (818) 980-1013 (FS-A)

Ambiance Agency: 901 Dove St., #235, Newport Beach (92660) (714) 720-7416 (FS-A)

Ambrosio/Mortimer: 9000 Sunset Bl., #900 (90069) 274-4274 (T-YA)

Amsel, Fred: 6310 San Vicente #407 (90048) 939-1188 (T-A)

Arthur Assoc., Irvin: 9363 Wilshire Bl., #212, BH (90210) 278-5934 (FS-A)

Artistic Enterprises Inc.: 6290 Sunset Bl., #403 (90028) 469-4555 (FS-A)

Artists Agency: 10000 Santa Monica Bl., #305 (90067) 277-7779 (T-A)

Artists Alliance Agency: 8457 Melrose Pl., #200 (90069) 651-2401 (FS-A)

Artists First Inc.: 8230 Beverly Bl. (90048) 653-5640

Artists Group Ltd.: 1930 Century Park West #403 (90067) 552-1100 (T-YA)

Askew L.A. Ltd.: 8619 Sunset Bl. (90069) 652-1234 (FS-A)

Associated Talent Intl.: 9744 Wilshire Bl., #312, BH (90212) 271-4662 (FS-A)

Atkins & Assoc.: 303 S. Crescent Heights Bl. (90048) 658-1025 (T-YA)

Atkins Talent Agency Sonya: 1636 Cahuenga Bl., #203 (90028) 469-7115 (FS-YA)

Avenue "C" Talent: 12405 Woodruff Ave., Downey (90241) 803-5775 (FS-YA)

Badgley/Connor: 9229 Sunset Bl. (90069) 278-9313

Baldwin Talent, Inc.: 1801 Avenue of the Stars #640 (90067) 551-3033 (FS-YA)

Ball, Bobby: 6290 Sunset Bl., #304 (90028) 465-7522 (FS-A)

Barr, Rickey: 1010 Hammond #202 (90069) 276-0887 (T-A)
Barskin Agency: 120 S. Victory Bl., Burbank (91502) (818) 848-5536 (T-A)
Bauer-Benedek Agency: 9255 Sunset Bl., #716 (90069) 275-2421 (T-A)
Bauman Hiller & Assoc.: 5750 Wilshire Bl., #512 (90036) 857-6666 (T-A)
BDP & Assoc.: 10637 Burbank Bl., Burbank (91601) (818) 506-7615 (T-A)
Belson & Klass: 144 S. Beverly Dr., #405, BH (90212) 274-9169 (T-A)
Bennett Agency Sara: 6404 Hollywood Bl., #329 (90028) 965-9666 (FS-YA)
Benson, Lois J.: 518 Toluca Park Dr., Burbank (91505) 849-5647 (T-A)
Berzon, Marian: 336 E. 17th, Costa Mesa (92627) (714) 631-5936 or (213) 207-5256 (FS-YA)
Beverly Hills Sports Council: 9595 Wilshire Bl., #711, BH (90212) 858-1872
Bikoff, Yvette: 9255 Sunset Bl., #510 (90069) 278-7490
Blanchard, Nina: 7060 Hollywood Bl., #1010 (90028) 462-7274 (C-A)
Bloom J. Michael: 9200 Sunset Bl., #710 (90069) 275-6800 (T-YA)
Borinstein-Bogart: 914 S. Robertson Bl., #101 (90035) 657-2050 (T-A)
Brandon & Assoc.: 200 N. Robertson Bl., #223, BH (90211) 273-6173 (T-A)
Bresler, Kelly & Kipperman: 15760 Ventura Bl., #1730, Encino (91436) (818) 905-1155 (T-A)
Brewis, Alex: 4717 Laurel Canyon, NH (91607) (818) 509-0831 (T-A)
Bridges Talent Agency Jim: 1607 N. El Centro #22 (90028) 874-3274 (FS-YA)
Brooke, Dunn & Oliver: 9165 Sunset Bl., #202 (90069) 859-1405
Burkett & Kear: 1700 E. Garry #113, Santa Ana (92705) (714) 724-0465 (FS-YA)
Burton, Iris: 1450 Belfast Dr. (90069) 652-0954 (FS-Y)
Bush & Ross Talents: 4942 Vineland Ave, NH (91601) (818) 762-0096 (FS-YA)
C.L. Inc.: 843 N. Sycamore Ave. (90038) 461-3971
Calder Agency: 17420 Ventura Bl., #40, Encino (91316) (818) 906-2825 (T-A)
Camden Artists: 2121 Avenue of the Stars (90067) 556-2022 (T-A)
Career Artists Intl.: 11030 Ventura Bl., #3, Studio City (91604) (818) 980-1315 or (818) 980-1316
Carol Mgmt/Talent Leslie: 316 N. Catalina, Burbank (91505) (818) 953-7224 (T-A)
Carroll William: 120 S. Victory Bl., Burbank (91502) (818) 848-9948 (FS-A)
Carter, Mary J.: 6525 Sunset Bl., #502 (90028) 467-2662 (FS-YA)
Castle-Hill: 1101 S. Orlando Ave. (90035) 653-3535 (FS-YA)
Cavaleri & Assoc.: 6605 Hollywood Bl., #220 (90028) 461-2940 (FS-YA)
Central Coast Model & Talent: 265 South St., #F, San Luis Obispo (93401) (805) 544-4500 (FS-YA)
Century Artists Ltd.: 9744 Wilshire Bl., #308, BH (90212) 273-4366 (T-A)
Charter Management: 9000 Sunset Bl., #1112 (90069) 278-1690 (T-A)
Chasin Agency: 190 N. Canon #201, BH (90210) 278-7505 (T-A)
Chiz, Terry H.: 5761 Whitnall Hwy., #E, NH (91601) (818) 506-0994 (T-A)
Chutuk & Assoc., Jack: 470 S. Beverly Dr., BH (90212) 552-1773
Circle Talent: 9465 Wilshire Bl., #725, BH (90212) 281-3765
Clark W. Randolph: 6464 Sunset Bl., #1050 (90028) 465-7140 (FS-YA)
Clarke, Kathy: 2030 E. 4th #102, Santa Ana (92705) (714) 667-0222
CNA: 1801 Avenue of the Stars #1250 (90067) 556-4343 (FS-A)
CPC & Assoc.: 733 N. La Brea Ave., #200 (90038) 662-5672
Coast to Coast: 12307-C Ventura Bl., Studio City (91604) (818) 762-6278 (FS-YA)
Colton Kingsley: 16661 Ventura Bl., #400, Encino (91436) (818) 788-6043 (T-A)
Comls Unltd, Inc., Sonjia W. Brandon's: 7461 Beverly Bl., (90036) 937-2220 (FS-YA)

Contemporary Artists: 132 Lasky Dr., BH (90212) 278-8250 (FS-YA)

Coppage Company: 11501 Chandler Blvd., NH (91601) (818) 980-1106

Coralie Jr.: 4789 Vineland Ave., #100, NH (91602) (818) 766-9501 (FS-YA)

Cosden, Robert: 7080 Hollywood Bl. (90028) 856-9000

Craig Agency: 8485 Melrose Pl., #E (90069) 655-0236 (T-A)

Creative Artists Agency: 9830 Wilshire Bl., BH (90212) 288-4545 (FS-YA)

Crown Agency: 5530 Corbin Ave., #355, Tarzana (91356) (818) 343-9199 (FS-YA)

Cumber, Lil: 6515 Sunset Bl., #300A (90028) 469-1919 (FS-YA)

Cunningham, Escott & Dipene: 261 S. Robertson Bl., BH (90211) 855-1700 (C-A, FS-Y)

Crow & Assoc., Susan: 1010 Hammond #102 (90069) 859-9784

Dade, Rosen & Schultz: 15010 Ventura Bl., #219, Sherman Oaks (91403) (818) 907-9877 (T-A)

De Grandcourt, Richard: 1216 State St., #706, Santa Barbara (93101) (805) 966-4848

Devroe Agency: 3365 Cahuenga Bl., (90068) 666-2666

Diamond Artists Ltd.: 9200 Sunset Bl., #909 (90069) 278-8146 (T-A)

Doty & Assoc., Patricia: 11969 Ventura Bl., #308, Studio City (91604) (818) 763-8488 (T-YA)

Douglass Addie J.: 4405 Riverside Dr., #105, Burbank (91505) (818) 980-3193 (FS-A)

Eastwest Model Mgmt: 6922 Hollywood Bl., #302 (90028) 463-7575 (FS-A)

Elias & Assoc., Thomas G.: 23501 Park Sorrento #218, Calabasas (91302) (818) 888-4608

Elite Model Mgmt/John Casablancas Inc.: 9255 Sunset Bl., #1125 (90069) 274-9395

Ellis Artists Agency: 119 N. San Vicente Bl., #202, BH (90211) 651-3032 (FS-YA)

Emerald Artists: 6565 Sunset Bl., #310 (90028) 465-2974

Estephan Talent Agency: 6018 Greenmeadow Rd., Lakewood (90713) 421-8048 (FS-A)

Farrell Talent Agency Eileen: 9744 Wilshire Bl., #309, BH (90212) 271-3400

Favored Artists: 4051 Beverly Bl., #201 (90048) 653-3191 (T-A)

Feature Players Agency: 4051 Radford Ave., Studio City (91604) (818) 508-6691 (T-A)

Felber, William: 2126 Cahuenga Bl. (90068) 466-7629 (FS-YA)

Fields Talent Agency Liana: 3325 Wilshire Bl., #749, Los Angeles (90010) 487-3656

Film Artists Assoc.: 7080 Hollywood Bl., #704 (90028) 463-1010 (FS-YA)

First Artists Agency: 10000 Riverside Dr., Toluca Lake (91602) (818) 509-9292

Flame Model Mgmt: 6565 Sunset Bl., #420 (90028) 465-2465 (FS-A)

Flick East-West Talents Inc.: 1608 N. Las Palmas (90028) 463-6333 (T-A)

Fontaine Agency Judith: 1720 N. La Brea Ave., 2nd Floor (90046) 969-8398

Fort Agency The: 5410 Wilshire Bl., #243 (90036) 965-7600

Fox, Beverly: 4655 Kingswell #203 (90027) 661-6347 (FS-YA)

Freed, Barry: 9255 Sunset Bl., #603 (90069) 274-6898

Frings Agency Kurt: 139 S. Beverly Dr., BH (90212) 277-1103

Gage Group The: 9255 Sunset Bl., #515 (90069) 859-8777 (T-A)

Garrett, Helen: 6525 Sunset Bl., #205 (90028) 871-8707 (FS-YA)

Garrick, Dale: 8831 Sunset Bl. (90069) 657-2661

Geddes Agency: 8457 Melrose Pl., #200 (90069) 651-2401 (T-A)

Geiff & Assoc., Laya: 18075 Ventura Bl., #225, Encino (91316) (818) 342-7247 (T-A)

Gerard Talent Agency Paul: 2918 Alta Vista Dr., Newport Beach (92660) (714) 644-7950 (T-A)

Gerler, Don & Assoc.: 3349 Cahuenga Bl., West (90068) 850-7386 (T-YA)
Gerritsen Intl.: 8721 Sunset Bl., #203 (90069) 659-8414 (T-A)
Gersh Agency The: 232 N. Canon Dr., BH (90210) 274-6611 (FS-YA)
Gibson J. Carter: 9000 Sunset Bl., #811 (90069) 274-8813 (T-A)
Gilly Talent Agency Georgia: 8721 Sunset Bl., #103 (90069) 657-5660 (T-A)
Global Talent: 12745 Ventura Bl., #C, Studio City (91604) (818) 766-4441
G.M.A.: 1741 N. Ivar #119 (90028) 466-7161
Gold, Harry Talent Agency: 12725 Ventura #E, Studio City (91604) (818) 769-5003
 (T-A, FS-Y)
Goldin Talent Agency Sue: 6380 Wilshire #1600 (90048) 852-1441 (FS-YA)
Gordon/Rosson Talent Agency: 12700 Ventura Bl., #350, Studio City (91604)
(818) 509-1900 (FS-YA)
Gores/Fields: 10100 Santa Monica Bl., #700 (90067) 277-4400 (T-A)
Gray Joshua & Assoc.: 6736 Laurel Canyon #306, NH (91606) (818) 982-2510
Gray/Goodman Talent Agency: 205 S. Beverly Dr., #210, BH (90210) 276-7070
Greenvine Agency: 110 E. 9th St., #C-1005 (90079) 622-3016 (T-A)
Gurian Agency The: 920 S. Robertson #4 (90035) 550-0400
Hamilburg, Mitchell J.: 292 S. La Cienga #212, BH (90211) 657-1501
Hanzer Holdings: 415 N. Barrington Ave (90049) 476-3089 (FS-A)
Harris & Goldberg: 2121 Avenue of the Stars #950 (90067) 553-5200 (T-A)
Hart, Vaughn D.: 200 N. Robertson Bl., #219, BH (90211) 273-7887 (T-A)
Heacock Literary Agency Inc.: 1523 Sixth St., Suite 14, Santa Monica
 (91401) 393-6227
Hecht Agency Beverly: 8949 Sunset Bl. (90069) 278-3544 (FS-YA)
Heller Agency: 7060 Hollywood Bl., #818 (90028) 462-7151 (T-A)
Henderson/Hogan Agency: 247 S. Beverly Dr., BH (90212) 274-7815 (T-A)
Howard Talent West: 11969 Ventura Bl., Studio City (91604) (818) 766-5300 (FS-A)
Hunter & Assoc., Ray: 1901 Avenue of the Stars #1774 (90067) 277-8161 (C-A)
Hunt & Assoc., George B: 121 E. Twin Palms Dr., Palm Springs (92264) (619) 320-6778
Intl., Contemporary Artists: 19301 Ventura Bl., #203, Tarzana (91356) (818) 342-3618
International Creative Mgmt: 8899 Beverly Bl. (90048) 550-4000
International Talent: 3419 W. Magnolia Bl., Burbank (91505) (818) 842-1204
InterTalent: 9200 Sunset Bl., (90069) 271-0600 (T-A)
It Model Management: 941 N. Mansfield Unit C, Los Angeles (90036)
962-9564 (FS-YA)
Jackman & Taussig: 1815 Butler #120 (90025) 478-6641 (FS-YA)
Jay, George: 6269 Selma Ave., #15 (90028) 465-0232
Jennings & Assoc., Tom: 427 N. Canon Dr., #205, BH (90210) 274-5418 (T-A)
Joseph, Helfond & Rix: 1717 N. Highland Ave., #414 (90028) 466-9111 (C-YA)
Joseph/Knight: 1680 N. Vine #726 (90028) 465-5474 (T-A)
Kaplan, Len: 4717 Laurel Canyon Bl., #206, NH (91607) (818) 980-8811 (T-A)
Kaplan-Stahler Agency The: 8383 Wilshire Bl., #923, BH (90211) 653-4483 (T-A)
Karg/Weissenbach & Assoc.: 329 S. Wetherly Dr., #101, BH (90211) 205-0435 (T-A)
Kassel Agency Carolyn: 2401 W. Magnolia Bl., Burbank (91506) (818) 761-1525
Kelman, Arletta: 7813 Sunset Bl. (90046) 851-8822 (FS-YA)
Kerwin Agency William: 1605 N. Cahuenga Bl., #202 (90028) 469-5155 (T-A)
Kjar, Tyler: 10653 Riverside Dr., Toluca Lake (91602) (818) 760-0321 (FS-YA)
Kohner Inc., Paul: 9169 Sunset Bl. (90069) 550-1060
L.A. Artists: 2566 Overland Ave., #600 (90064) 202-0254 (T-YA)
L.A. Models: 8335 Sunset Bl. (90069) 656-9572 (C-A)

L.A. Talent: 8335 Sunset Bl. (90069) 656-3722 (FS-A)
Labelle Agency: El Paseo Studio #110, Santa Barbara (93102) (805) 965-4575 (FS-YA)
Lane, Stacy: 13455 Ventura Blvd., #223, Sherman Oaks (91423) (818) 501-2668 (FS-Y)
Lani Talent Agency Moya: 1589 East Date St., San Bernardino (92412) (714) 882-5215 (FS-YA)
Lantz Office Inc., The: 9255 Sunset Bl., #505 (90069) 858-1144 (T-A)
Lawrence Agency: 3575 Cahuenga Bl., West #125-3 (90068) 851-7711 (T-YA)
Lawrence, Fred & Assoc: 9044 Melrose Ave., (90069) 273-5255 (T-A)
Leading Artists: 445 N. Bedford, BH (90210) 858-1999
Levin, Sid: 1680 N. Vine St., #821 (90028) 461-4789
Liberty Glennis Agency: 10845 Lindbrook Ave., #203A (90024) 824-7937 (FS-A)
Lichtman, Terry: 12456 Ventura Bl., #1, Studio City (91604) (818) 761-4804 (T-A)
Light Agency Robert: 6404 Wilshire #800 (90048) 651-1777
Light Company The: 901 Bringham Ave. (90049) 826-2230 (FS-YA)
Lindner & Assoc., Ken: 2049 Century Park East #2717 (90067) 277-9223 (T-A)
Lloyd Talent Agency Johnny: 6404 Hollywood Bl., #219 (90028) 464-2738
Lockwood Agency The: 8217 Beverly Bl., #5 (90048) 658-8087 (T-YA)
Loo Agency Bessie: 8235 Santa Monica Bl., #202 (90046) 650-1300 (FS-YA)
Lovell & Assoc.: 1350 N. Highland Ave. (90028) 462-1672 (T-A)
Lynne & Reilly: 6290 Sunset Bl., #326 (90028) 461-2820
Major Clients Agency: 2121 Avenue of the Stars #2450 (90067) 277-4998 (T-YA)
Maris Agency: 17620 Sherman Way #8, Van Nuys (91406) (818) 708-2493 (T-A)
Marshak, Wyckoff & Assoc.: 280 S. Beverly Dr., #400, BH (90212) 278-7222 (T-A)
Marshall, Alese Model & Coml.: 24050 Vista Montana, Torrance (90505) 378-1223
Martel Agency: 1680 N. Vine St., #203 (90028) 874-8131 (FS-A)
M.A.X.: 275 S. Beverly Dr., #210, BH (90212) 550-8858
Maxine's Talent Agency: 4830 Encino Ave., Encino (91316) (818) 986-2946 (FS-A)
McCartt, Oreck & Barrett: 10390 Santa Monica Bl., #300 (90025) 553-2600 (T-A)
McHugh Agency James: 8150 Beverly Bl., #303 (90048) 651-2770 (FS-A)
McMillan Hazel: 8217 Beverly Bl., #6 (90048) (818) 788-7773 (FS-YA)
M.E.W. Inc.: 151 N. San Vicente, BH (90211) 653-4731 (FS-A)
MGA/Mary Grady: 150 E. Olive Ave., #111, Burbank (91502) (818) 843-1511 (FS-YA)
Miller Gilbert: 21243 Ventura Bl., #243, Woodland Hills (91364) (818) 888-6363 (T-A)
Miller Lee: 5000 Lankershim #5, NH (91601) (818) 505-0077 (T-A)
Minkoff Agency The: 12001 Ventura Place Suite 335, Studio City (91604) (818) 760-4501
Miramar Talent: 1210 W. Orange Grove #8 (90046) 656-6906
Mishkin Agency: 2355 Venedict Canyon, BH (90210) 274-5261
Mitchell F. Sterling: 6115 Selma Ave., #211 (90028) 203-0738 (FS-YA)
Morris William: 151 El Camino Dr., BH (90212) 274-7451
Moss Agency Burton: 113 San Vicente Bl., #202, BH (90211) 655-1156 ((T-A)
Moss & Assoc., H. David: 8091 1/2 Melrose #3 (90046) 653-2900 (T-A)
Murphy Talent Agency Mary: 12001 Ventura Place #304, Studio City (91604) (818) 506-3874
Nathe Susan & Assoc., C.P.C.: 8281 Melrose Ave., #200 (90046) 653-7573 (FS-A)
New World Artists: 6777 Hollywood Bl., #530 (90028) 851-0769 (T-A)

212

Nicklin Group The: 9478 W. Olympic Bl., #304, BH (90212) 277-5272 (T-A)
Pacific Artists: 515 N. La Cienega #1. (90048) 657-5990 (FS-A)
Parness Agency The: 9220 Sunset Bl., #204 (90069) 272-2233 (T-A)
Pearson Agency Ben: 606 Wilshire Bl., #614, Santa Monica (90401) 451-8414
Perseus Modeling & Talent: 3807 Wilshire Bl., #1102 (90010) 383-2322 (FS-YA)
Prieto & Assoc.: 12001 Ventura Pl., #340, Studio City (91604) (818) 506-4797
Prima Model Mgmt Inc.: 832 N. La Brea Ave. (90038) 465-8511 (FS-YA)
Privilege Talent: 8344 Beverly Bl. (90048) 658-8781 (FS-A)
Progressive Artists: 400 S. Beverly Dr., BH (90212) 553-8561 (T-A)
Rainford Agency: 7471 Melrose #14 (90046) 655-1404 (T-A)
Ray Rappa Agency: 7471 Melrose Ave., #11 (90046) 653-7000 (C-A)
Rissky Business: 10966 Le Conte #A (90024) 208-2335 (T-A)
Robinson-Weintraub & Gross: 8428 Melrose Pl., #C (90069) 653-5802
Rogers & Assoc., Stephanie: 3855 Lankershim Bl., #218, NH (91604) (818) 509-1010
Rose Agency Jack: 6430 Sunset Bl., (90028) 463-7300 (FS-YA)
Rosenberg Office Marion: 8428 Melrose Pl., #C (90069) 653-7383 (T-A)
Rosson Agency Natalie: 11712 Moorpark St., #204, Studio City (91604) (818)
508-1445 (FS-YA)
SAI Talent Agency: 4924# Lankershim Bl., NH (91601) (818) 505-1010 (FS-YA)
Sanders Agency The: 8831 Sunset #304 (90069) 652-1119 (FS-A)
Savage Agency The: 6212 Banner Ave. (90038) 461-8316
Scagnetti Talent Agency Jack: 5330 Lankershim Bl., #210, NH (91601)
 (818) 762-3871 (FS-A)
Schaefer Peggy: 10850 Riverside Dr., NH (91602) (818) 985-5547 (C-A)
Schechter Co., Irv: 9300 Wilshire Bl., #410, BH (90212) 278-8070 (T-A)
Schiowitz & Assoc.: 291 S. La Cienega, BH (90211) 657-0480 (T-A)
Schnaar, Sandie: 8281 Melrose Ave., #200 (90046) 653-9479 (C-A)
Schoen & Assoc., Judy: 606 N. Larchmont Bl., #309 (90004) 962-1950 (T-A)
Schut Agency Booh: 11350 Ventura Bl., #206, Studio City (91604) (818) 760-6669
(FS-YA)
Schwartz & Assoc., Don: 8749 Sunset Bl., (90069) 657-8910 (FS-YA)
Screen Children's Agency: 12444 Ventura Bl., Studio City (91604)
(818) 985-6131 (FS-Y)
Sekura John/A Talent Agency: 1680 N. Vine (90028) 962-6290 (T-A)
Selected Artists Agency: 13111 Ventura Bl., #204, Studio City (91604)
(818) 905-5744 (FS-A)
Shapira & Assoc., David: 15301 Ventura Bl., #345, Sherman Oaks (91403)
(818) 906-0322 (FS-A)
Tisherman Agency: 6767 Forest Lawn Dr., (90068) 850-6767 (FS-YA)
Tobias-Skouras & Assoc.: 1901 Avenue of the Stars #840 (90067) 277-6211 (T-A)
Triad Artists: 10100 Santa Monica Bl., 16th Floor (90067) 556-2727
Turtle Agency The: 15010 Ventura Bl., #219A, Sherman Oaks (91403)
(818) 907-9892 (T-YA)
Twentieth Century Artists: 3800 Barham Bl., #303 (90068) 850-5516 (T-YA)
Vanity Models & Talent Agency: 7060 Hollywood Bl., #1216 (90028)
461-0987 (FS-YA)
Variety Artists Int'l Inc.: 9073 Nemo St., 3rd Floor (90069) 858-7800
Vaughn Agency: 500 Molino St., #213 (90013) 626-7434
Wain Agency Erika: 1418 N. Highland Ave., #102 (90028) 460-4224

Wallack & Assoc: 1717 N. Highland Ave., #701 (90028) 465-8004
Watt & Assoc., Sandra: 7551 Melrose #5 (90046) 653-2339 (FS-A)
Waugh, Ann: 4731 Laurel Canyon Rd., #5, NH (91607) (818) 900-0141 (T-A)
Webb Ent. Inc., Ruth: 7500 Devista Dr. (90046) 874-1700 (FS-YA)
Weiss Talent Agency Richard: 1680 N. Vine St.,#503 (90028) 856-9989 (C-A, FS-Y)
Wilder Agency: 3151 Cahuenga Blvd., West #310 (90068) 969-9641 (FS-A)
Wilhelmina Artists' Representative Inc.: 6430 Sunset Blvd., #701 (90028)
464-8577 (FS-A)
Wilson Agency, Shirley: 291 S. La Cienga Blvd., #306, BH (90211)659-7030 (FS-Y)
Witzer, Ted: 1900 Avenue of the Stars #2850 (90067) 552-9521
World Class Sports 9171 Wilshire Bl., #404, BH (90212) 278-2010 (FS-A)
Wright Talent Agency Carter: 6533 Hollywood Bl. (90028) 469-0944 (FS-A)
Writers & Artists Agency: 11726 San Vicente Bl., #300 (90049) 820-2240 (FS-A)
Zadeh & Assoc., Stella: 11759 Iowa Ave. (90025) 207-4114 (T-A)
Zimring Co., The: 9171 Wilshire Bl., #530, BH (90210) 278-8240
Zolton Talent: 1636 Cahuenga Bl., #206 (90028) 871-0190 (FS-YA)

NEW YORK
Area code is (212) unless otherwise noted.

Abrams Artists & Assoc., Ltd: 420 Madison Ave., 14th Floor (10017)935-8980
Actors Group Agency: 157 W. 57th St., #600 (19919) 245-2930
Adams Ltd., Bret: 448 W. 44th St. (10036) 765-5630
Agency for Performing Arts: 888 7th Ave. (10106) 582-1500
Agency for the Arts Inc.: 1650 Broadway #306 (10019) 247-3220
Allen Talent Bonni: 250 W. 57th St., #1001 (10107) 757-7475
Amato Theatrical Ent., Michael: 1650 Broadway #560 (10019) 247-4456
Ambrose Co.: 311 W. 43rd St., #401 (10036) 586-9110
Ambrosio/Mortimer & Assoc: 165 W. 46th St., #1109 (10036) 719-1677
American Intl., Talent: 303 W. 42nd St., #608 (10036) 245-8888
Anderson Agency Beverly: 1501 Broadway #2007 (10036) 944-7773
Andreadis Talent Agency: 119 W. 57th St., #711 (10019) 315-0303
Associated Booking: 1995 Broadway (10023) 874-2400
Astor Agency Richard: 1697 Broadway (10019) 581-1970
Avenue Talent Ltd.: 35 E. 21st St., 7th Floor (10010) 473-1900
Barry Agency: 165 W. 46th St (10036) 869-9310
Bauman Hiller & Assoc.: 250 U. 57th St., #2223 (10107) 757-0098
Bellin Agency Peter: 230 Park Ave. (10169) 949-9119
Bethel Agencies: 513 W. 54th St., #1 (10019) 664-0455 or 664-0462
Bloom J. Michael: 233 Park Ave., S., 10th Floor (10003) 529-6500
Bookers Inc.: 150 W. Fifth Ave., #834 (10011) 645-9706
Bresler, Kelly & Kipperman: 111 W. 57th St., #1409 (10019) 265-1980
Buchwald & Assoc., Don: 10 E. 44th St. (10017) 867-1070
Carson/Adler Agency: 250 W. 57th St., #729 (10107) 307-1882
Cataldi Agency Richard: 180 7th Ave., #1C (10011) 741-7450
Celebrity Talent: 247 Grand Ave., 2nd Floor (10002) 925-3050
Coleman-Rosenberg: 210 E. 58th St., #2F (10022) 838-0734
Cooper Assoc., Bill: 224 W. 49th St., #411 (10019) 307-1100
Cunningham, Escott & Dipene: 118 E. 25th St. (10010) 477-1666

214

Deacy Agency Jane: 181 Revolution Rd., Scarborough, NY (10510) (914) 941-1414
Despointes/Casey Artists: 75 Varick St., #1407 (10013) 334-6023
Diamond Artists: 119 W. 57th St. (10019) 247-3025
Dicce Talent Ginger: 60 E. 42nd St., #1352 (10165) 661-8840
Douglas, Gorman, Rothacker & Wilhelm Inc.: 1650 Broadway #806 (10019) 757-5500
David Drummond Talent Rep.: 102 W. 75th St. (10023) 677-6753
Eisen Assoc., Duicina: 154 E. 61st St. (10021) 355-6617
Entertainment Assoc.: Lakeview Commons #103, Gibbsboro, NJ (08026) (609) 435-8300
Faces Talent: 567 3rd Ave. (10016) 661-1515
Fields Inc., Marje: 165 W. 46th St. (10036) 764-5740
Flick East & West: 881 7th Ave., #1110 (10019) 307-1850
Ford Talent Group: 344 E. 59th St. (10022) 688-8628
Foster-Fell: 90 West St., Penthouse (10006) 571-7400
Frontier Booking Intl.: 1776 Broadway (10019) 265-0822
F.T.A.: 401 Park Ave., South Penthouse (10016) 541-5250
Funnyface: 440 E. 62nd St., #1B (10021) 752-4450
Gage Group: 1650 Broadway #406 (10019) 541-5250
Gersh Agency: 130 W. 42nd St., #1804 (10036) 997-1818
Gilchrist Talent Group: 310 Madison Ave., #1003 (10017) 692-9166
Hadley Enterprises Peggy: 250 W. 57th St. (10019) 246-2166
Harter/Manning & Assoc.: 111 E. 22nd St. (10010) 529-4555
Hartig Agency Michael: 114 E. 28th St., #203 (10016) 684-0010
Henderson/Hogan: 405 #. 44th St. (10036) 765-5190
Hunt, Diana; Royalton Hotel: 44 W. 44th St. (10036) 391-4971
H.V. Talents: 18 E. 53rd St., (10022) 751-3005
Iannone-Day Agency: 311 W. 43rd St., #1405 (10036) 957-9550
Intl., Creative Mgmt.: 40 W. 57th St., (10019) 556-5600
Jan J. Agency: 328 E. 61st St., (10021) 759-9775
Jacobson Wilder Kesten: 419 Park Ave., South (10016) 686-6100
Jordan, Joe: 156 5th Ave., #711 (10010) 463-8455
Jovano Agency: 2320 Main St., Bridgeport, CT (06606) (203) 336-0597
Kahn Jerry: 853 7th Ave. (10019) 245-7317
Kearney/Bishop: 1697 Broadway #801 (10019) 581-6200
Kerin Assoc., Charles: 360 E. 65th St., #11J (10021) 288-6111
King, Archer: 420 Lexington Ave. (10017) 210-8740
Kingman Agency: 1501 Broadway #2100 (10036) 354-6688
Kirk Artists Roseanne: 161 W. 54th St., #1204 (10019) 315-3487
KMA Assoc.: 211 W. 56th St., #17E (10019) 581-4610
Kroll Agency Luch: 390 West End Ave. (10024) 877-0627
Kronick, Kelly & Lauren: 420 Madison Ave., 14th Floor (10017) 684-5223
Lally/Rogers & Lerman: 37 E. 28th St. (10016) 889-8233
Lantz Office: 888 7th Ave. (10106) 586-0200
Larner, Lionel: 130 W. 57th St., (10019) 246-3105
Leach, Dennis A.: 160 5th Ave., #615 (10010) 691-3450
Lewis Assoc., Lester: 400 E. 52nd St., #11D (10022) 758-2480
L'Image Talent Group: 35 E. 21st St., 7th Floor (10010) 477-2100
Mannequin Models: 150 E. 58th St., #3500 (10155) 755-1428
Martinelli Attractions John: 888 8th Ave. (10036) 586-0963

McDermott Enterprises Marge: 216 E. 39th St. (10036) 889-1583
Meredith Model Mgmt: 10 Furler St., Totowa, NJ (07512) (201) 812-0122
MMG Enterprises: 250 W. 57th St. (10107) 246-4360
Morris William: 1350 Avenue of the Americas (10019) 586-5100
News & Entertainment: 221 #. 57th St., 9th Floor (10019) 765-5555
The New York Agency: 1650 Broadway #504 (10019) 245-8860
Noble Talent: 250 W. 57th St., #1501 (10107) 581-3800
Oppenheim-Christie Assoc.: 13 E. 37th St. (10016) 213-4330
Oscard Assoc., Fifi: 19 W. 44th St. (10036) 764-1100
Ostertag, Barna: 501 5th Ave., #1410 (10017) 697-6339
PGA: 1650 Broadway #711 (10019) 586-1452
Packwood Talent Harry: 250 W. 57th St., #1416 (10107) 586-8900
Palmer Agency Dorothy: 235 W. 56th St., #24K (10019) 765-4200
Phoenix Artists: 250 W. 57th St., #2530 (10107) 956-7070
Premier Talent Assoc.: 3 E. 54th St. (10022) 758-4900
Professional Artists Unltd.: 513 W. 54th St. (10019) 247-8770
RadioActive Talent: 476 Elmont Rd., Elmont, NY (11003) 315-1919
Rascals Untld.: 135 E. 65th St. (10021) 517-6500
Rea Agency Edith: 156 Fifth Ave., #417 (10010) 989-5221
Reich Agency Norman: 65 W. 55th St., #4H (10019) 399-2881
Revelation Entertainment: 601 Halstead Ave., Mamaroneck, NY (10543)
(914) 381-5207
Roos Ltd., Gilla: 16 W. 22nd St., 7th Floor (10010) 758-5480
Ryan Enterprises Charles Vernon: 1841 Broadway #907 (10023) 245-2225
Sames & Rollnick Assoc.: 250 W. 57th St., #703 (10107) 315-4434
Sanders Agency Ltd.: 1204 Broadway #306 (10001) 779-3737
SEM & M: 156 5th Ave., #523 (10010) 627-5500
Schill William: 250 W. 57th St., #1429 (10107) 315-5919
Schuller Talent: 276 5th Ave., 10th Floor (10001) 532-6005
Selected Artists Rep.: 337 W. 43rd St. (10036) 586-4300
Silver Agency Monty: 145 W. 45th St., #1204 (10036) 391-4545
Smith & Assoc., Susan: 192 Lexington Ave., 12th Floor (10016) 545-0500
Spotlite Enterprises Ltd.: 221 W. 57th St., 9th Floor (10019) 586-6750
Starkman Agency: 1501 Broadway (10036) 921-9191
STE Representation: 888 7th Ave. (10019) 246-1030
Stewart Artists Corp.: 215 E. 81st St. (10018) 249-5540
Strain & Jennett Assoc.: 1501 Broadway (10036) 391-0380
Stroud Mgmt.: 119 W. 57th St., #1511 (10019) 315-3111
Talent Representatives: 20 E. 53rd St. (10022) 752-1835
The Artist's Agency: 230 W. 55th St., #29D (10019) 245-6960
Thomas Agency Michael: 305 Madison Ave., #4419 (10165) 867-0303
Tranum Robertson & Hughes: 2 Dag Hammarskjold Plaza (10017) 371-7500
Triad Artists: 080 7th Ave., #1602 (10106) 489-8100
Troy Talent Gloria: Kaufman-Astoria Studios 34-12 36th St., Astoria, NY (11106)
(718) 392-1290
Universal Talent Agency: 505 5th Ave., 10th Floor (10017) 661-3888
Van der Veer People: 401 E. 57th St. (10022) 688-2880
Waters Agency Bob: 1501 Broadway #705 (10036) 302-8787
Webb Enterprises Ruth: 701 7th Ave., #9W (10036) 757-6300
Wilhelmina Artists Rep.: 9 E. 37th St. (10016) 889-9450

Wolters Theatrical Agency Hanns: 10 W. 37th St. (10018) 714-0100
Woo, Patricia Agency: 156 5th Ave., #1111 (10011) 989-7171
Wright Rep., Ann: 136 E. 56th St., #2C (10022) 832-0110
Writers & Artists: 70 W. 36th St., #501 (10018) 947-8765
Zoli Mgmt.: 146 E. 56th St. (10022) 319-0327

ARIZONA
Area code is (602).

Black Agency Robert: 725 S. Rural Rd., #C201A, Tempe (85281) 966-2537 (FS-YA)
Fosi's Talent Agency: 2777 N. Campbell Ave., #209, Tuscon (85719) 795-3534
Grissom Agency: 4811 E. Grant Rd., #261, Tuscon (85712) 327-5692 (FS-YA)
Kristi's Talent Agency: 5705 N. Scottsdale Rd., #125, Scottsdale (85253) 946-9000
Leighton & Goodwin Talent & Model Mgmt., Inc.: 3333 E. Indian School Rd., Phoenix
(85018) 224-9255 (FS-YA)
Premier Talent: 4603 N. 16th St., #6, Phoenix (85016) 468-1292 (FS)
Talents: 4501 N. 22nd St., #100, Phoenix (85016) 468-1292 (FS)
Tor/Ann Talent & Booking: 6711 N. 21st Way, Phoenix (85016) 263-8708

BOSTON

Maggie, Inc.: 35 Newbury St., Boston (02116) (617) 536-2639 (FS-YA)

CHICAGO
Area code is (312) unless otherwise noted.

A Plus Talent Agency Corp.: 666 N. Lake Shore Dr., #1520 (60611) 642-8151 (FS-YA)
Ambassador Talents: 203 N. Wabash Ave., #2212 (60601) 641-3491
Boncher, Mary: 575 W. Madison #802 (60606) 902-2400
David & Lee: 70 W. Hubbard St., #200 (60610) 670-4444 (FS-YA)
Durkin Talent: 743 N. La Salle #250 (60610) 664-0045
E.T.A. Inc.: 7558 S. Chicago Ave., (60619) 752-3955
Ferrer Agency: 300 W. Grand #440 (60610) 467-0021
Geddes Agency: 188 W. Randolph #2400 (60611) 263-4090
Green & Green Model & Talent: 213 W. Institute Pl., #406 (60610) 649-9555
Hall Talent Nancy: 980 N. Michigan Ave., #1400 (60611) 280-4784
Hamilton Inc., Shirley: 333 E. Ontario #B (60611) 787-4700
Jefferson & Assoc.: 1050 N. State (60610) 337-1930
Johnson Talent Agency Ltd., Susanne: 108 W. Oak St. (60610) 943-8315 (FS-A)
Lily's Talent Agency: 10 S. Main Park Ridge (60068) 698-6364
Lorence Ltd., Emilia: 619 N. Wabash (60611) 787-2033
Mercury Inc., C.J.: 1330 Lake Ave., Whiting, Indiana (46394) (219) 659-2701
National Talent Network Inc.: 101 E. Ontario St., #760 (60611) 280-2225 (FS-YA)
Nouvelle Talent Mgmt.: 210 W. Kinzie (60610) 828-9246
Philbin Talent Agency: 6301 N. Kedvale (60646) 777-5394
Phoenix Talent Ltd.: 332 S. Michigan #1847 (60604) 786-2024
Salazar & Navas, Inc.: 868 N. Wabash #101 (60611) 751-3419
Schucart Ent., Inc., Norman: 1417 Green Bay Rd., Highland Park (60035)
433-1113 (FS-YA)

Stewart Talent Mgmt., Corp.: 212 W. Superior #406 (60610) 943-3131 (FS-YA)
Wilson Talent Arlene 414 N. Orleans (60610) 644-6699

DALLAS
Area code is (214).

Bock Agency Harold: 1420 Dragon Suite 101 (75207) 744-4411 (FS-YA)
Eisenberg Agency Vicki: 4514 Travis St., #217 (75205) 521-8430
Mary Collins/Agent C. Talent: 4220 Herschel #3 (75219) 528-7890
Dawson Agency Kim: 6309 N. O'Connor Rd., #113-IB22, Irving (75039) 556-0891
Farson/Cobb: 2727 Oak Lawn #217 (75219) 521-7978
Industry/Dallas: 4319 Oak Lawn (75219) 520-1135
J & D Talent: 1420 Dragon #101 (75207) 744-4411
Norton Agency The: 3900 Lemmon Ave. (75219) 528-9960
Taylor Peggy: 4300 N. Central Expwy., #110 (75206) 826-7884
Townsend Agency J.: 2600 Stemmons #200 (75207) 637-5700
Wyse Agency Joy: 2720 Stemmons Freeway #504 (75207) 638-8999

DENVER
Area code is (303) unless otherwise noted.

Barbizon Agency: 7535 E. Hampden (80231) 337-6952
Collage: 1444 Wazee #330 (80202) 623-2544
Concepts Talent Mgmt.: 150 W. 1st (80223) 733-2100
Images Inc., J.F.: 5251 DTC Parkway #1100, Englewood (80111) 779-8888 (FS-YA)
Kristi's Agency: 720 S. Colorado Bl., #160A (80222) 756-3046
Look Agency: 8101 E. Prentice Ave., #L110, Englewood (80111) 740-2224
M.T.A.: 1026 W. Colorado Ave., Colorado Springs (80904) (719) 577-4704

DETROIT
Area code is (313) unless otherwise noted.

Affiliated Models Inc.: 28860 Southfield Rd., #100 (48076) 559-3110 (FS-YA)
C.L.A.S.S. Model & Talent: 1625 Haslett Rd., Haslett (48840) (517) 339-2777
Gail & Rice Production: 11845 Mayfield, Livonia (48150) 427-9300 (FS-YA)
Haney & Assoc., Marce: 1150 Griswold Ave., #2300 (48226) 961-6222 (FS-YA)
Jeffrey Model & Talent Michael: Arbor Atrium #110 315 W. Huron St., Ann Arbor (48103) 663-6398
Production Plus Inc.: 5665 W. Maple #C W. Bloomfield (48033) 855-8115
Talent Shop: 30100 Telegraph Rd., #116, Birmingham (48010) 644-4877 (C-YA)
T.L.C. Unltd: 2737 W. 12th Mile Rd., Berkley (48072) 399-8787

FLORIDA

A-1 Peg's Modeling & Talent Agency: 133 E. Lauren Court Fern Park (32730) (407) 834-0406
Act 1 Agency: 2157 SW 13th Ave., Miami (33145) (305) 856-0005 (FS-YA)
Azuree Model & Talent: 140 N. Orlando Ave., #120, Winter Park (32789) (407) 629-5055

218

Berg Talent: 8313 W. Hillsborough Ave., Tampa (33615) (813) 886-5157
Best One Int'l Modeling: 626 Ocean Dr., Miami Beach (33139) (305) 531-1090
Bravo Talent & Modeling Agency: 4237 Henderson Blvd., Tampa (33629)
(813) 289-4511
Burns, Dott: 478 Severn Davis Island, Tampa (32606) (813) 251-5882 (FS-YA)
Cassandra Models Theatrical Agency: 513 W. Colonial Dr., Orlando (32803)
(407) 628-8803
Coconut Grove Talent Agency: 3525 Vista Court, Miami (33133) (305)
858-3002 (FS-YA)
Dimensions III: 5025 S. Orange Ave., #209, Orlando (32809) (407) 851-2575 (FS-YA)
Eastern Talent: 3121 Ponce De Leon, Coral Gables (33134) (305) 444-4114
Green & Green: 21404 W. Dixie Hwy., N. Miami (33180) (305) 931-0085
Haley Talent Agency Suzanne: 618 Wymore Rd., #2, Winter Park (32789)
(407) 740-5700
Just For Kids: 1995 NE 150th St., #C, N. Miami (33181) (305) 940-1311 or 462-6730
Just For Kids: 5850 Lakehurst Dr., #290-4, Orlando (32819) (407) 345-8503
L'Agence: 804 Ocean Dr., Miami Beach (33139) (305) 672-2160
MarBea Agency: 6100 Hollywood Bl., #428, Hollywood (33024) (305) 964-7401
Marks, Herbert: 924 Lincoln Road Bldg., Miami Beach (33139) (305)
534-2119 (FS-A)
Marie Agency Irene: 2400 E. Commercial #430, Ft. Lauderdale (33308)
(305) 771-1400 (FS-YA)
Marie Irene Agency: 4201 W. Cypress Ave., Tampa (33607) (813) 968-8795
Paramount: 1 Corp Dr., #119, Clearwater (33520) (813) 577-0006
Polan Talent Agency Marian: 10 NE 11th Ave., Ft. Lauderdale (33301)
(305) 525-8351 (FS-YA)
Pommier Models, Inc., Michele: Biltmore Hotel #100 1200 Anastasia Ave, Coral Gables
(38134) (305) 667-8710 (FS-YA) also at Cavalier Hotel #101 1230 Ocean Dr., Miami
Beach (33139) (305) 531-5475
Stellar Talent Agency: 195 SW 15th Rd., #201, Miami (33129) (305) 285-0079
Stewart's Modeling & Talent Agency Evelyn: 12421 N. Florida Ave., #D-218, Tampa
(33612) (813) 935-2208
Talent Network: 200 S. Andrews Ave., #B12 Ft. Lauderdale (33301) (305) 527-5578
Vermillion Models: 1211 N. Westshore Bl., #416, Tampa (33607) (813) 289-3311
Wellington: 823 E. Las Olas Bl., Ft. Lauderdale (33301) (305) 728-8003 or 944-6608
Young Faces: 612 Atlantic Shore Bl., Hallandale (33009) (305) 454-7711

GEORGIA
Area code is (404).

Atlanta Models & Talents Inc.: 3030 Peachtree Rd., NW #308, Atlanta (30305)
261-9627 (FS-YA)
Borden & Assoc., Ted: 3384 Peachtree Rd., #101 NW, Atlanta (30326) 266-0664
Burns Agency The: 3210 Peachtree Rd., NW #9, Atlanta (30305) 233-3230
Elite Model Mgmt.: 3060 Peachtree Rd., NW #1465, Atlanta (30305)
262-3422 (FS-A)
Kennedy Models & Talent Glyn: 990 Hammond Dr., #880, Atlanta (30328) 395-3736
(FS-YA)
L'Agence Models: 26 Perimeter E. #264, Atlanta (30346) 396-9015

Serindipity: 2989 Piedmont Rd., Atlanta (30305) 237-4040 (FS-YA)
Shragers People Store Rebecca: 3110 Maple Dr., #407A NE, Atlanta (30305) 237-3740
Summer's, Donna: 1961 N. Druid Hills Rd., #204B, Atlanta (30329) 321-6825
Take One: 244 Fairground St., Marietta (30060) 423-7009

HAWAII
Area code is (808).

ADR: 431 Kuwil St., Honolulu (96817) 524-4777
Kotomori Agency Service Amos: 1018 Hoawa Lane (96826) 955-6511 (FS-YA)
Morgan Talent Ent.: 1750 Kalakaua Ave., #901 (96826) 944-2035
Muller, Kathy: 619 Kapahulu Ave., Penthouse (96815) 737-7917
Woodhall Agency Ruth: 1223 Kamaile St. (96814) 947-3307

HOUSTON
Area code is (713).

Actors Etc., Inc.: 2630 Fountainview #300 (77057) 623-2275 (FS-YA)
Creative Talent: 1445 N. Loop West #975 (77008) 863-7188
Hamil Neal: 7887 San Felipi #227 (77063) 789-1335
Intermedia Models & Talent: 5353 W. Alabama #222 (77056) 622-8282 (FS-YA)
Mad Hatter Inc.: 7887 San Felipe #227 (77063) 974-2888
Pastorini-Peterson Talent Assoc.: 1800 Augusta Dr., 4th Floor (77057) 266-5800 (FS-YA)

MISSOURI

Backstage Workshop Talent Agency: 8025 Ward Parkway Plaza, Kansas City (64114) (816) 363-0808
Talents Plus: 3663 Lindell Bl., #100, St. Louis (63108) (314) 531-4800

NEVADA
Area code is (702).

Baskow & Assoc., J.: 4503 Paradise Rd., #1, Las Vegas (89109) 733-7818
Lenz Agency: 1630 Aztec, Las Vegas (89109) 733-6888 (FS-YA)
Mack Agency Jess: 1111 Las Vegas Bl., #209, S. Las Vegas (89104) 382-2193 (FS-A)
Morris Agency Bobby: 1629 E. Sahara Ave., Las Vegas (89104) 733-7575 (FS-YA)
Supreme Agency: 6250 Mountain Vista St., #L1 Henderson (89015) 456-4118 (FS-YA)

NEW MEXICO
Area code is (505).

Aesthetics Inc.: 308 Read St., Santa Fe (87501) 982-5883 (FS-YA)
Mannequin Agency: 3701 San Mateo NE Suite J, Albuquerque (87110) 888-2935 or 888-2933 (FS-YA)

Plaza Three Talent & Model Agency: 4206 Louisiana, NE #12, Albuquerque (87109) 884-8333

PENNSYLVANIA
Area code is (215) unless otherwise noted.

Askins Talent Agency Denise: New Market Suite 200 Head House Square, Philadelphia (19147) 925-7795
Claro Agency The: 1513 W. Passyunk, Philadelphia (19145) 334-8704
Expressions Model & Talent: 104 Church St., Philadelphia (19106) 923-4420
Greer, Lange: 7 Great Valley Parkway #129, Malvern (19355) 647-5515 or 647-5425
Midiri Models: 621 S. 4th, Philadelphia (19147) 238-8887
McCullough & Assoc.: 8 S. Hanover, Margate, NJ (08402) (609) 822-2222 (FS-A)
Plaza 7: 160 King of Prussia Plaza, King of Prussia (19406) 687-4759
Reinhard Agency: 2133 Arch (19103) 567-2008
Tiffany Talent: Commerce Plaza 2 Blackwood/Clementon Rd., Clementon, NJ (08021) 784-0050

UTAH
Area code is (801).

Button & Perkins Agency: 1800 SW Temple #103 (84115) 485-9253
C.T.A.: 4646 S. Highland Dr., #203 (84117) 272-9543
Lasting Impressions Modeling & Talent Agency: 1120 S. State St., Orem (84058) 224-1837 (FS-YA)
McCarty: 150 W. 500 South (84101) 359-9292
Saxton House Agency: 175 W. 200th South #1010 (84101) 537-1847

SAN DIEGO
Area code is (619).

Agency II Model & Talent: 2725 Congress St., #1H (92110) 291-9556
Artists Mgmt., Agency: 835 5th Ave., #411 (92101) 233-6655
Fields Liana Talent Agency: 2103 El Camino Real #107-B, Oceanside (92054) 295-9477
Nina Blanchard: 1133 Columbia St. (92101) 234-7911 (C-A)
Lily Talent Agency Beatrice: 7724 Girard Ave., #300, La Jolla (92038) 454-3579 (FS-YA)
Patterson Agency Janice: 2251 San Diego Ave., #A217 (92110) 295-9477
Real Tina: 3108 5th Ave. (92103) 298-0544 (FS-YA)
Shamon Freitas & Co.: 2400 Kettner Bl. (92109) 234-3043 (FS-YA)

SAN FRANCISCO
Area code is (415) unless otherwise noted.

Agency on the Island: 1361 Park St., #200, Alameda (94501) 521-9295
Best Model & Talent: 500 Sutter St. (94102) 392-2378
Brebner Agencies Inc.: 185 Berry St., #144 China Basin Bldg., #2 (94107) 495-6700
Dell Talent Marla: 1996 Union St. (94123) 563-9213

Dorie Int'l.: 2421 Lombard St. (94123) 563-4747
Film Theatre Actors Exchange: 271 Columbus Ave., #2 (94133) 433-3920
Frazer Agency: 4300 Stevens Creek Bl., #140, San Jose (95129) (408)
554-1055 (FS-YA)
Grimme Agency: 207 Powell St., 6th Floor (94102) 421-8715
L'Agency: 1875 Bascom, Campbell (95008) (408) 433-2612 and 870 Market #1215,
San Francisco (94102) 559-3929
Legends Model & Talent Agency: 1624 Franklin St., #1202, Oakland (94612)
832-5233
Look Model & Talent: 166 Geary St., #800 (94108) 781-2841
Los Latinos Modeling: Dyer Bldg., 2801 Moorpark Ave., #11, San Jose (95128)
(408) 296-2213 and (408) 295-2842
Panda Talent Agency: 3721 Hoen Ave., Santa Rosa (95405) 543-9049
Perseus Modeling & Talent: 100 Spear St., #1435 (94105) 543-9049
Quinn-Tonri Talent Agency: 601 Brannan St. (94107) 543-3797
Stars The Agency: 777 Davis St. (94111) 421-6272
City Models & Talent: 2325 3rd St., #431 (94107) 431-1132
Take One Talent: 340 Brannan St., #404 (94107) 956-3859
Visions Model Agency: 1055 Old Country Rd., San Carlos (94070) 581-9652

SEATTLE
Area code is (206).

Actors Group The: 219 1st Ave., S. #205 (98104) 624-9465
Hallowell Agency Lola: 1700 Westlake Ave., N. #436 (98109) 281-4646
James Agency Carol: 117 S. Main St. (98104) 447-9191 (FS-A)

TENNESSEE
Area code is (615).

Bruce Agency The: 1022 16th Ave., So Nashville (37212) 255-5711
Chaparral Talent Agency: P.O. Box 25, Oltewah (37363) 238-9790 (FS-YA)
Lee Buddy Attractions: 38 Music Square East (37203) 244-4336
Morris William: 2325 Crestmoor, Nashville (37215)
Talent & Model Land: 1501 12th Ave., Nashville (37203) 385-2723

WASHINGTON D.C.

Central Agency: 623 Pennsylvania Ave., SE, Washington D.C. (20003) (202) 547-6300
Central Agency: 2229 N. Charles St., Baltimore, MD (21218) (301) 880-3200
Taylor Royall Agency: 2308 South Rd., Baltimore, MD (21209) (301) 466-5959

DEPARTMENT OF LABOR OFFICES

ALABAMA
Department of Labor
Industrial Relations Building
Montgomery, AL 36130
(205) 832-6753

ARIZONA
State Labor Department
800 W. Washington St., #102
Phoenix, AZ 85005
(602) 255-4515

ARKANSAS
Department of Labor
Wage & Hour Division
Little Rock, AR
(501) 371-1401

CALIFORNIA
Department of Labor
P.O. Box 603
San Francisco, CA 94101
(415) 557-4070

CONNECTICUT
Department of Labor
200 Folly Brook Building
Wethersford, CT 06109
(203) 566-4550

GEORGIA
Department of Labor
254 Washington St. SW., #682
Atlanta, GA 30334
(404) 656-3017

IDAHO
Department of Labor
Boise, ID 83702
(209) 334-2327

INDIANA
Department of Labor
1013 State Office Building
Indianapolis, IN 46204
(317) 232-2675

LOUISIANA
Division of Labor
State Capitol
Baton Rouge, LA 70804
(504) 342-5363

CALIFORNIA
Division of Labor Standards
107 S. Broadway #5015
Los Angeles, CA 90012
(213) 620-5130

COLORADO
Department of Labor
State Capitol
Denver, CO 80203
(303) 866-4704

FLORIDA
Division of Labor
1320 Executive Center Dr.
Tallahassee, FL 32301
(904) 488-8396

HAWAII
Department of Labor
Division of Labor
Honolulu, HI 96813
(808) 548-4071

ILLINOIS
Labor Law Enforcement
Chicago, IL 60604
(312) 793-2804

IOWA
Division of Labor
1000 E. Grand Ave.
Des Moines, IA 50319
(515) 281-3606

MAINE
Bureau of Labor Standards
Augusta, ME 04330
(207) 289-3331

MARYLAND
Department of Licensing
501 St. Paul Place
Baltimore, MD 21202
(301) 659-2261

MICHIGAN
Department of Labor
7150 Harris Dr.
Lansing, MI 48909
(517) 322-1825

MISSOURI
Department of Labor
P.O. Box 449
Jefferson City, MO 65106
(314) 751-3403

NEVADA
Department of Labor
Capitol Complex
Carson City, NV 89710
(702) 885-4850

NEW MEXICO
State Labor Board
1596 Pacheco St.
Santa Fe, NM 87501
(505) 827-9870

NORTH CAROLINA
Department of Labor
Raleigh, NC 27601
(919) 733-2152

OHIO
Department of Industry Relations
Columbus, OH 43215
(614) 466-3271

MASSACHUSETTS
Department of Labor
State Capitol
Boston, MA 02202
(617) 727-3478

MINNESOTA
Department of Labor
444 Lafayette Road
St. Paul, MN 55101
(612) 296-6107

NEBRASKA
Division of Labor
44601 S. 50th St.
Southwest Plaza #214
Omaha, NE 68117
(402) 554-3095

NEW JERSEY
Department of Labor
Office of Wage & Hour
Trenton, NJ 08625
(609) 292-2337

NEW YORK
Department of Labor
80 Lafayette St.
New York, NY 10013
(212) 553-5681

NORTH DAKOTA
Division of Labor
Bismarck, ND 58505
(701) 224-2660

OREGON
Division of Labor
240 Cottage St. SE.
Salem, OR 97310
(503) 229-5750

PENNSYLVANIA
Department of Labor
Harrisburg, PA 17120
(717) 787-5279

SOUTH CAROLINA
Department of Labor
Columbia, SC 29201
(803) 758-7794

TENNESSEE
Division of Labor
501 Union Building
(615) 741-2582

UTAH
Utah Industrial Commission
160 E. 300 South
Salt Lake City, UT 84110
(801) 533-5874

VIRGINIA
Department of Labor
P.O. Box 12064
Richmond, VA 23241
(804) 786-2387

WEST VIRGINIA
Department of Labor
1800 Washington St. East
Charleston, WV 25304
(304) 348-7890

WYOMING
Labor Department
Cheyenne, WY 82002
(307) 777-7262

RHODE ISLAND
Division of Labor
Providence, RI 82983
(401) 277-2734

SOUTH DAKOTA
Department of Labor
Pierre, SD 57501
(605) 773-3681

TEXAS
Department of Labor
Austin, TX 78767
(512) 475-7003

VERMONT
Department of Labor
Montpelier, VT 05602
(802) 828-2157

WASHINGTON
Department of Labor
General Administration Bldg.
Olympia, WA 98504
(206) 753-2474

WISCONSIN
Department of Labor
Madison, WI 53707
(608) 266-6860

FEDERAL INFORMATION CENTERS

ALABAMA
Birmingham (205) 322-8591
Mobile (205) 438-1421

ALASKA
Anchorage (907) 271-3650

225

ARIZONA
Phoenix (602) 261-3313

ARKANSAS
Little Rock (501) 378-6177

CALIFORNIA
Los Angeles (213) 894-3800
Sacramento (916) 551-2380
San Diego (619) 557-6030
Santa Ana (714) 836-2386
San Francisco (415) 556-6600

COLORADO
CO Springs (303) 471-9491
Denver (303) 844-6575
Pueblo (303) 544-9523

CONNECTICUT
Hartford (203) 527-2617
New Haven (203) 624-4720

FLORIDA
Ft. Lauderdale (305) 522-8531
Jacksonville (904) 354-4756
Miami (305) 536-4155
Orlando (305) 422-1800
St. Petersburg (813) 893-3495
Tampa (813) 229-7911
West Palm Beach (305) 833-7566

GEORGIA
Atlanta (404) 331-6891

HAWAII
Honolulu (808) 551-1365

ILLINOIS
Chicago (312) 353-4242

INDIANA
Gary (219) 883-4110
Indianapolis (317) 269-7373

IOWA
From all points in Iowa
1 (800) 532-1556

KANSAS
From all points in Kansas
1 (800) 432-2934

KENTUCKY
Louisville (502) 582-6261

LOUISIANA
New Orleans (504) 589-6696

MARYLAND
Baltimore (301) 962-4980

MASSACHUSETTS
Boston (617) 565-8121

MICHIGAN
Detroit (313) 226-7016
Grand Rapids (616) 451-2628

MINNESOTA
Minneapolis (612) 370-3333

MISSOURI
St. Louis (314) 425-4106
From all points in MO
1 (800) 392-7711

NEBRASKA
Omaha (402) 221-3353
From all points in NE
1 (800) 642-8383

NEW MEXICO
Albuquerque (505) 766-3091

NORTH CAROLINA
Charlotte (704) 376-3600

OHIO
Akron (216) 375-5638
Cincinnati (513) 684-2001
Cleveland (216) 522-4040
Columbus (614) 221-1014
Dayton (513) 223-7377
Toledo (419) 241-3223

PENNSYLVANIA
Philadelphia (215) 597-7042
Pittsburgh (412) 644-3456

TENNESSEE
Chattanooga (615) 265-8231
Memphis (901) 521-3285
Nashville (615) 242-5056

UTAH
Salt Lake City (801) 524-5353

VIRGINIA
Norfolk (804) 441-3101
Richmond (804) 643-4928
Roanoke (703) 982-8591

WISCONSIN
Milwaukee (414) 271-2273

NEW JERSEY
Newark (201) 645-3600
Trenton (609) 396-4400

NEW YORK
Albany (518) 463-4421
Buffalo (716) 846-4010
New York (212) 264-4464
Rochester (716) 546-5075
Syracuse (315) 476-8545

OKLAHOMA
Oklahoma City (405) 231-4868
Tulsa (918) 584-4193

OREGON
Portland (503) 221-2222

RHODE ISLAND
Providence (401) 331-5565

TEXAS
Austin (512) 472-5494
Dallas (214) 767-8585
Fort Worth (817) 334-3624
Houston (713) 229-2552
San Antonio (512) 224-4471

WASHINGTON
Seattle (206) 442-0570
Tacoma (206) 383-5230

DEPARTMENT OF EDUCATION OFFICES

COUNCIL OF CHIEF STATE SCHOOL OFFICERS

379 Hall of the States
400 North Capitol St., NW
Washington, DC 20001
(202) 393-8161

ALABAMA
501 Dexter Ave.
481 State Office Building
Montgomery, AL 36130
(205) 261-5156

ARIZONA
1535 West Jefferson
Phoenix, AZ 85007
(602) 255-4361

ARKANSAS
721 Capitol Mall
Little Rock, AR 72201
(501) 371-1464

CALIFORNIA
P.O. Box 944272
Sacramento, CA 94244
(916) 445-4338

COLORADO
201 E. Colfax
Denver, CO 80203
(303) 866-6806

CONNECTICUT
165 Capitol Ave.
Room 308, State Office Bldg
Hartford, CT 06106
(203) 566-5061

DELAWARE
P.O. Box 14002, Townsend Bldg.
Dover, DE 19901
(302) 736-4601

DISTRICT OF COLUMBIA
415 Twelfth St., NW
Washington, DC 20004
(202) 724-4222

FLORIDA
Capitol Bldg., Room PL 116
Tallahassee, FL 32301
(904) 487-1785

GEORGIA
2066 Twin Towers East
Atlanta, GA 30334
(404) 656-2800

HAWAII
P.O. Box 2360
Honolulu, HI 96804
(808) 548-6405

IDAHO
650 West State St.
Boise, ID 83720
(208) 334-3300

ILLINOIS
100 North First St.
Springfield, IL 62777
(217) 782-2221

IOWA
Grimes State Office Bldg.
Des Moines, IA 50319
(515) 281-5294

KENTUCKY
1725 Capitol Plaza Tower
Frankfort, KY 40601
(502) 564-4770

MAINE
State House, Station No. 23
Augusta, ME 04333
(207) 289-5800

MASSACHUSETTS
1385 Hancock St.
Quincy, MA 02169
(617) 770-7300

MINNESOTA
712 Capitol Square Bldg.
550 Cedar St.
St. Paul, MN
(612) 296-2358
MISSOURI
P.O. Box 480
Jefferson State Office Bldg.
Jefferson City, MO 65102

NEBRASKA
P.O. Box 94987
301 Centennial Mall, South
Lincoln, NE 68509
(402) 471-2465

INDIANA
State House, Room 229
Indianapolis, IN 46204
(317) 232-6612

KANSAS
120 East Tenth St.
Topeka, KS 66612
(913) 296-3201

LOUISIANA
P.O. Box 44064
Baton Rouge, LA 70804
(504) 342-3602

MARYLAND
200 West Baltimore St.
Baltimore, MD 21201
(301) 659-2200

MICHIGAN
P.O. Box 30008
115 West Allegan St.
Lansing, MI 48909
(517) 373-3354

MISSISSIPPI
P.O. Box 771, High St.
Jackson, MS 39205
(601) 359-3513

MONTANA
State Capitol
Helena, MT 59620
(406) 444-3654

NEVADA
400 West King St.
Capitol Complex
Carson City, NV 89710
(702) 885-3100

NEW HAMPSHIRE
101 Pleasant St.
State Office Park South
Concord, NH 03301
(603) 271-3144

NEW MEXICO
State Capitol 300
Santa Fe, NM 87503
(505) 827-6516

NORTH CAROLINA
Education Bldg., Room 318
Edenton and Salisbury St.
Raleigh, NC 27611
(919) 733-3813

OKLAHOMA
2500 North Lincoln Blvd.
Oklahoma City, OK 73105
(405) 521-3301

PENNSYLVANIA
333 Market St., 10th Floor
Harrisburg, PA 17126
(717) 787-5820

SOUTH CAROLINA
1006 Rutledge Bldg.
1429 Senate St.
(803) 758-3291

TENNESSEE
100 Cordell Hull Bldg.
Nashville, TN 37219
(615) 741-2731

UTAH
250 E. 500 South
Salt Lake City, UT 84111
(801) 533-5431

NEW JERSEY
225 West State St.
Trenton, NJ 08625
(609) 292-4450

NEW YORK
111 Education Bldg.
Albany, NY 12234
(518) 474-5844

OHIO
65 S. Front St., Room 808
Columbus, OH 43215
(614) 466-3304

OREGON
700 Pringle Pkwy., SE
Salem, OR 97310
(503) 378-3573

RHODE ISLAND
22 Hayes St.
Providence, RI 02908
(401) 277-2031

SOUTH DAKOTA
Education Kneip Bldg.
Pierre, SD 57501
(605) 773-3243

TEXAS
1702 N. Congress Ave.
Austin, TX 78701
(512) 463-8985

VERMONT
State St.
Montpelier, VT 05602
(802) 828-3135

VIRGINIA
P.O. Box 6Q
Fourteenth and Franklin St.
Richmond, VA 23216
(804) 225-2023

WEST VIRGINIA
1900 Washington St.
Bldg., B, Room 358
Charleston, WV 25305
(304) 348-3644

WYOMING
Hathaway Bldg.
Cheyenne, WY 82002
(307) 777-7675

WASHINGTON
Old Capitol Bldg.
Mail Stop FG-11
Olympia, WA 98504
(206) 753-6717

WISCONSIN
125 South Webster St.
P.O. Box 7841
Madison, WI 53707
(608) 266-1771

NOTES